CW00925187

From the

Underground

Church to

Freedom

TOMÁŠ HALÍK

From the Underground Church to Freedom

Translated by

GERALD TURNER

University of Notre Dame Press

Notre Dame, Indiana

The work was supported by the European Regional Development Fund-Project "Creativity and Adaptability as Conditions of the Success of Europe in an Interrelated World (No. CZ.02.1.01/0.0/0.0/16_019/0000734)."

Published in the United States of America

Library of Congress Cataloging-in-Publication Data

Names: Halík, Tomáš, author. | Turner, Gerald, translator.
Title: From the underground church to freedom / Tomáš Halík ; translated
    by Gerald Turner.
Other titles: To že byl život? English
Description: Notre Dame, Indiana : University of Notre Dame Press, [2019] |
    Translation of: To že byl život? : z podzemní církve do labyrintu svobody.
Identifiers: LCCN 2019021443 (print) | LCCN 2019981271 (ebook) |
    ISBN 9780268106775 (hardback) | ISBN 9780268106799 (epub) |
    ISBN 9780268106805 (pdf)
Subjects: LCSH: Halík, Tomáš. | Catholic Church—Czech Republic—Clergy—
    Biography. | Theologians—Czech Republic—Biography. | Intellectuals—
    Czech Republic—Biography. | Czechoslovakia—Politics and government—
    1968–1989. | Czechoslovakia—Church history.
Classification: LCC BX4705.H137 A3 2019 (print) | LCC BX4705.H137 (ebook)
    | DDC 282.092 [B]—dc23
LC record available at https://lccn.loc.gov/2019021443
LC ebook record available at https://lccn.loc.gov/2019981271

. . . with all my ways you are familiar.

—Psalm 139:3

And I have always been unwilling to ask the way—it was never to my taste! Instead I sought and tried out the ways myself. My entire journey has been an experimental questioning.

—Friedrich Nietzsche, Thus Spoke Zarathustra

Contents

ONE

Are You Writing about Yourself?

Human life is ongoing self-interpretation. If I wish to present myself to someone else or to understand myself, I start to tell my own story. This is me in time. Unlike animals or things, we are not simply "now": I myself am observing events. I unfold from a past that I carry with me, and at the same time, in a certain sense, I already "have" the future: in the form of hopes, wishes, plans, and fears.

Sometimes the derivation of the Latin word for religion—*religio*—is given as *re-legere*—re-reading. Yes, faith is reading our own story anew, reading it from another viewpoint, in a broader context, with detachment and deeper understanding. Our life, viewed with the eyes of faith, is not a "tale told by an idiot, signifying nothing," as Shakespeare's Macbeth says. It is a story whose hidden author and director is God. But he does not move us like puppets on strings; the drama in which he has placed us is more like commedia dell'arte—a play in which we are given enormous scope for improvisation. We recognize God's writing style by its infinite generosity and its incomprehensible trust in our freedom. Wherever human

1

freedom is not deformed and caricatured by indiscipline and willfulness, wherever it is realized in love and creation, there, in that freedom of human self-transcendence, can we glimpse perhaps the purest image and illustration of God, who is very freedom and generosity.

Confessions, the title of Augustine's best-known book, can denote both confession of sins and confession of faith, or credo. Confession, the honest narration of one's own life journey with all its faults and misgivings, is certainly closely linked to confession in the sense of confession of faith, confessing to God. During the Mass we confess our sinfulness and our faith. Before confessing to God in the confession of faith, we go to confession to confess our sins and doubts and confess our humanity.

In confessing our sins and weaknesses we confront the person within us whom we would rather leave outside the church door—but it is that person who is truly invited to the feast. When you give a banquet, invite the poor, the crippled, the lame, and the blind. That is what God does also: he does not invite the wealthy, just, and pious side of our being in its Sunday dress, the side that wants to reward God—or thinks it can. God invites what is blind, lame, weeping, poor, and hungry within us. Not in order to condemn this "less attractive" side of our being, but in order to feed and cheer it. The rabbi from Nazareth never failed to speak about it in his arguments with the Pharisees.

People often tend to be proudly locked up in their "virtues," certainties, and strengths. What is fundamental in them opens up through their thirst, their yearning, and their wounds. What is fundamental in us is that very "openness," openness to what is fundamental, to what is "the only needful thing," which does not open itself to us at our moments of our satiated, self-sufficient, self-assurance. The openness of the human heart and the openness of the Kingdom of God are one and the same openness.

Who am I actually? "I have become a question to myself," Augustine says. Yes, our self—like our God—must be for us the subject of continuous questioning, doubting, and seeking. We seek ourselves, and God also, by telling our story, and in telling it we do not conceal our trembling. Only the heart that has not ceased to tremble in holy restlessness can, in the end, find rest in the sea of God's Peace.

▌ "ARE YOU WRITING ABOUT YOURSELF AGAIN? Do you think people have the time or inclination to read about your life?," my associate Scarlett asked today in my study as she took a casual glance at the manuscript I had just handed to her for her critical comments. Scarlett has been at my side for forty years in good times and bad. She is the first person to read my texts, and a severe critic of everything I say, write, and do. No one on earth is capable of upsetting me the way she does; no one on earth has been of benefit and assistance to me the way she has. When several of my friends were appointed to high office after 1989, I could see that they desperately needed someone to give them systematic feedback, instead of the yes-men and lickspittles who surrounded them. The mature and good-natured side of myself I owe chiefly to Scarlett. The Bible says that a woman of fortitude is worth more than rubies; it requires a lot of fortitude, patience, and an unflagging hurricane of energy to stand by me.

What am I to say in response? I am writing about myself but also about a half century of history of a country in the heart of Europe, and particularly about the history of the sorely tested Czech Catholic church. I'm not a historian, that's for sure, and my testimony will be a "subjective" one. How else? Naturally I am also writing my story for the readers of my books, and for those who have attended my lectures. When I read a book or listen to someone's talk I frequently ask myself: How did this person come to the views they expound? Have they derived them mainly from books, from their study of specialist literature, or are their opinions also backed by the gold of their own personal life experience? Has their vision of the world undergone trials and crises? Did they have to revise or radically reassess their former views sometimes? When I know an author's life story and how their personality and opinions have evolved, their writings become more vivid, meaningful, credible, and immediate. My readers and listeners also have the right to know the internal context of my writing, as well as the external one, not just the historical circumstances and the social and cultural context, but also my life story and the drama of spiritual seeking and the process of maturity; should they wish to, they will find here the key to a deeper understanding of what I try to convey to them in my books and lectures. Before describing what one sees, one should declare where one stands, what is one's standpoint, and why one has adopted it.

"Are you writing about yourself?" I could also reply that I am writing about God. But is it possible to speak about God and not invest one's life in that account? Were I to speak about God "objectively" without investing myself in it, I would be speaking about a pallid abstraction. Wouldn't such an "external God" be merely an idol. Conversely, is it possible to speak about oneself and say nothing about God? Were I to speak about myself and say nothing about God, I could attribute to myself what is his and become stuck for eternity in a trap of self-centeredness or drown myself in narcissistic superficiality. When Narcissus leans over the surface of the lake he sees only himself, and his eye remains fixed to the surface and his own image there. This superficiality turns out to be fatal for him. The gaze of the believer must penetrate deeper. Only then will the depth not become a malignant trap.

Two realities, crucial for our life, are *invisible*: our self and God. We see many manifestations that can be attributed to our self and others to God, but neither our self nor God presents themselves to us things that we can point to and which we can localize with certainty. The mystics—and particularly my beloved Meister Eckhart— have asserted one very profound thing that is also extremely dangerous: God and I are one and the same.

This position can indeed be dangerous. When, from our standpoint, God has coalesced with our self, in the sense that we have substituted God for our self, then we have lost our soul. When we rigorously separate the two and start to regard God as something entirely external and separate from our soul, we have lost the living God, and all we have left is an idol, some thing, just "a thing among things." The abiding task of theology is to point to that dynamic intermingling of immanence and transcendence. Perhaps we could speak about the link between our self and God in the terms used by the Council of Chalcedon to describe the relationship between the human and the divine in Christ: they are inseparable and yet unmixed. If I take seriously the mystery of the Incarnation—the heart of the Christian faith—and comprehend it not as some chance occurrence in the past but as the key to understanding the entire drama of the history of salvation, the history of the relationship between God and people, then I cannot think of humanity and divinity separately. When I say "I," I am also saying "God," *because the human being without God is not whole.*

It is only in relation to God that we can start to sense that our self is structured somewhat differently than it seems when viewed with the superficial, naive gaze of everyday life. Beyond our "ego" we sometimes get a glimpse of something for which the mystics and modern depth psychology strive to find an adequate expression— "the inner man," the "deep self," *das Selbst.* Meister Eckhart used to speak about the "inner God," the "God beyond God"; some modern and postmodern theologians (and a-theists) speak about "God beyond the God of theism." Perhaps it is not until we come to see the naive, objectified understanding of God and the similarly naive understanding of the "self" as illusions that we will be capable of grasping Eckhart's statement: "God and I are one"; we will comprehend that it is neither blasphemous self-deification nor covert impiety. "The eye with which I see God is the same eye with which God sees me," wrote Meister Eckhart. And we find something similar in the writings of St. Augustine: "The love with which you love God and the seeking whereby you seek Him, are the love and seeking whereby God seeks and loves you."

Augustine wrote countless tracts about God, but what may be most inspirational to those who still dare to talk about God is his boldness to present candidly his own life story and say to the reader: Seek, friend. The solution to the puzzle, the key to the meaning of this story, is God. You will find God only by knowing yourself; you will find yourself only by seeking God. Augustine thereby invented a new literary genre and a new way to reflect on faith: autobiography as a framework of philosophical theology.

■ WHEN MARIE AND MIROSLAV HALÍK BROUGHT their first-born son home from the maternity hospital in Prague it felt like a dream to them. My mother was almost forty-five years old and my father almost fifty, and they had previously reconciled themselves to childlessness. And for a while, that day at the beginning of June 1948 remained dreamlike for them. Scarcely an hour later, just as they were passing through the Baroque gateway into the Vyšehrad fortress complex, bells rang out all over Prague, there was a cannonade salute, and the archbishop intoned the Te Deum in St. Vitus Cathedral.

But there the fairy tale ended and the dream gave way to the harsh reality: those bells tolled the knell of freedom and democracy in Czechoslovakia. They announced that Gottwald, leader of the Communist Party, had succeeded Masaryk and Beneš as president of the republic and was now installed in Prague Castle. It was the finishing touch to the putsch that occurred in February of that year.

The new president had ordered a celebratory Te Deum for that day from Archbishop Beran. A year later he ordered the same archbishop, a former inmate of the Nazi concentration camp at Dachau, to be placed under house arrest for many years. The following year he had the regime's first political opponents executed, and they were followed to the gallows by a number of Gottwald's comrades who had helped him take power. The promises of the "democratic road to socialism" that enabled the Communists to win the elections in the postwar euphoria—in the aftermath of disillusion with the Western allies' deal with Hitler over Czechoslovakia at Munich—were entirely forgotten.

Many of my parents' friends started to disappear. Some went into exile, others to prison. Had they not had such a small child at the time, perhaps my parents would also have opted for a hazardous escape via the Bohemian Forest marshes from this country, where darkness had fallen and the ice age of Stalinist terror had begun.

Three days after my birth, while still at the maternity hospital, I was baptized in the hospital chapel (which was closed soon afterward and converted into a storeroom for the next forty years). When I look at the photograph of that event I can see four men leaning over me. Where was faith at that moment? As an infant I had no idea what was happening to me. My father left the Catholic Church at the age of seventeen after the fall of the Habsburg monarchy in 1918 under the influence of the "Away from Vienna—away from Rome" campaign. Both my godfathers, uncles from my mother's and my father's side of the family, had probably not attended a church service since their secondary school years. Frankly speaking, I wouldn't even vouch for the faith of the priest who christened me, who shortly afterward became an official of the Peace Movement of the Catholic Clergy, which collaborated with the Communist regime.

The baptismal seed was sown in extremely fallow soil. The religion of our family—like that of the great majority of Czech intellectuals who reached adulthood at the end of World War I and then linked their lives with Masaryk's interwar democracy—was belief in humanity, a moral code, scientific progress, and democracy. There wasn't much talk at home about religion. My parents were not practicing Catholics and had only had a civil marriage, and they didn't attend church. Neverthess, that secular humanism, influenced by Karel Čapek and Tomáš Masaryk, still retained many Christian elements, and the ethical and aesthetic cultural atmosphere of our family was still influenced by Christianity. In those days the external pressure from Communism tended to bring decent people closer to that foundation of Christian values rather than distance them. On the day I was born, my father lit a large candle before the altar of the Infant of Prague, and it was always important to him that we should celebrate

Christmas and Easter at home with great care and in a beautiful way, and he also told me about the folk customs and traditions associated with the celebrations. But the *Christianness* of that culture tended to remain "anonymous" and implicit; it tended to be folkloric and aesthetic rather than "devotional," separated by a high wall from everything that happened within the confines of the church.

By then many people of that generation invited clergy only to christenings and only rarely to weddings or funerals. And during the years that followed my birth, it was neither easy nor without risk to meet with a priest. Priests too began to disappear in those years—to prisons and work camps, some to the gallows. The persecution of the church and the omnipresent brutal propaganda against the church and religion became much more intense than in any of the surrounding countries of the "socialist camp," even including the Soviet Union itself.

It would seem that the Stalinists had chosen Czechoslovakia as soil to experiment with the total atheization of society. In a sense they had favorable conditions for the experiment. The country's dramatic religious history—the burning at the stake of Jan Hus at the Council of Constance in 1415, the five crusades against the heretical Czechs, the violent re-Catholicization of Bohemia in the seventeenth century, and the Catholic Church's alignment with the Habsburg monarchy—all left its trace. Whereas the Poles regarded the Catholic Church as the main pillar of their national identity (in opposition to Orthodox Russia and Protestant Germany), modern Czech nationalism—an ideology created to fight for the emancipation of the Czech lands from Vienna, in other words, also from "Austrocatholicism" and Rome—regarded Czech identity as scarcely compatible with Catholicism ("Romanism"). By the end of the Austro-Hungarian monarchy, and particularly in the interwar years, the Czech lands, in contrast to agrarian Slovakia, could boast advanced industrialization and a high level of general education—circumstances naturally favorable to secularization. Traditional rural communities—a biosphere of a popular church and piety—retreated in the face of modern urban culture, and the Catholic Church was incapable of putting down roots in this new environment.

■ SEVERAL TIMES DURING MY CHILDHOOD, when someone heard my parents say my name, they would come over and stroke my head and say, with a knowing smile at my parents, "You have a very nice name!" I didn't understand until much later that the Christian name my parents gave me was a sign of resistance. When someone born in the years following the Communist putsch in 1948 was named Tomáš, it was a clear sign that their parents were "reactionaries." By choosing the name, they wanted to declare their loyalty to the ideals of the First Republic and of its founder, Tomáš Masaryk.

For at least two generations, Tomáš Garrigue Masaryk was regarded as the nation's chief mentor. His "religion of humanity" was an amalgam of Kantian ethics, Comtian positivism, Toquevillian political philosophy, liberal Protestantism, a romantic interpretation of Czech Protestantism, and the Unitarianism of his American wife. Masaryk was undoubtedly a profoundly pious man, influenced in his youth by Catholic modernism, who affirmed to the very end of his life that, like Goethe's Faust, "his heart was Catholic and his head was Protestant." However, he had been deeply disillusioned by the Catholic Church of his time. After the fall of the Austrian monarchy, a delegation of Czech Catholics, representing a considerable part of the Czech Catholic clergy, demanded reformist changes from Rome, including the democratization of the church, the introduction of the national language into the liturgy, the rehabilitation of Jan Hus, and voluntary celibacy. Rome's response was resolute and took the form of a single word: "Numquam!" Never! Most of the reform-minded clergy accepted it with clenched teeth, but a small percentage of clergy and laity left the Catholic Church at that time.

The Czech Communists subsequently built into their ideology an older anticlerical tradition while radicalizing it and exaggerating it ad absurdum. When they were preparing to implement their plan to build a new society as a city without God, the Communist minister of culture at the time declared, "Let us awaken the Hussite instincts of our people!"

For years I sought an answer to the question why a country that had, in the distant past, burned with religious fervor, one from which the sparks of reforming ideas had leapt to all corners of the earth, is now regarded, along with the areas of the former German Democratic Republic, as one of the most atheistic regions of Europe if not the whole world. Of course, much is explained by the historic tragedy of the Communist regime's attempt to systematically eradicate religion from public life and from the hearts and minds of two generations; and the social structure of Czech society also played a role.

But how true is the assertion that the Czechs are an atheistic nation? I have studied the spirituality of individuals who shaped Czech culture in the nineteenth and twentieth centuries, such as František Palacký, Tomáš Masaryk, F. X. Šalda, Karel Čapek, Jan Patočka, and Václav Havel. They represented a broad range of opinions, but not one of them was an atheist. On the contrary, they all had a profound connection to what transcends us. Nevertheless, each of them maintained a distance from traditional religious terminology. Václav Havel, for instance, used to speak in Heideggeresque terms about the "horizon of horizons" or the "absolute horizon." I dubbed that phenomenon "shy piety" on the basis of a passage from a travelogue by the Czech Catholic writer Jaroslav Durych, in which Durych compares the dramatic religious comportment of the Spanish and other Latin nations to the shy and discreet comportment of Czechs at prayer—as if Czech believers constantly felt the ironic gaze of the nonbeliever. Czech expressions of faith are discreet; they avoid grand words and spectacular gestures. I think it also has something to do with the Czechs' aversion to pathos. Pathos seems ridiculous to us. Czechs suspect pathos of insincerity, hypocrisy, or hollow superficiality, and they resist it by using irony. I would add that the reserved nature of Czech piety is not just due to fear of mockery but also to an attempt to protect something rare and fragile.

The roots of Czech secularization and anticlericalism are too deep to be simply regarded as the result of Communist ideological brainwashing. First of all, it is a much older phenomenon, which emerged historically as a defensive reaction to the church's links with power, as well as to Counter-Reformation triumphalism and the formalism of "Austro-Catholicism." Second, when we study this phenomenon carefully, we can see its positive aspect: a certain inward modesty out of aversion to shallow piety.

The "shy piety" of intellectuals seeking a somewhat abstract expression for their humanism—a humanism open to the "transcendental," outside the boundaries of ecclesiastical terminology—has a popular parallel in what I term "somethingism": I don't believe in God, I don't go to church, but I know there is *something* above us. I believe in "my own God." I often say that somethingism is the most widespread religion among the Czechs. Maybe this phenomenon, which has existed here for a long time already, anticipated a similar development in a number of other European countries. For me as a theologian and a Czech Catholic priest, the hermeneutics of this shy piety and of many forms of somethingism is a pastoral duty. However, it is also an interesting topic with respect to my academic research into the psychological and sociological aspects of religion's transformations.

And indeed anticlericalism may be conceived as an expression of a love-hate relationship, an unconscious manifestation of unrealistic expectations of the church that were disappointed. Of course, the Communists deliberately misused the "Hussite instincts of our people" in their propaganda, but maybe the church should take such "instincts" seriously, because they are a sign of the opposite of what it should fear more than hatred: indifference.

With hindsight, the impression I have is that Communist persecution in this country actually helped the church in a way. Its solely formal aspects fell away. A major role was played by the life testimony of imprisoned priests; very many of those who endured Communist prisons and labor camps in the 1950s either underwent conversion as the result of the influence of those priests or at least acquired for the rest of their lives a great respect for priests and the church, and for faith. Czechs often instinctively sympathize with the persecuted. Paradoxically, when atheistic propaganda was forced on people, sympathy for the church increased, particularly among the intelligentsia and young people, and this reached its peak just before the fall of Communism.

There is one area in which the Communists were successful: most Czechs born under the Communist regime virtually never encountered the living church, and that shy piety never directly encountered Christian culture. Somethingism is burdened by religious illiteracy. That is why my country might appear to be atheistic to a superficial glance. But if I have been placed here by the Lord, isn't it part of my task to be dissatisfied with superficial glances?

But doesn't this represent a challenge for a Christian, and particularly for a priest and theologian? I must admit that I would not like to be a priest in a traditional Catholic setting. I would feel out of place among people who take religion for granted. Jesus compared Christians to salt. I don't feel at ease where society is "oversalted" with Christians and Christianity. One doesn't need much salt; but if there is a complete lack of salt, or the salt has lost its savor, the food is tasteless.

I am enormously grateful to God that I was born in the Czech lands and for over half a century I have lived through the troubled history of the church. I'm glad to be a priest in an environment in which religion is not taken for granted by any means.

So the seed of my christening fell onto very stony soil that time before the threshold of the 1950s. The land was beginning to freeze in a disturbing fashion, due to the icy blasts from the East. And yet, at the age of eighteen—almost at the age at which my father left the church—I discovered a path to faith and then into the family of the church. Twelve years later I was ordained a priest clandestinely in a foreign country; not even my mother, with whom I lived, was allowed to know I was a priest. I spent the next eleven years in the service of the underground church and in a milieu of cultural and political dissent. It was a time of a rigid police state, which, while it was not as harsh as the Stalinism of the 1950s, was more sophisticated and hence more dangerous for the moral health of Czech society. I was already forty when a completely new chapter of my life opened: I could work publicly in the church and in academia, as well as take part in founding a number of initiatives and institutions within the church, the university, and political life. During those dramatic years of the difficult transition from a police state to a new democracy and free society, I worked closely with leading representatives of church and state. For many years I was close to President Václav Havel and to Pope John Paul II. After being prevented, for almost two decades, from traveling anywhere outside the Communist bloc, over the next twenty years I visited every continent on the planet, including the Antarctic. After being excluded from academia for twenty years, I had the opportunity to lecture at universities on the five continents.

After my fiftieth birthday I returned to literary creation, the favorite activity of my early youth. It seemed to me presumptuous to write a book of any substance before I reached fifty. It was first necessary to acquire some experience, to study, to reflect, to travel, and to suffer, before offering it to others for their consideration. Every year I travel to a contemplative monastery in the Rhineland and spend four or five weeks there on my own in the silence. All my books came into being there as a by-product of my private spiritual exercises, of that time of prayer, meditation, study, and reflection in the course of long walks through the deep forest. In my sixtieth year my books started to be translated into various languages and reach readers and commentators in different parts of the world; I also began to receive numerous foreign awards, prestigious prizes, and honorary doctorates. For someone who for years had not been allowed to publish a single line, who wrote his first small-scale texts "for the desk drawer," texts that could read by only a few friends, or possibly sent to samizdat journals under a pseudonym, this was a source of great satisfaction. These, then, are the main divisions of the story I shall try to relate in this book.

I have already made available some of these reminiscences to my Czech readers in a book of interviews with the journalist and laicized priest Jan Jandourek, which was published to mark my fiftieth birthday.

Even in the case of that book I resisted the publisher's proposal for a long time. What often happens in such negotiations is that one indulges others' subconscious expectations and also the dictates of one's own narcissism and presents oneself as an example for others—that's if one doesn't succumb to the other extreme: exhibitionist self-flagellation. I like Einstein's witticism that "the only rational way of educating is to be an example—of what to avoid, if one can't be the other sort." I truly do not regard myself as a model and example for anyone. The lives of all people without exception—with their searching, their gifts, and their mistakes—are unique and are of infinite value in God's eyes.

So be it, I eventually said. One should probably write one's reminiscences at an age when one's memory still functions, when one is still capable of remembering many things, and when eyewitnesses to those events are still alive.

Why should I tell my story once more now? I am standing on the threshold of old age and am becoming less and less concerned about what others might find interesting in my life. Instead I am starting to be more concerned about what will interest God when I stand before his judgment seat. And at that moment, what matters are the fruits of those years rather than the events of one's life; in other words, what one has matured into, what conclusions one has reached, what insights one has acquired, what one has learned, and, above all, in what way one has enriched the lives of others.

My Path to Faith

When the Communist regime fell in Czechoslovakia I moved to a new apartment close to one of the most beautiful bridges in Europe, Charles Bridge, in the very heart of Old Prague, a Gothic bridge flanked by Baroque sculptural groups. The place had long been dear to me: it recalled not only the glorious history of our country and city but also a bit of family history.

Charles Bridge, or rather the Clementinum, the former Jesuit college that stands directly opposite the Old Town bridge tower of Charles Bridge, has connections with my father's life. It is there, in the original seat of the Arts Faculty of Charles University, that my father studied in the late 1920s and early 1930s and where, in the 1950s, he worked as a bibliographer in the National Library. As a child, I would visit him there, most memorably on the morning of Christmas Eve. From there, every year, we would walk to some wine restaurant in the Old Town for lunch, stopping on the way to view the Christmas Crib at the Church of the Holy Savior. I expect I would have been more than amazed if someone had told me then that I would minister as a Catholic priest in that very church in forty years' time.

■ I AM DESCENDED FROM TWO OLD CHOD families on both my mother's and my father's side.* Both families came from Bavaria in the Middle Ages, and almost all of my ancestors—up to my parents' marriage—were settled in the town of Domažlice, close to the border with Bavaria. Nevertheless, several interesting individuals from both families made their names in Prague: from one of the families came the philosopher and natural scientist Emanuel Rádl and from the other Antonín Randa, "Privy Counsellor and Minister to His Majesty the Emperor," president of the Czech Academy of Sciences and the Arts, rector of Charles University, and founder of Czech jurisprudence. And during the revolution of 1848, my great-grandfather Jan Halík fought in the student legions against the troops of General Windischgrätz on the barricade under the Old Town bridge tower of Charles Bridge.

There is a legend in our family that some girl on the barricade, in a passionate gesture, pressed a dagger into my great-grandfather's hand and called on him to "avenge the nation." After the defeat of the revolution, Jan Halík was arrested and spent some time in prison. He then returned home to Domažlice and found unrevolutionary employment as a confectioner. He subsequently founded one of the oldest firms in Domažlice, became a respected burgher, and fathered ten children. Even so, he kept in touch with patriots and revolutionaries to the end of his days. After the defeat of the Great Poland Up-

---

* "The . . . Chods were a small community of peasant farmers who played a significant role along the south-western stretch of the Bohemian-Bavarian borderland between the fourteenth and the seventeenth centuries. Acting as pre-modern 'border guards' the Chods regulated trade and travel through the border region and engaged in the military defence of the frontier. Their loyalty was assured by a series of royal documents granting them a significant degree of political autonomy, economic prosperity and social stature. This privileged status, coupled with the relatively isolated nature of their existence, combined to facilitate the development of a distinct borderland identity among the Chods." Dr. Kelly Hignett, paper originally presented at the conference "From Borderland to Backcountry: Frontier Communities in Comparative Perspective," University of Dundee, July 5–7, 2009.

rising, he helped some Polish patriots escape across the border; the poet Mickiewicz might have been among them. Jan was also a friend and patron of the writer Josef Tyl, who wrote the words of the Czech national anthem.

■ MY FATHER FELT NO GREAT ATTACHMENT to the family confec-
tionery firm, and as a boy he had more of an intellectual bent. He edited student magazines, wrote verse, and was a regular public speaker
at the unveiling of memorial plaques and other cultural events in
the Chod region. His young years coincided with the beginnings
of the Czechoslovak Republic, and after its proclamation he even left
the Catholic Church, like many others. However, toward the end of
his life, he told me that the dean of the parish did not take the fleeting passions of adolescent boys too seriously and did not record his
decision in the parish register, so it wasn't validated. My father studied philosophy, Czech literature, and French at Charles University,
where his professors included F. X. Šalda and Josef Pekař, and Jan
Patočka and Julius Fučík were fellow students. He wrote his doctoral
thesis on the literature of the Czech Revival. After his studies in the
1930s he remained in Prague. It was not easy for intellectuals to find
work in those days, and he was no exception. My mother intervened
and helped find him a job as a librarian in the Prague Municipal Library; she was a very refined lady but could be forceful and strong-
minded when necessary. And so they were able to get married in the
mid-1930s, when they were both over thirty years old. My parents
moved into an apartment at Pankrác, in Prague, where I would spend
the first forty-two years of my life.

Father's closest friend was Count Zdeněk Bořek Dohalský, who
also hailed from the Chod region and came from an ancient noble
family with Hussite roots. Zdeněk introduced him to Prague's intellectual society. The entire Dohalský family had close ties with the cultural and political elite of the First Republic. Zdeněk was on the editorial board of the daily *Lidové noviny*, whose contributors included

the foremost Czech writers and journalists. His brother Antonín was a canon of Prague Cathedral and chancellor of the archbishopric, and his third brother, František, was a diplomat in London. During the Nazi occupation the entire family was persecuted. Zdeněk Bořek Dohalský was executed at the Theresienstadt concentration camp, and Antonín, the priest, died at Auschwitz.

It was Zdeněk who introduced my father to the most important Czech writer, playwright, and journalist of the day, Karel Čapek. Čapek died at Christmas 1938, shattered by the demise of Czechoslovak democracy, to which he had devoted his life. That year he was nominated for the Nobel Prize for Literature, but he died before the decision was made. On a proposal from Čapek's closest friend, Ferdinand Peroutka—a journalist and future director of Radio Free Europe in New York—my father was entrusted with processing Čapek's literary estate, and he became the editor of Čapek's works. This would become his main occupation for the rest of his life. He worked on Čapek's literary output for almost forty years, until his death in 1975. My mother assisted him enormously in this work, searching for articles in the archives and typing many texts. The times were not at all favorable for such activity. Several months after Čapek's death, the country was occupied by the Nazis, who closed down the archives and introduced restrictions in libraries. Thanks to his wide circle of acquaintances, my father was able to visit the archives in spite of the Nazis' ban and search there for texts by Čapek, which had been published in various journals under various pseudonyms and initials, so it was like detective work. On several occasions he seemed to hear Čapek whispering the names of journals to him, and this led to surprising discoveries. When he was preparing material for books, he would sometimes spread out all the texts in front of him and imagine Čapek advising him how to assemble them all. It was an extraordinary example of loyalty to a single personality, to a single author. Many of the books that are known to the world under the name Karel Čapek were never seen by the author during his lifetime. Had it not been for my father's lifelong dedication, most of those texts would have remained in the literary graveyards of old journals or in the Čapek archive of unpublished manuscripts. And yet my father's name was hidden in tiny type in editorial notes. There were some unexpected adventures related to that work. During the war, part of the Čapek archive was kept safe in a bank and part of it was kept at home by my father. After an air raid toward the end of the war, an unexploded bomb remained close to our home and all the residents were obliged to leave their apartments. Nevertheless, my father managed to sneak home and save Čapek's manuscripts and notes. So for him it was not cold scholarly interest but rather a sort of personal creed for which he was willing to sacrifice himself.

A great day in my life was the inauguration of the Čapek Brothers Museum at Malé Svatoňovice in June 1946, attended by President Beneš, which turned into a national demonstration and a demonstration of freedom after the war. My parents often recalled it as the most wonderful day of their lives. After a short postwar thaw came the 1950s, when Čapek virtually ceased to be published in Czechoslovakia. Only when a signal was received from Moscow that Soviet literary historians had started to study him were the Czech comrades obliged to treat the "bourgeois humanist" with greater tolerance and to have him published. Nonetheless, some of his writings could not be published until the Prague Spring of 1968, and some only after 1989. Thanks to my father's care, a score of volumes were published from Čapek's posthumous writings. They were translated into many languages and won readers all over the world; a Japanese princess, for instance, was one of the enthusiastic admirers of Čapek's works.

■ MY FATHER WAS AN ERUDITE, SLIGHTLY TIMID, modest, and extremely diligent man. Immersed from morning until night in his Čapek research, he was able to devote himself fully to me chiefly on Sundays and during holidays. From quite an early age I traveled around on his shoulders to Czech castles and other monuments, as well as to galleries, museums, and exhibitions, avidly lapping up the guides' commentaries, supplemented by my father's explanations. I expect that is why I have always had a penchant for history and everything connected with it. On one occasion we visited the town of Klatovy, where my father showed me the miraculous painting of the Black Madonna, who was said to have shed tears of blood. I was a little boy then, and I found that story very exciting. For the first time in my life I sensed something fascinating and also terrifyingly mysterious, something that Rudolf Otto would call a numinous feeling. Were I to try to reconstruct my earliest religious experience, I expect it would be that moment.

My father was by conviction a Masarykian humanist with positivist leanings, and he had a typical First Republic detachment regarding anything that went beyond the orbit of reason. He had one remarkable gift, however, the gift of intuitive perception and astonishing insights about future events. Our relatives used to relate that, in the middle of the Nazi occupation, my father predicted—and had it written down—that the war would end on May 8, 1945. Later, with a tinge of shy self-deprecation, he intimated to me what the Fates had told him about my future in a dream he said he had had on the day of my birth. So far it looks as if they were not far wrong.

Two years before my father's death in 1973, when I was on military training, we exchanged letters summing up our relationship. I thanked him for helping me find faith, in spite of being an "atheist," and for giving me the best religious upbringing by having been a good father. When I say the first words of the Lord's Prayer, or meditate about the father-son relationship in the Trinity, I know what the words mean. Their power derives from the deep experience of my father's relationship with me. "In that way you did more for me than if you had drummed the catechism into me," I wrote to him.

I valued the sincerity with which my father parted company with the church as a young man in the turbulent year 1918. Had he not done that, and instead simply observed tradition for social reasons and tried to hand on to me something he himself did not believe in, I would probably have been unable to accept such a formal religion or would have soon abandoned it. His sincere abandonment of the church gave me the space in which to sincerely discover faith and the church half a century later. I also wrote that to him and added that although faith is a very personal matter, I have a certain sense of receiving this gift "on his behalf."

After that, we tended to maintain a reserved mutual silence about such matters; such declarations are more easily made in writing than spoken, and probably only once in a lifetime. But I recall that shortly before his death my father attended Mass with me at St. Ignatius Church, and when I glanced back on my way out I saw my father kneeling for the first time in my life; I made no comment. And we both maintained silence about it.

My father and I often paid visits to Karel Čapek's widow, the actress Olga Scheinpflugová. What always particularly attracted me in Čapek's villa was the Friday Circle room, in which intellectuals associated with President Masaryk would meet every Friday. Since Masaryk's death no one had been allowed to sit in his armchair, and a vase of flowers was always placed on it. After the war Mrs. Scheinpflugová tried to revive the tradition, and in place of President Masaryk it was attended by his son Jan, who was then foreign minister. My father would also attend those meetings. He told me that several days before the Communist putsch in February 1948, Jan Masaryk came there and begged everyone to stick together, because things could happen that would be worse for Czech history than the battle of White Mountain in 1620. That was the last time my father saw him alive; on March 10, 1948, he died tragically in mysterious circumstances, his body found beneath the window of his office at the Foreign Ministry. Before my father died, he once told me a secret that Olga Scheinpflugová had divulged to him in 1948. She said that shortly after Jan Masaryk's death his valet had telephoned her and just managed to tell her it wasn't suicide before being cut off.

My parents never became involved with the Communist regime. After my mother's death I came upon an entry in her diary where she recorded something that happened when I was barely four years old. I had apparently responded to her announcement that we were going to the dentist by asking, "Are we going legally or illegally?" My mother's comment was, "The radio!" That diary entry isn't as amusing as it might seem: in those days the state radio used to broadcast for hours on end direct transmissions from the show trials of members of "illegal groups," in which tortured individuals confessed to the most dreadful crimes and asked to be given the severest sentences. What might seem amusing could have caused my parents enormous problems in those days. During the years of my early childhood, the Communists sent hundreds of innocent people to the gallows and hundreds of thousands to prison and labor camps. Fortunately my family avoided direct persecution. My father worked all his life as a librarian. Libraries initially were under the control of the Ministry of Information, where he started to work after the war, but in the early 1950s he transferred to the National Library at the Clementinum. The library was also a kind of "depository" for politically unreliable people; one of my father's colleagues was the widow of the executed Communist leader Vladimír Clementis. When my father told me this, I always felt the presence of the executioner when I was in her company. For a long time I had no idea that not far from our house, behind the imposing building of the Supreme Court, was Pankrác prison and its execution yard, where they executed a close acquaintance of our family, Dr. Milada Horáková, a hero of the anti-Nazi resistance, who had shortly afterward become a heroic opponent of the Communists. My home was an oasis of calm, however.

I grew up in a beautiful, large apartment full of books, sculpture, and pictures. I lived entirely among adults. My father's only brother was childless, and although my mother came from a family of six children, three of her siblings had not married. Only one of my mother's brothers, a member of the anti-Nazi resistance, who was tortured to death by the Gestapo during the war, left behind just one small son. Such a family case history suggests an atypical childhood.

I was happy in the world of adults. The many attempts to send me out to play with other children soon ended with my returning home bored. The year I spent in kindergarten, where I was supposed to become accustomed to other children, was a dreadful time of boredom for me; I hated the uniform sweatpants we wore and the group games. I would stand for hours looking out the window, impatient for my mother to take me home. In later years I would instinctively close my eyes when we passed by on a tram.

The bountiful and multicolored world I loved was the family drawing room surrounded by interesting visitors and the conversations of adults, which reverberated in my dreams and fantasies. I loved it when he had visitors. Only later, when I was in high school, did I realize that the people who formed part of my father's circle of friends and acquaintances, or whom I met when I was out with him, were among the great names of Czech culture: Vladimír Holan, Jaroslav Seifert, František Langer, Adolf Hoffmeister, František Kupka, Adolf Branald, and many others. Many researchers on Čapek's life and writings would also visit our apartment: from Poland and Russia and later from Japan and America. Professors from famous universities and young Czech students who were preparing their graduation theses or wanted to consult something from his Čapek archive were treated with equal concern by my father. It must have been around that time that I first met Václav Havel in person. I don't recall him from those days, but when Havel became a well-known playwright in the mid-1960s, my father recalled how he had visited us at home several times as a very modest young man with an interest in the work of Karel Čapek and of Čapek's brother Josef.

My parents bestowed on me an enormous amount of love and care, but they were wise and mature enough to make sure they didn't spoil me too much. From my earliest years I was provided with plenty of stimulus not only to make me think but also to encourage my emotional and aesthetic growth. They awoke in me a passion for learning that I have never lost, and they allowed me to enjoy the safety and beauty of the home. I never witnessed a quarrel between my parents. I expect that is the reason coarse behavior always makes me feel uneasy, and I don't know how to react to it. In fact, I am always ashamed on behalf of such people. Throughout my life I have truly found it very hard to abide vulgarity and bad manners.

My mother never worked outside the home. She was of great assistance to my father, but she chiefly devoted herself to housework and to my upbringing. At a time of "emancipation," her femininity was not contaminated by any masculine trait. I don't recall her ever wearing trousers, smoking, or using a swear word. Mom was a beautiful and generous woman, and a lady in the true sense of the word. She was also a person with a great social conscience. As a young child I already recognized one particular attribute: she was able to listen with her heart, to empathize with others, and to comfort and encourage everyone, so people would often confide their personal problems to her. It truly was unusual, because often these people were total strangers on a tram car who out of the blue would begin to recount their life stories and troubles to her.

My mother's brother, Uncle Josef, was a great influence on me. He was a bachelor, and he focused on me his longing to pass on something of worth to the next generation. I regarded the freedom of his bachelorhood, which he would sometimes boast about, as something like an aristocratic title: it was quite possibly an unconscious model for my future celibacy. Although he had not attended university, he was widely educated, and I learned to appreciate the value of Austrian-style classical Gymnasium schooling. Long before I started school I was able to read and write a bit, and my uncle helped me take my first small steps in Latin and Greek. He recounted old Czech legends to me, and the myths of the ancient world.

He also tried hard to compensate for the overemphasis on the arts in my upbringing on my father's side by encouraging my interest in nature and natural science. We used to go on long forest walks together, during which he would tell me about plants and animals. He would also take me to see the natural history collections of museums, and on our return home we would spend hours browsing through Brehm's *The Life of Animals* and encyclopedias of birds, fish, animals, plants, and minerals. However, history always interested me much more than nature, literature more than biology, and art galleries more than mineral collections. From my early years, we would go to the theater and the cinema together, and he would teach me from memory lots of poems, arias, and speeches from plays. He identified most of all with Cyrano de Bergerac and warned me against superficiality by quoting the unforgettable line, "I may not cut a stylish figure, but I hold my soul erect."

When a boy is growing up, it is particularly important for him to have a positive male role model in addition to his father, someone in whom he can confide about matters—particularly at a certain age—that he can't speak about with his parents. My uncle had a greater inclination than my parents to treat me as an adult and an equal, and I very much appreciated that. Only later did I discover in medieval chivalric literature the important role often played in a young man's life by his mother's younger brother. I think my uncle Josef was the first embodiment of the ideal of chivalry, which has been, in a sense, a pivotal image for me throughout my life.

He was also probably the first person to talk to me about religion. He was not a practicing Catholic, but he had fond memories of one of his catechists and of his time as an acolyte. I even fancy that he once mentioned that his mother would have liked him to go into the priesthood. Like many who grew up around 1918 he used to criticize the church in my presence, but he didn't become an atheist. I remember his words: "Some call it God, others nature, but let us respect one another." That was in the 1950s, when the regime's mouthpieces called religion an expression of mental backwardness and a tool of reactionaries. So he helped me take a small step toward a more positive attitude to faith and to believers.

My uncle was an ardent patriot, and I expect he was the first person to tell me about Jan Hus, as well as about the Hussite leader Jan Žižka and Jan Amos Komenský (Comenius), the Protestant bishop and pedagogue known as the "teacher of nations." We also talked about politics, and we regularly listened to the BBC's broadcasts in the depths of the 1950s, despite the risk that I might blurt out something at school. He even taught me some prayers from the Latin Mass because it was "part of a general education." Much later, when I was about twenty, he was very cross with me for converting to Catholicism. However, he became reconciled to it over the years, and in one of our last conversations he urged me solemnly, now that I belonged to the church, to do what I could to make the church tolerant of others' opinions and to stop Catholics from regarding Hus as a heretic. Having been an avid reader all his life, his eyesight became steadily worse with age, and he died in an institute for the blind when I was twenty-six. I deeply regret not having devoted as much time to him in his declining years as he did to me when I was a boy.

WHEN A WOMAN JOURNALIST ONCE ASKED ME if I already wanted to be a priest when I was a child, I told her I had wanted to be a polar bear. Later in my childhood I made a slight concession and opted for polar explorer. I had scarcely learned to read than I was already devouring books about expeditions to the world of eternal ice, and scarcely had I learned to write than I was writing a fictional travelogue titled "Science of the North." I really had no inkling at the time that almost fifty years later I would unexpectedly be given the opportunity to take part in an adventurous journey to the world of icebergs—but to the south, to Antarctica. We should be careful about what we earnestly wish for, because such wishes have a habit of coming true but mostly at a different time and in a different way from what we imagined and planned.

Then for a while I had an interest in astronomy and would attend a club at the planetarium where I learned to recognize the constellations. My parents and my uncle supported all my interests, so I attended drawing classes and took private singing lessons, and so on. They accepted my aversion to sports and games; I found physical education classes the most grueling part of school, because I was extremely clumsy. I confess that I have never been to a football match or any other sporting event in my life. Only once, in January 1969, did I watch an ice hockey match on television, when Czechoslovakia was playing against the Soviet Union, but that had nothing at all to do with sports: it was several months after the Soviet invasion, and it was a political sociodrama with a psychotherapeutic effect. That match was followed by turbulent all-night celebrations on the street. As a result of that explosion of people's real feelings about the Soviet occupation forces, the Soviets reacted immediately by replacing the general secretary of the Communist Party, Alexander Dubček, who symbolized the Prague Spring, with the acquiescent pro-Soviet Gustáv Husák.

Sometime when I was in the fourth grade, I developed a passion for history, which lasted many years. In those days I devoured historical novels, both Czech and foreign, including Jirásek and Sienkiewicz. As a child the Hussite movement was the subject that interested me most. From my earliest years Uncle Josef had told me stories about Jan Hus with great passion. Then I became fascinated with the atmosphere of the Hussite wars. This was all reflected in my first literary experiments, from the fifth grade until I graduated from high school. I adopted as my watchword *nulla dies sine linea*—"not a day without a line"—and for a good number of years while I was in school I would sit down and write at least one symbolic line at home every day regardless of how much homework I had, and I would do so not only on schooldays. I actually wrote a historical novel in five parts titled "Ripening," which was set in the Hussite period. That was also when I made my "debut" in the media. At the age of eleven I read from from my novel on a young people's radio show, and I talked about my hobbies. Every July 5, on the eve of the anniversary of Hus's execution, I would put together a small display of pictures and books and hold a kind of private viewing for my parents, neighbors, and classmates, at which I would give a speech. I can even remember as a young boy staying awake on the night of July 5, trying to empathize with what Master Jan endured before he was burned to death. Looked at in hindsight, I must have been a romantic screwball as a child.

For years, all my father's acquaintances, as well as my teachers and fellow pupils, took it for granted that this pubescent boy was destined to be a historian of the Hussite movement and a writer of historical novels. I started to prepare myself systematically for my "writing activity," and my father was a great supporter of my interests; in fact, he introduced me painlessly to the scientific method. He taught me how to create card files and archives, so as a small boy I was compiling card files of facts about the Hussite movement and its leading figures. When I discovered my childhood archive twenty years later, I was astounded to see how detailed it was. I used to visit places linked with Hussism, cut out and paste items, arrange postcards, and even collect soil from Hussite battlefields. I also bought a dictionary of Old Czech and became engrossed in it. I almost lived in a fictional world. Matters subsequently took a very different course, but in a certain sense I have never betrayed the boy of those days.

In some ways, my literary activity was a means of coping with the problems of growing up. Around the age of puberty I found the writings of Sigmund Freud in my father's library, as well as a popular textbook on psychoanalysis; I became immersed in the latter, and it engaged my attention even more than when I had previously come across a magazine with nude pictures. It's hard to say how much I understood about psychoanalysis at the time, or whether it had any influence on my psychosexual development. Throughout my youth I was an introvert. I tended to be shy in my contacts with girls and unlikely to take the initiative. Eventually I learned to overcome my embarrassment by witty conversation and became quite popular with girls. I would treat them with a kind of chivalrous gallantry, which most of them were unaccustomed to in those days, so they were the ones who ended up embarrassed. I used to fall in love, of course, and it was always a fairly dramatic experience for me. However, because of all the things I have already said about myself, it tended to be platonic in character and usually ended that way too.

At school I was already inspired by opposition figures: "dissidents" who were opposed to the crowd mentality, the majority viewpoint, and the powers that be; those who rejected prejudice, "public opinion," and official ideologies. I expect that is how, as a boy, I perceived Hus and how I later viewed Masaryk in his struggle against anti-Semitism during the Hilsner affair (the Czech parallel of the Dreyfus case) and Karel Čapek in the period toward the end of his life when he was hounded by the public and by the right-wing nationalist and Catholic press. Maybe one of the first seeds of my conversion was the English film *Becket*. I was captivated by the figure of Thomas à Becket as a bishop standing up courageously to the king, the barbarous noblemen, and the collaborationist, self-serving clergy. I could never bear injustice, and at school I stood up for the those who were treated unfairly. The teachers used to call me the "poor man's lawyer."

With an atypical childhood like mine, I have had to cope throughout my life with a certain sense of exclusiveness and a tendency to excessive self-preoccupation. It wasn't until many years later, during my psychotherapeutic training, that I started to make a bit of progress with it. I had never been selfish in a primitive way. Indeed my parents had taught me to be kind to others, and my mother endowed me with the ability to empathize with others and feel genuine sympathy. But as an only child I never had that spontaneous feeling for others and their needs that children of large families naturally have. The experience of sharing with siblings opens up the world in a different way. I was always self-centered, and I expect I have never completely rid myself of that, although I would later become very aware of it, and it always distressed me. In spite of our lifelong efforts to free ourselves from them, there are failings and limitations that, to our shame, we encounter in ourselves over and over again and that we must bear as a cross.

Although my family surroundings offered me so much in terms of cultured thinking, behavior, and experience, I also lacked the experience of solidarity with my peers. Perhaps membership in a scout troop would have helped me, but scouting was banned in those days— the leaders of the scouting movement were in jail—and the compulsory children's organization—the Pioneers, the children's section of the Communist youth movement—was no substitute of course.

Around puberty I started consciously to protest against the socialist drabness of life in those days by the way I behaved and dressed. I tried to act the English gentleman and liked wearing a three-piece suit and tie and a hat and carrying an umbrella. I dreamed of having a full beard when I grew up and smoking a pipe, like a proper intellectual. I must have cut a fairly comical figure. I discovered how small children could be allergic to difference, but when I reached high school the other children started to appreciate my nonconformist taste, and as the years passed they not only tolerated it, but actually supported me.

■ I HAVE A VAGUE MEMORY OF TELEVISION IMAGES of the suppression of the Hungarian Uprising in November 1956, when I must have been in the second grade. My father spoke about how the Communist regime would one day collapse, and Mom scolded him for talking about it in my hearing. Politics was not spoken about much at home in those days. I suspected that my parents' attitudes conflicted with the school's ideology, but it did not interest me too much during my childhood.

I first became avidly interested in politics when I was sixteen or seventeen. I started to listen regularly to Western radio stations, particularly Voice of America and Radio Free Europe, and read Masaryk's writings on democracy. I put an American flag in my bedroom (one that my parents had acquired in spring 1945 when the U.S. Army liberated western Bohemia and had later hidden away), together with a photograph of Winston Churchill. There was a group of us at school; we used to lend each other banned literature and debate about a future democratic system in Czechoslovakia, and we even dreamed of establishing secret opposition parties. On the anniversary of Masaryk's death we would visit his grave at Lány near Prague; later, during the Prague Spring, in March 1968, I organized a hike to Masaryk's grave by several hundred students. That interest in politics was one of the factors that pushed my childhood fascination with Hussism into the background.

At high school I started to take a great interest in philosophy, and it is possible that I originally came to it thanks to my interest in Masaryk and politics. That was one of the reasons why, just before my final examinations, I rather surprised people by opting to study sociology and philosophy instead of history. At that time I started to read Nietzsche, and I have returned to his writings repeatedly at various periods of my life.

That was the beginning of the 1960s. A breath of freedom started to be felt in cultural circles in spite of the regime. New films were appearing, along with small-scale theaters and exhibitions of abstract art. The occasional lecture on sociology, modern literature, or philosophy took place—something previously unheard of. There was a wave of interest in Kafka and existentialism. Prague's intellectual circles were increasingly coming alive. Articles with critical barbs started to appear in *Literární noviny* (Literary News), attacking the "personality cult," as Stalinism was called in those days. People read articles and books by Ludvík Vaculík, Milan Kundera, Ivan Klíma, and Ladislav Mňačko. I had little interest, however, in the new wave of pop music, and the Beatles, the Beatnik movement, and hippies didn't particularly appeal to me.

I attended one of the first performances of plays by Václav Havel, including "The Memorandum" and "The Garden Party." My fellow students from those days still recall how provocative I was in high school: I would give enthusiastic reports of Havel's plays, and in one literature lesson I actually read Karel Čapek's essay "Why I Am Not a Communist." After John F. Kennedy's assassination I came to school with a black armband and went to the U.S. embassy to sign the book of condolence. I also put an obituary of Kennedy on the notice board in our classroom, which led to a scandal, of course. But by then a number of the high school teachers sympathized with the opposition. The regime of President Antonín Novotný became the butt of hundreds of political jokes, and people were losing their fear of the Communists. This was no longer the 1950s. The regime was no longer "the iron fist of the proletariat" but seemed instead to consist of ludicrous bloated bureaucrats confronted by long-haired and bearded intellectuals in black sweaters with feelings of alienation in their heads and the books of Franz Kafka under their arms.

The balance of power in society had altered considerably. Of course, there was still the secret police, but at least we youngsters did not come into conflict with them much, and they did not make their presence felt to the same degree as in former years. There were fewer cases of political imprisonment, and it was mostly writers who had problems with them. Some high-profile writers' congresses were held, and speeches by opposition authors, as well as other interesting texts, began to circulate among the people. However, the phenomenon of samizdat (clandestine publication of books and magazines) did not exist yet, nor did political dissent of great influence as there would be in the 1970s and 1980s.

At that time an unauthorized student May Day gathering used to take place every year in the gardens at the top of Petřín hill in Prague. Antiregime slogans were chanted, and the gatherings often developed into a demonstration, which would be dispersed by the police. I took part in it several times between the ages of fourteen and seventeen. It caused a lot of fuss at home because it involved some risk, of course. Once, when I was about fifteen, I insisted on attending, so my mother accompanied me, although by then she was elderly. She walked behind me at a discreet distance, but then the police arrived with dogs and water cannons and attacked us with truncheons. We were lucky enough to escape unscathed.

My teens were hardly idyllic: the spirit of my revolutionary great-grandfather and the heritage of proud Chod rebels sometimes rose up within me. But my youthful conflict with Communism chiefly took the more peaceful form of private study of philosophy, whereby I yearned to develop my own, independent viewpoint.

■ WHEN I STARTED TO WRITE YOUTHFUL philosophizing essays (which gave way to historical novels in the course of my time at high school), religious themes spontaneously emerged for the first time. I began to acknowledge some transcendent life principle, although it was still far removed from the gospel and the Catholic Church in particular.

I was about seventeen when I started to show an avid interest in religions of every kind. But it was quite a long time before I opted for Christianity. I had absolutely no experience of the living church. However, I was well informed about the historical facts; I had a long-standing fascination with the Middle Ages and its spiritual world, but for a long time I viewed Catholicism "with Hussite eyes" as negative. And I totally failed to take into account that the Catholic Church was alive in my country. Indeed, as far as I was concerned, the church was something exotically medieval that possibly survived somewhere, in the same way that rare examples of practically extinct species of flora or fauna survived somewhere. I possibly overheard something on the radio about the opening of some council or other in Rome, and I saw on television a shot of the funeral of John XXIII, but I didn't relate to it in any way.

When "some kind of God" started to appear more frequently in my essays on philosophical texts—such as Rádl's *Consolation from Philosophy*, some of Plato's dialogues, and Unamuno's *Tragic Sense of Life*—it did not occur to me that it had anything in common with the church or that I perhaps ought to seek out a priest and discuss it with him. That first phase of my "conversion" took the form of a kind of shift toward a philosophical life.

There was one powerful experience associated with it. I remember one evening on a school trip to the mountains, our teacher broke into peals of laughter that someone would bring a book called *The Tragic Sense of Life* on a ski trip. The next morning during skiing lessons I slipped away, removed my skis, and went for a walk alone in the snowy landscape. As I trudged along, it struck me that this solitariness, in the sense of an inability to join in collective merrymaking, would perhaps be my fate for the rest of my life. But what started as an oppressive feeling was immediately transformed into a sort of blissful realization that at the very center of that solitude there was Someone with me, who would lead me and never abandon me—and in a certain way I entrusted my life to him. Later, when I read the *Confessions* of St. Augustine, or Thomas Merton's autobiography *The Seven Storey Mountain*, that experience of a vague rudimentary prayer came strongly to mind again.

A friend and I were in northern Bohemia during one vacation and I started to read the Bible—from the very beginning. This is the usual mistake of potential converts. They have no one to tell them that the Bible is not "a book" but rather a library, and so, without any explanation of its structure, they start to read it as a novel and generally give up somewhere in those interminable passages of liturgical regulations in Leviticus. They have no one to tell them that if they are seeking an answer to the question whether there is a God, they should not seek it in the Bible, because the Bible neither poses nor answers the question whether God exists.

Nevertheless, the Lord would seem to have understanding of this gesture of first reaching for the Bible. And so such fledgling readers of scripture, even if they seldom learn much from their own reading, begin on their own to reflect more on God and relate to him, and these reflections lead to the first tentative steps along the path of prayer and contemplation.

That is what happened to me. I discovered that there was a pilgrimage site in that beautiful but abandoned Sudeten countryside not far away, and I made a whole-day pilgrimage to it. I took just a loaf of bread and spent the day traveling to a ruined and padlocked hilltop church and back again. During my journey I wanted to decide whether or not I believed in God. Maybe something really did happen during that walk, some sort of transition from intellectual interest to personal faith. On that hilltop I said the Lord's Prayer and asked God to give me light. I returned with the feeling that I truly believed in God.

■ IN RETROSPECT I ASK MYSELF to what extent my first turning toward religion was part of the political protest of those days. Of course, like many other young people, I too started to sympathize a priori with everything that the Communists railed against. I looked for all available literature about St. Augustine and Thomas Aquinas, and no doubt what attracted me to them in the first instance was the fact that they were called religious obscurantists by the Marxists.

In the mid-1960s I eagerly read Chesterton's *Orthodoxy* during a Christmas vacation. The very fact that he was a friend of Čapek's appealed to me, but there was also my fondness for the culture of the English-speaking world, with its intellectual humor, mental games, and love of paradox. Chesterton delighted me with his provocative treatment of modern prejudices, his polemical art, and his brilliant ability to look at things from a surprisingly different angle. That book showed me I could find a home in Christianity, and it helped me to articulate my own philosophy. "Dogma" ceased to be a bugaboo and a synonym for mental rigidity and became instead an interesting and exciting world.

Sometime before I completed high school, I started attending organ concerts at St. James's Church with a friend. The large attendance of young people at such concerts was certainly an expression of ideological and cultural opposition, albeit not entirely conscious in most cases. But at the same time it was also—and not just for me, I'm sure—fascination with a world of mystery, beauty, and the spirit—everything that the drabness of the "real socialism" of those days could not offer us.

Concerts also took place as part of the Mass, and although the music dominated and the liturgy was something distant and incomprehensible (preconciliar, sotto voce, in Latin, in the depths of the choir, backs to the congregation), it nonetheless took place in a church context. I wanted to understand what was happening in the church. At home I even dug out an old Latin missal and started to read about the structure of worship. But my interest still tended to be cultural rather than an expression of my own religious belief.

■ AT THAT TIME, ONE OF MY CLASSMATES informed me that there was an interesting priest at the Týn Church on the Old Town Square who gave terrific, witty sermons in which he even quoted Karel Čapek. That took me aback. What was a Catholic priest doing quoting Čapek? So I started leaving St. James's Church before the end of Mass in time to catch the sermon at the nearby Týn Church. I had an immediate liking for Fr. Jiří Reinsberg, the priest in question. If he had gone around in a clerical collar like some "reverend father" in old films we would have immediately written him off. But because he was unconventional we started to wonder what actually constituted priesthood, what was the X factor that turned that modern man, who always wore everyday clothes and with whom we could largely identify, into a priest? It was clearly not a black clerical gown, a reserved tone of voice, or a pious inclination of the head.

Although a political thaw of sorts was under way at that time, priests were still under strict surveillance. Any contact with young people could immediately lead to the cancellation of their official permission to perform clerical activity and choosing between manual labor or attending regular police interrogations involving blackmail and coercion to collaborate with the secret police. The Týn Church, however, was an exception, in a certain sense; it was one of those "display windows" for tourists, allowing them to see a functioning church in the center of Prague and conclude we had religious freedom.

Although he was diligently spied on, Father Reinsberg had never been sent to prison, unlike many of his colleagues and friends. Maybe it was because of the "display window" factor, or because the police took account of the fact that Reinsberg's brother was a prewar Communist who was tortured to death in a concentration camp. Possibly the police wanted to have one place under close surveillance where they could take note of goings-on without intervening, or maybe Father Reinsberg had a capable guardian angel. It's hard to say. His sermons always displayed an intellectual style and humor, and from time to time they had an antiregime slant, or at least we wanted to perceive it as such. And the liturgy was not the same as at St. James's Church, where it tended to be a supplement to the music.

Gradually, Sunday by Sunday, I shifted from my safe distance near the church door, pillar by pillar, closer and closer to the pulpit and the altar. Today I smile when I see someone who comes just for the sermon standing with arms folded near the door before leaving. The next time they come a little closer and stay longer, and then a little closer. Just like I did fifty years ago.

I remember the first time I knelt during Mass. When I tell it these days to young converts they smile, because they are all familiar with it. It takes enormous courage for new believers to kneel or make the sign of the cross in public; they feel as if the entire congregation is looking at them and judging them.

▮ BY 1966, THE YEAR I GRADUATED from high school and moved on to the Arts Faculty of Charles University, the church was no longer simply a romantic appurtenance of the Middle Ages but had assumed the form of Father Reinsberg and the young people at the Týn Church. I was gradually making up my mind to take the next step of faith: to go to confession and communion. I didn't know much about any of it; I had many questions and personal concerns: the need for a life change, for cleansing, a need to go deeper. It seemed to me that a whole-life confession could be the threshold to the new way of life that I longed for.

But in those days none of my friends was a truly practicing Christian. I mixed with "sympathizers," who noticed with surprise that my interest in religion was rather more than fashionable protest and was assuming a more personal character. My conversion continued to proceed more through books and reflection than under the influence of a specific person and through their witness and example. Father Reinsberg, whom I observed from a distance, inspired my confidence that the church could have a human face, but it was not he who "converted" me in the true sense of the word. I don't how much I was aware at that time that conversion means something quite different, that it is more profound than simply deciding that Christian teaching is true and wanting to be part of that tradition, wanting to attend church and do the things that Catholics usually do, including moderate observation of the Ten Commandments.

Only much later did I recognize the truth of the simile that conversion is something like sunrise. After all, sunrise is not simply experiencing some new object—the orb of the sun—appearing in the sky before our eyes, but rather suddenly seeing everything differently than at night. Similarly, when God enters our lives, he is not simply a quantity to be added to the "things" that we have become aware of in some way; rather we suddenly see everything in a different light, and our understanding of the world is totally changed.

During the long vacation after graduation from high school I finally made up my mind, and in mid-September 1966 I went to see Father Reinsberg. I gathered my courage and entered the sacristy after Mass. I told him I would like to go to confession and communion for the first time. "Well, that's one for the book!," was his reply. He invited me into the parish office and asked me about my studies, and then we talked for a while about philosophy and Freud. We agreed that I would come the following Wednesday, which happened to be the Feast of St. Wenceslas, the main patron saint of the Czech nation, and the day before my official matriculation at the university.

That afternoon I went to confession and then walked up to the castle, and I took communion for the first time after the Mass for St. Wenceslas at St. Vitus Cathedral, which was celebrated by Bishop Tomášek. I clearly remember praying in the St. Wenceslas chapel after Mass and how the Gothic statue of St. Wenceslas in knightly armor had a new meaning for me. "Yes, I want to be a knight for Christ," I said to myself at that moment; I want to remain faithful, come what may. I realized how poorly prepared I was, in fact. I was a bit like Abraham setting out on his journey without knowing where I was heading. But I had a very vivid sense of something—or rather Someone—entering my life, that a gate had opened and I had crossed a new threshold.

■ JIŘÍ REINSBERG MADE A DEEP IMPRESSION on my life. I would visit him at the sacristy of the Týn Church with my friends, particularly Pavel Bratinka. In between hundreds of anecdotes and humorous stories he imparted to me in dribs and drabs the truths of faith, so I was able to complete a kind of informal preparation for communion. He was a truly joyful person, although I had the impression that he would tell those well-known cascades of anecdotes when he wanted to draw a curtain between himself and other people, in order to think his own thoughts.

Throughout his life Father Reinsberg was surrounded by intellectuals, and maybe he was convinced for some reason of the need to rebuke them incessantly. I expect he didn't want them to become too proud: spare the rod and spoil the child. At that time he treated us beginners and students with indulgence, but subsequently I was treated to more than a fair share of his criticism, and especially after I became a priest, for which he above all was responsible. But at the same time I knew he had a paternal fondness for me and prayed for me, and whenever anyone started to criticize me in his presence, they would get a more severe dressing down than I used to get. Later I served him as an acolyte and was thus introduced to the liturgy by someone who loved it and was a great authority on it, as he was one of the pioneers of postconciliar liturgical reforms in our country. During my years at the faculty I would drop by after midday Mass and accompany him to Podolí, where he lived, in our immediate neighborhood.

On the way he would tell me so many things about the faith and the church—accompanied, of course, by many anecdotes and stories—that it amounted to my first course in theology and a seminar to boot, and it was pretty good. It was nice watching how he was constantly greeted by people and how he would react to them in a lively and witty fashion, having become, over those many years, a distinctive figure, a fixture of Old Prague, knowing the history of every house. When someone gives me a friendly wink, nod, or greeting, I realize that I too am now a fixture of Old Prague, and in many respects I continue to plow the same furrow as "Father Jiří." It is not my custom to imitate people but sometimes during the canon of the Mass, or during my sermon, or at confession, I catch myself spontaneously using his intonation or turn of phrase, and I can't help smiling. I no longer live alone, Reinsberg lives in me!

IN 1967 I WAS CONFIRMED AT VYŠEHRAD at Pentecost by Bishop Tomášek. It was a day of enormous significance for me. There was a full moon the night after my confirmation. I awoke in the middle of the night, knelt down, and started to pray. And I had the feeling that I had previously only had a naive notion of what prayer is. There is an enormous difference between pious reflection on a religious topic and the moment when one addresses God from the depth of one's heart. Similarly, but many years later, I was to discover another enormous difference: between addressing God and silently reposing in God—in the silence of God. On that occasion, on the night after my confirmation, I simply realized, with a somewhat surprised smile, that these sacraments really work.

THREE

The Spring That Turned into Winter

In the mid-1960s, the years before I completed my high school education, I abandoned my plan to study history. I no longer spent my time exclusively in the archives and in Old Prague but also started to frequent the student pubs in the Malá Strana district below the castle. Everywhere we drank a modicum of beer and engaged in highly intellectual conversation, often also about politics, philosophy, and belief. Occasionally some mysterious and interesting individuals would find their way into our pubs and tell us students all sorts of things, such as about the prisons and concentration camps in Czechoslovakia in the 1950s. It's hard to say how many secret police informers were around in those days. I vividly remember how, in the famous U Fleků pub—it happened to be first day of May just before the student May celebrations—an unassuming old fellow joined us; he suddenly turned to me and said, although he had never set eyes on me before, "You must study sociology! Here's a name for you to remember: Max Scheler, an interesting author!"

When I arrived home afterward I said to myself that it was actually a good idea. Sociology answers the questions I was then asking, which were related to philosophy, history, politics, and religion. And wasn't Masaryk a professor of sociology? When I discovered in the dictionary that Max Scheler was a Catholic thinker who concerned himself with the philosophy of values and that he was one of the founders of the sociology of knowledge, there was no more to be said. Sociology suddenly seemed to me an appropriate synthesis of all my previous interests.

I silently thanked the venerable soothsayer, and the Lord for sending him, and in 1966 I applied to the sociology faculty, which had only recently reopened. We were the first real students of the discipline, which for a long time had been declared a bourgeois pseudo-science. I passed the entrance exam—oral tests had never troubled me—and was overjoyed to be accepted into the Arts Faculty, majoring in sociology and philosophy.

The mid-1960s were a time when Marxism-Leninism was quietly neglected. Our teachers first converted from *Das Kapital* of the older Marx to the economic and philosophical writings of the younger Marx, and then they mostly deviated into existentialism, psychoanalysis, phenomenology, and other "Western" philosophical schools, although officially these studies were presented as "a critique of bourgeois philosophy and sociology." Discussion took place about Parsons, Bell, Dahrendorf, Schelsky, Fromm (who later gave a lecture at our faculty), Marcuse, and the Frankfurt school. At that period of ideological thaw in the second half of the 1960s, when I was at university, official Marxism was either transformed into Euro-Marxism or openly ignored. Later, during "normalization" after the Soviet-led invasion of August 1968, pragmatists and opportunists hid behind Marxist clichés while believing in nothing. By then Marxism, the regime's official doctrine, was no more than a commodity for which there wasn't the least demand, having long lost any attraction or worth. By the 1960s, there were far fewer convinced Marxist intellectuals in the "East" than there were in the West.

I enjoyed the golden age of the Arts Faculty—probably its most productive period of the past half century. Heading the chair of philosophy in those days were the esteemed professors Karel Kosík and Milan Machovec. I attended Machovec's Marxist-Christian dialogue seminar, which was visited by well-known theologians, including, if I'm not mistaken, Gustav Wetter and Klemens Tillmann; in spring 1968 it also received a visit from Karl Rahner. During my first years at university, the Arts Faculty was already one of the most fertile seedbeds of the Prague Spring.

In my first year I fulfilled a dream I had had in high school: I set up a debating club and was elected its first chairman. Even before 1968 its first foreign guests were young members of the Polish opposition, including Adam Michnik, with whom I would form a firm friendship thirty years later. If my memory serves me right, there was also a brief visit from Rudi Dutschke or someone else from his New Left circle. In autumn 1967, I started to move in student opposition circles. The student opposition, which subsequently played a major role in the events of 1968, had ties with intellectuals associated with the writers' union weekly, *Literární noviny*, and the literary magazine *Tvář*, particularly Václav Havel.

■ SPRING 1968 WAS THE SPRING OF MY LIFE, the spring of my faith, and a new spring for the church in the wake of the Second Vatican Council. Everything around us and within us was imbued with the intoxicating springtime scent of hope for a loosening of the political system and greater freedom. The fact that we were around the age of twenty meant we were more disposed to resonate with the spirit of the times that bubbled like new wine, permeated with all sorts of radical notions and postadolescent naïveté.

Only much later did many of us realize the international significance of 1968, which we chiefly perceived in the light of the dramatic local events associated with the Prague Spring and the subsequent Russian occupation. Preoccupied by what was of immediate concern to us, we tended to be only marginally aware of the student unrest in Western Europe, the assassinations of Martin Luther King Jr. and Robert Kennedy, or the escalation of the Vietnam War.

We chiefly read what was briefly available thanks to more liberal local censorship, but we were only vicariously aware of the cultural mentality of the "second Enlightenment," which started to emanate from art and philosophy around that year. In hindsight it strikes me that the yearning to shake the existing order and breathe deeply of freedom, which inspired students in particular on both sides of the Iron Curtain in such different ways, was the dying breath of European modernity, which had dominated the West since the French Revolution. It was probably Marxism's last chance to present itself without the Stalinist straitjacket. In Czechoslovakia it took the form of "socialism with a human face," while in the West it inspired the New Left, as part of that remarkable antiauthoritarian trinity Marx-Nietzsche-Freud, which led students—disciples of Sartre and Marcuse—to the barricades. The outcome was paradoxical: many of the slogans, values, and symbols of that revolt against the world of consumption and old systems soon became consumer goods.

If there is anywhere that we can trace the shift from modernity to postmodernity, then it is probably 1969, after the debacle of liberalization tendencies in the Soviet bloc and the pacification of the student revolts in the West. Later, in the underground seminars of the 1970s, we read with great sympathy the French "new philosophers," who emerged from the ranks of disenchanted former Marxists. We were very interested to see what would come out of that rejection of Marxism, and of the entire Enlightenment tradition of European modernity, and whether it would not simply be nostalgia for premodern culture.

◼ I ENCOUNTERED ECUMENICAL INITIATIVES not long after my conversion. Prior to the Prague Spring, I attended regular ecumenical meetings in the Protestant theological seminary in Prague, where leading Protestant and Catholic intellectuals discussed with each other. That unique island of freedom existed only because it had the blessing of the renowned Protestant J. L. Hromádka, who was for years dean of the Comenius Theological Faculty and had received a Lenin Prize. Although (at least formally) Catholics constitute over 90 percent of professing Christians in the Czech lands, the cultural mentality and consciousness of national identity are strongly influenced by Protestant tradition. One cannot understand Czechs—including Czech Catholics—without understanding Hussism and Utraquism. "Shake a Czech priest, and a Hussite will fall out," Slovak priests used to say. That is an extreme exaggeration, and a ridiculous generalization, of course, but the assertion does contain a small grain of truth.

Under the Communist regime, the Czech Protestant churches—and particularly the largest of them, the Evangelical Church of the Czech Brethren—enjoyed relatively greater freedom than the majority Catholic Church. The Communists always concentrated their harassment on the majority church, and in their eyes the Catholic Church was particularly dangerous because its leadership was in Rome; in other words, it was out of their reach and could not be manipulated. The Protestant church, which seemed less of a danger to the lords and masters and much more loyal—particularly in the person of Professor Hromádka, one of its leading authorities—was allowed to pursue various activities not permitted to the Catholic church, such as different kinds of meetings, youth fellowships, and Bible classes, and some clergy were allowed to study at theological faculties abroad. Many Protestant pastors generously opened their doors to Catholics, even at the risk of difficulties and harassment. So many of the activities that could not take place within the framework of the Catholic Church took place in semi-legality in an ecumenical spirit. As a result, it is possible that in those days I had a better idea of modern Protestant theology than I had of contemporary Catholic "new theology" (which was inaccessible and unfamiliar to us). I started to read the writings of outstanding Protestant theologians, particularly Bonhoeffer and Tillich, which greatly influenced me.

The first Catholic authors I read after Chesterton were Jacques Maritain and Romano Guardini. It wasn't until the Prague Spring that I had access to books published by the exile Czech Christian Academy in Rome or books smuggled to us through various channels—by Teilhard de Chardin, Karl Rahner, Hans Küng, Thomas Merton, and others.

My more systematic study of theology commenced with Ratzinger's *Introduction to Christianity* and Kasper's *Coming to Faith*. But for many years I was escorted along my journey to faith by novels rather than theological writings: the books of Graham Greene, Heinrich Böll, Francois Mauriac, and Georges Bernanos. And when I introduced others to the world of faith I also preferred to lend them similar literature rather than the catechism.

■ JUST BEFORE THE PRAGUE SPRING ARRIVED I made my first trip to the West. Although I have used the metaphor of a bridge to characterize my life, I don't like people speaking about my country as "a bridge between East and West"—as President Beneš was wont to do after World War II. In terms of my entire mentality, cultural focus, and political and spiritual makeup I belong to the West, and I have never concealed my unequivocal pro-Western inclinations. I have always believed it my task to make every effort to make at least a small contribution so that my country would assume its proper place within Europe, and within Western culture.

My first direct contact with the West was not particularly encouraging, however. It was a student exchange with the Catholic university of Tilburg in autumn 1967—a harbinger of the relaxation that would arrive the following spring. I was greatly looking forward to experiencing a Catholic university for the first time. When we arrived in Holland we found ourselves right at the center of post-Vatican II ferment. I subsequently heard that little, traditional Holland had been chosen with Vatican consent to be a sort of laboratory for a bold pastoral experiment in the spirit of Vatican II. For the first time in my life I saw modern churches and libraries full of religious literature and discovered names of authors I had never heard of before. I had already read Jacques Maritain and his *Integral Humanism* at home; it was published by the Christian Academy in Rome. Those were the ideas I was familiar with at that time. I immediately asked the Dutch students if they had any books by Maritain and Mounier. They burst out laughing, saying that such authors had not been read for thirty years. They reeled off the names of the new theologians, such as Schillebeeckx, Chenu, Küng, and others of whom I hadn't the slightest inkling. They also told me that there was to be a discussion that very evening on the topic, "God Is Dead and Has Now Left His Mausoleum: The Catholic Church." Their student chaplain had married, and they were organizing a demonstration against the bishop in his support. That was all really too hard for me to take.

It was a classic case of culture shock like the one that many Czech Catholics—clergy and laity alike—suffered a quarter of a century later, when the borders opened after the collapse of Communism. A similar shock continues to color the attitude of some Christians in the East to the Western churches. Psychology also played a role: those Dutch colleagues were also trying to provoke me a bit, and my resentful reaction was not solely a defense of the church's tradition but also self-defense in a way, because in the face of an unfamiliar world I felt a bit like a hayseed. They had long since read and knew the authors that I had only just enthusiastically discovered and knew other things that were unfamiliar to me. Faced with the unknown, one often has a tendency to take distrustful umbrage in defense of one's own identity. But they also blocked the possibility of dialogue by failing to ask about my church and its experience. They assumed a priori that a foreigner from the "Eastern bloc" was a trifle primitive.

But would I have been capable in those days of reflecting on the situation of my own church and explaining it in a comprehensible fashion? After all, self-awareness calls for knowledge of the other, which is a condition for understanding the identity of one's own surroundings and accepting oneself, without any need to argue one's side or belittle the other. "They should take a lesson from us, not we from them," I said to myself that time. I now know that we must learn from each other, but it is necessary first of all to break down the wall of mutual prejudice.

It is not surprising that the young wine of Catholic neomodernism shocked me in those days. Naturally those of us who had lived under the pressure of the Communist regime were not at all accustomed to students of a Catholic university criticizing bishops, the authority of the church, or the Vatican. When the church is subjected to harsh external pressure it understandably behaves like an army unit in the trenches: it is not the right moment to criticize the captain. It was only much later, after 1989, that I realized how much our rather artificial unity had cost us. We had never developed what the Germans call *Streitkultur*—the culture of disputation. We had no experience of a free society or church, in which different currents naturally coexist and in which polemic—including a critical attitude to church authorities—need not give rise to personal animosity and accusations of heresy. In the face of an external enemy, we underestimated and subconsciously concealed from ourselves the fact that there existed many marked differences of opinion and mentality among us.

After I returned from Holland I encountered certain Catholic circles who offered me a simple interpretation of my first experience of the post–Vatican II church in the West, which was that the Council had been the work of "Trojan horses" in the church—Jews and Freemasons working to undermine the church from within. These were the results! It was necessary to stick closely to tradition and the magisterium as much as possible and prevent all attempts to introduce the Vatican II spirit into our church.

I think that my brief experience with that milieu helped me understand the attitudes and psychology of Catholic integrism. For a while I really believed those opinions. I would read various publications by Catholic traditionalists, and since I was a zealous convert and an opponent of the regime, who was psychologically trained for opposition and defense, I was all too ready to be a defender of the church in the face of threat. Moreover, there was something non-conformist about that counterculture of revolt against the "spirit of the times." For some young people radical conservatism is just as attractive as left-wing extremism is for others. It suits their need to define themselves negatively vis-à-vis their surroundings in their search for their own identity. There are always young people to be found among "Conservatives." Some of them suffer from childish anxiety, and they seek in religion something to protect them from the complicated world and their inner confusion; they want to find within the church people of a similar outlook who won't harm them. But they also include highly intelligent, distinctive, and nonconformist young people, as well as truly ardent Christians, whose conservativism is a deliberate protest against the mediocrity of their surroundings. They are part of that segment of young people that is unwilling to swim with the current. Even now some of my students spend all their spare time in one particular Prague monastery, wearing white robes and inhaling the sweet smell of incense along with neo-Thomist syllogisms and mysticism, neatly systematized according to Garigou-Lagrange. Others seek a similar safe haven in the conservatism of certain "new church movements." Maybe it is good for a young Catholic to experience something like this, just as I did. But I would not like to build the academic parish as that kind of reservation, and I think I can only really start to serve them when the majority have grown out of that stage of development.

Only later did I realize that Czech Catholics' mature acceptance and understanding of Vatican II was hindered by our paltry knowledge of the theology that inspired it. When many of our clergy in public ministry—who, of course, knew virtually nothing about such authors as Karl Rahner, Urs von Balthasar, Joseph Ratzinger, Henri de Lubac, Pierre Teilhard de Chardin, Edward Schillebeeckx, Hans Küng, and others—had to put into practice the decisions of the Council, they by and large perceived it solely as an order from above. That resulted in purely formal changes, such as turning the altar toward the people and celebrating the liturgy in the national language. But the mentality, theology, and preaching of most priests in public ministry were fixed in the spiritual climate of the period long before Vatican II. So long as changes—mostly just changes in the liturgy—were not accompanied by reflection on their own experience, or by theological study, they remained shallow and artificial. Although those clergy mostly fulfilled "the letter" of the Council's changes, at least formally, they never properly understood the Council or accepted it in their hearts.

I am not even surprised that some young clergy and seminarians today reject that superficial form of the post–Vatican II church. Unfortunately, instead of thoroughly studying the tradition and spiritual renewal, they sometimes react by throwing in their lot with superficial traditionalism, which is often an unintentional tragicomic caricature of Catholicism of the renovation period.

One attempt to overcome the intellectual isolation of Czech Catholicism and to present not only the documents of Vatican II but also its theological roots was the course "Living Theology" led by Josef Zvěřina during the Prague Spring and the magazine *Via* run by Ota Mádr. Unfortunately, those two experiments fell victim to the first wave of repression after the Russian occupation and shifted to clandestinity and the underground church, where I also followed them.

I was personally cured of that brief influence of Catholic integrists by what happened in 1968, and for three reasons. First, I came to maturity, and this was thanks to my dramatic personal experience that year. Second, I heard the message of Vatican II from the mouths of priests who had proved their fidelity to Christ, the church, and the pope by their years in prison, and no one could suspect them of being closet enemies or "Trojan horses" in the church. Third, I was able to spend some time in the West toward the end of 1968 and form a more objective opinion.

▌I regarded Jiří Reinsberg as a father, as the first of my fathers in the faith. However, around the time of the Prague Spring in 1968 I came to know a number of other excellent priests, some of whom had only recently returned from many years in prison.

The first of these I should mention was Dr. Antonín Mandl ThD. Like Reinsberg, Antonín Mandl was a protegé of Fr. Metod Klement, a Benedictine monk from the Emmaus Monastery in Prague. Before World War II, Father Klement trained many priests from wealthy and educated Prague families. A number of them went on to study at the Nepomucenum, the Czech college in Rome. Some, including Mandl and Reinsberg, were there when war broke out. They would later join the Czechoslovak army in England and learn much about life from their experience of war. Mandl subsequently pursued postgraduate study in France, where he became acquainted with the new theology, and the new pastoral methods, particularly through the Young Christian Workers movement (and its counterpart for Catholic students, the Young Christian Students movement), which was involved in the great postwar European revival movement. When he returned to Czechoslovakia he naturally started from scratch, as a chaplain in a small parish outside Prague, but before long he became a director of Catholic Action and one of Archbishop Josef Beran's closest assistants. He also celebrated Mass for students at the university church of St. Salvator. Soon the Communists would hold that against him, and he was among the first to be jailed, enduring many years of imprisonment in the harshest conditions. He was not only a highly educated, wise, and genteel person; he was also very good-looking. With his fine features and aquiline nose, he bore a striking resemblance to Teilhard de Chardin, with whom he also had a spiritual affinity. I discovered later that his appearance and innate gentility aroused the sadism of the guards at the time of his arrest, and as a result he suffered cruelty and dreadful humiliation at their hands. They knocked out his teeth and hung him up for hours by his feet, burning his body with lighted cigarettes. In the 1950s, nobody endured worse beatings in custody than Father Mandl. He was a man of great vision and bold theological thinking.

He was one of those who didn't regard prison as a dreadful wrong on the part of the Communists but as a God-given school, in which the church was to cleanse itself and be regenerated. In prison he came to know many people with different ideologies; he even baptized one of the leading Communists condemned to death in the trial of Rudolf Slánský and associates (a show trial masterminded by agents of the Soviet KGB, which was the largest purge of their own ranks carried out by the Stalinists at the beginning of the 1950s).

When Father Mandl returned from prison he was pleased to learn about the Second Vatican Council; the Council had started to regenerate the church precisely along the lines he and his friends had envisaged in their meditations in prison. In place of Austro-Catholic pomp there would be simplicity; in place of power, service. He wanted not only a legal system, ritual, and morality but also deep spirituality and a vigorous liturgy, inspiring human freedom and joy. The church was no longer to be a bunker, resisting hostile encirclement, but a paternal home and a place for dialogue. But what was dearest to his heart was ecumenism: the reconciliation and unity of Christians of different denominations. He was also an acquaintance of the composer Olivier Messiaen, who made him a gift of a long black scarf, which he jokingly called "my Olivier Messiaen scarf." After Father Mandl died I obtained a similar scarf for myself in his memory.

I also often remember with fondness the Franciscan Bonaventura Bouše, who was an intimate friend, particularly in the brief period of political thaw at the end of the 1960s and into 1970. At that time, he created one of the most remarkable parish communities in Prague, in a small church on the edge of the city. It was a meeting place for many interesting and thoughtful people, particularly arts-oriented intellectuals and artists. Bonaventura was a spellbinding preacher and an outstanding authority on liturgy. He was a radically oriented theologian with a precise and penetrating mind, but most of all he was an extremely sensitive and decent person. In the course of his life, his thinking had evolved in quite a dramatic fashion. His friends told me that as a young man he had been a sternly conservative and even inflexible member of the Franciscan order. Only later, when he ministered to a young woman as she died a long and painful death, did he abandon the world of simple pious answers to difficult life problems. I was gratified to see that in the little book rack on his desk there were always to be found, side by side, the Bible, the Fioretti of Saint Francis, stories of the Desert Fathers, Nietzsche's *Thus Spoke Zarathustra*, and the novels of Franz Kafka. That was his spiritual world, which I found congenial.

I recall my disappointment when a certain Dominican priest, whom I respected, told me how he had been outraged by an exhibition of Picasso's paintings; I realized that there was a yawning gulf separating his world of St. Thomas's *Summa* and the handbook of Dominican asceticism from the vision of the world of modern art and philosophy, and that people like him could never cross it. It was clear to me that even after my conversion I could not cease to be a modern thinking and feeling person and that my faith, if it is to be sincere, cannot turn its back on the disquiet and multifariousness of life reflected in the work of Picasso and Salvador Dalí, not to mention that of Kafka, James Joyce, Fellini, or Ingmar Bergman. Bonaventura Bouše was a priest who understood modern art and the modern world, although he never conformed uncritically to the spirit of the times. His face, which bore a striking resemblance to a portrait of Savanarola, had something of the somber prophet about it, and that applied even more to his spiritual physiognomy. With enormous fervor and conviction he would proclaim Jesus's radical newness, in contrast to the legalistic world of Judaism and religious systems in general; in that respect his thinking was quite close to the dialectical theology of post-Barthian Protestantism. He was reminiscent in some way of the prophetic figure of John the Baptist, and he would preach with passion in his Advent addresses about the Baptist's words: "Even now the ax lies at the root of the trees."

Bouše was an ecumenical person through and through, who wanted the church's catholicity to permit acceptance of the great fruits of the Protestant tradition. He wanted to show solidarity with all who arduously seek love, where the cautious men of church institutions seldom go. In his pastoral activity he was generously accommodating toward people who were in difficult moral and spiritual situations. He knew that in doing so he often followed paths that greatly diverged from what was customary in the church in those days—and still is. Because he was someone who was utterly incapable of taking things lightly, this caused him great suffering. The only thing I had a slight problem with was his somewhat somber tenacity, lacking the humorous detachment that I had known with Father Reinsberg. But he was a man who thirsted after justice, and I was not surprised when his name appeared among the first signatories of the Charter 77 human rights movement. He sincerely agonized over the state of the Czech church, writing several radically critical and prescient texts on the subject, whose prophetic acuity earned him hostility and rebuffs in the church. When the secret police closed down his parish and banned him from continuing his ministry, the church establishment—including Bishop Tomášek in those days, alas—heaved a sigh of relief at having gotten rid of a bothersome nonconformist cleric. I admired and loved him as a person, although at the time I regarded his theological views as too radical and occasionally argued with him. Even now my thinking has taken a slightly different direction, but I understand him now much better than I did then, and I am very grateful to him for the experience of the church community that he founded and embodied.

I have often meditated on the story of the Grand Inquisitor in Dostoyevsky's *Brothers Karamazov*, which, in my view, should be compulsory meditational reading for all candidates and holders of church office. I asked myself before God whether in that situation I would have enough courageous love and inner freedom to reject the "time-tested" position of the Inquisitor and stand fully on the side of Jesus. And on meeting priests and members of the hierarchy I have often asked myself what position they would have taken. To be honest, I would not hazard a guess in the case of many esteemed and meritorious priests (and monsignors). Bonaventura Bouše, together with Mandl and Zvěřina, were people about whom I was firmly convinced that they would not hesitate for a moment to take Christ's side in the dispute between the freedom of the gospel and institutional pragmatism.

I have now mentioned a third name, Josef Zvěřina. For many Czech Catholics, that name is tantamount to a program: Zvěřina became a symbol of striving for the moral and intellectual regeneration of Czech Catholicism. He was probably the most significant Catholic theologian we had in the twentieth century. But even more important than his writings and extensive teaching activity was his character, his courage, and the prescience with which, at all dramatic moments in our nation's history over half a century, he always stood in the front rank of those who championed the greater good. Interned during the Nazi occupation and imprisoned for many years under the Communist regime, he was the first of those who introduced Vatican II's ideas of renewal into the Czech context and strove for the church to play an honorable role in the efforts in favor of freedom during the Prague Spring. During the years of normalization after the Soviet occupation, he assumed the main burden of clandestine education in the church, traveling literally from the Bohemian Forest to the Tatra mountains in Slovakia, "often in danger," in the words of the Apostle. He was among the first signatories of Charter 77, and in November 1989 he was active in the Civic Forum, the coalition of opposition groups that emerged in the course of the Velvet Revolution.

There is one more name I must mention: Oto Mádr. I first met Oto Mádr in March 1968 at a momentous meeting of several dozen Catholic intellectuals in the house of Josef and Marie Kaplan and their large family. That meeting virtually marked the beginning of the Prague Spring for the Czech Catholic Church. The Catholics there agreed that the movement was not simply a question of changes within the Communist Party, but concerned society as a whole, and the church could not stand aside. It was also the first larger gathering at which Czech Catholics had an opportunity to get together, make one another's acquaintance, and consider their needs, capacity, and opportunities.

My first contact with Mádr was not particularly auspicious. I was approached by a slim, elderly man with a very refined and ascetic face, strongly reminiscent of Pope Pius XII. He immediately looked me over with an eagle's gaze and "interrogated" me "in the form of a friendly chat"—as he immediately noted in his notebook. "You can finally consider yourself a Catholic," some friends told me later. "That was Father Mádr whose notebook lists all Czech and Moravian Catholics with coded details about what they can be used for." Mádr was a soldier of the church, a born general, organizer, and conspirator. He was quite different from Zvěřina, Mandl, and Reinsberg. Unlike them, he came from humble origins, and that marks a person. He lacked their "wit," their magnanimous and slightly bohemian levity and humor. Indeed such characteristics always irritated him and made him nervous, as I noticed; in fact, I never saw him completely at ease. It struck me that his hyperactivity compensated for his great inner tension, which also had to do with his permanently fragile health.

I met with him on several occasions at that time and was immediately given tasks and directives. I became worried when I felt that he wanted to involve me in his arrangements and interfere in my private life. When he found out that I was involved both in the activities of Catholic students and in the activities of the student opposition on campus, he wanted me to abandon my "political" activities and become a proper Catholic activist according to his way of thinking. I had never wanted to be a pawn in anyone's game. I wanted to retain the freedom to choose my friends and activities as I saw fit, so I tended to avoid contact with Mádr. He respected this and probably understood what I eventually realized, years afterward, namely, that inner freedom is an absolute necessity in my life. But he probably never stopped monitoring me. When fate brought us together again some fifteen years later, this time for close and serious cooperation, he knew, remarkably, a great deal about me, even things that the regime's secret police hadn't discovered, however much they tried. On that occasion Oto Mádr also appeared to me in quite a different light, and I not only appreciated his true greatness and enormous merits, but I also began to like him and understand him as a person.

His passion was organizing and linking people. He was constantly weaving conspiratorial networks, always preparing and planning something, collecting and assessing information. Apparently he was also engaged in these activities when he was in prison, which brought the risk of a death sentence, and then for years, clandestinely, until 1968. During the Prague Spring he proved to be practically the only one who had a perfect overview of the situation and of "reserve forces"; he was prepared and had a detailed plan. He set about organizing publishing and educational activities and became the chief adviser to the episcopate, and as an eminence grise he coordinated virtually every activity in the church. In addition, he started to give lectures at the theological faculty and was one of the first who, cautiously and diplomatically but in an erudite and systematic fashion, started to introduce candidates for the priesthood to the new style of theological thinking and to the wealth of new emphases in post–Vatican II theology.

Antonín Mandl died in 1972. At the end of the 1970s Bonaventura Bouše moved out of Prague and went into retirement. Zvěřina and Mádr started to play a decisive role in the underground church—and in my own life—chiefly from the early 1980s.

IN JANUARY 1968 THINGS STARTED to move on the Czechoslovak political scene, and at the Arts Faculty we followed events closely. At the end of that month I was invited to take part in a TV program in which a group of students were to discuss the question of democracy with Professor Eduard Goldstücker, an expert on the work of Franz Kafka. The show was due to be broadcast at the end of February and was intended as a sort of litmus test to see how far one could go and what the censor would permit. It turned out that what we had considered extremely revolutionary at the end of January seemed tame a month later. The ice had broken, and the pace quickened week by week.

One thing I remember vividly from spring 1968 was the return of professors who had been expelled from the university in the purges of the 1950s. Every such return was a major event. I remember in particular the literary historian Václav Černý giving a talk in the style of a big show in the main hall, in which he spoke about his life and sarcastically settled scores with his opponents—various Czech "mini-Stalins."

The following week it was the turn of Professor Jan Patočka, philosopher and student of Husserl, who was expelled from the university in the 1950s, and we expected a similar show from him. Instead, however, he picked up a piece of chalk and said, "In his first book of the *Metaphysics*, Aristotle defined philosophy as follows," and he started to write on the blackboard in Greek. None of us knew Greek to any extent, and it soon became clear to us how little we knew of philosophy. Patočka's lectures were attended not only by students: the benches in the lecture hall were also filled by lecturers from the faculty. We realized that previously we had heard about philosophy, but here at Patočka's lectures we were "doing" philosophy. I remember after one such lecture walking through the blossoming gardens on the bank of the River Vltava as if in a trance, "high on phenomenology." Completely new worlds were opening up to me, a new type of thinking, and I drank my fill of it all.

If I had to name two of my many teachers whom I recall at moments of important decision making in my life, at moments when one asks oneself what one's teacher would do in the circumstances, then it would be Josef Zvěřina and Jan Patočka. Both of those wise and courageous men opened up new modes of thinking and new spiritual horizons to me, and they were also examples of moral strength and civic courage. In addition, they were compatible in terms of ideas. Patočka initiated me into Husserlian phenomenology and Heidegger's fundamental ontology, while Zvěřina introduced me to Rahner's theology, which would have been inconceivable without Heidegger. However, I only fully appreciated Heidegger at the beginning of my own teaching career at university, when I would compare various interpretations of Nietzsche's idea of the death of God and when I dealt with the relationship between the writing of Meister Eckhart and Heidegger's ideas.

Patočka was my rigorous examiner when I took my final examination in philosophy. It was just before he was forcibly retired at the beginning of the normalization era of the Husák regime. I subsequently attended his lectures in private apartments. I will never forget our last meeting. It must have been shortly before his death, sometime at the end of February or the beginning of March 1977. It was a cold and rainy afternoon on one of Prague's busiest thoroughfares, I. P. Pavlov Square. I was waiting in a crowd for a bus when I suddenly heard someone call out to me with unmistakable diction: "Hello! Colleague Halík!" At that time Professor Patočka was a spokesman for Charter 77, and the media campaign and police persecution of those who had signed that manifesto of human rights defenders was reaching its climax; he was undoubtedly under police surveillance. The time was out of joint, as Shakespeare would have said. But as if the situation was totally normal, Jan Patočka started to talk to me about philosophy, asking me what I was doing, what I was reading, and what I was working on. I mentioned that I had read his *Heretical Essays*, and the professor invited me to come to see him some time and share my views on them. His bus arrived, and before the doors closed he said the last words I was to hear from his lips: "Thinking people have to get together, don't they?"

Three weeks later he was dead. He died, like Socrates, at the age of seventy, after eleven hours of continuous interrogation by the secret police. His funeral, which I attended, was an orgy of police harassment, and a sign of how much the regime feared him. Behind every tree in the cemetery stood a secret policeman with a camera, while police on motorcycles circled the graveyard, and a police helicopter hovered overhead, the din from the engines drowning out the words of the priest over the coffin.

Whenever in subsequent years I hesitated over whether I should attend a clandestine lecture in a private apartment—because I was tired or concerned about my personal security—I would recall Patočka's parting words: Yes, thinking people must get together.

■ I SCARCELY SLEPT IN 1968. During the spring months of that year our student group from various faculties of Charles University was very active. We would make trips to factories and discuss with the workers. It was a great experience for me. The workers would always be assembled in one of the factory workshops, and we would argue heatedly in their presence with the local Communists from the factory management, who would bitterly attack us and the entire "renewal process." There was a lot of shouting; the young workers would back us up. The Communists were divided into Stalinists and "progressives," those who supported the reform program of Alexander Dubček. However, by then many of us were looking far beyond the horizon of "socialism with a human face" and longing for genuine pluralist democracy with opposition parties. There were discussions in Prague involving writers and journalists. Because I was a keen debater from the faculty's debating club, I was elected chair of the Students' Academic Board for a certain period during the Prague Spring and represented the Arts Faculty on the university-wide students' council.

Thanks to my efforts, students from the Cyril and Methodius Theological Faculty were also invited to that university-wide gathering. After February 1948, that faculty had been excluded from Charles University and uprooted to Litoměřice in northern Bohemia. After the meeting I went with one of those seminarists to a student tavern not far from the faculty. Although he was fifteen years older (and had previously graduated from the Arts Faculty), we soon became friends and he told me about his future plans. He said he was due to be ordained in a year's time, after which he would go to Jerusalem for postgraduate Old Testament studies. I told him that my life's dream was to lecture at the Arts Faculty one day, and I also confided to him my efforts to find a priest who would play a pastoral role for the university students. If someone had shown us our futures in a magic mirror at that time, we would have scarcely believed it. A few months later Russian tanks crushed our plans. The two of us would enter Jerusalem together but not until twenty-four years had passed, by which time I was the university chaplain and the student at that tavern, Miloslav Vlk, was my superior, the archbishop of Prague.

CATHOLIC BELIEVERS WERE IN THE MINORITY among students in those days—although a very lively and active minority. We formed a group to organize the establishment of a student church. We considered the Church of St. Salvator, which had traditionally been a university student church until the beginning of the 1950s, but it was then in use by the Slovak parish. So in the end we found a home at St. Thomas's Church in Malá Strana. We invited speakers and organized lectures on various topics. We did not limit ourselves to lectures and discussions, however. Later, when many doctors and medical staff emigrated after August 1968 and the health service was in great difficulties, we would act as unpaid volunteer orderlies on night shifts in hospitals.

From May 1968 we organized literary and musical programs at St. Thomas's as part of religious services. I remember one evening in May when a leading actor from the National Theater recited verse by the Catholic poet Jan Zahradníček, who had spent years in Communist prisons. The poet's son Jan also attended; they had drummed into his head at school that his father was a criminal, and suddenly he saw a church full of young people listening intently to his father's poems.

■ In 1968, the documents of the Second Vatican Council started to circulate in the Czech lands, and here and there the first steps were taken toward implementing the post-Council renewal of the liturgy. Thus liberalization of political life and the post–Vatican II aggiornamento reached us at the same time; they were both seen as a breath of freedom and hope. The reform-minded Communists talked about "socialism with a human face," while some reform-minded Catholics talked about "Christianity with a human face." The Second Vatican Council was a child of the 1960s, and therein lay its charm, as well as certain limitations.

On May 20, 1968, a congress was held at Velehrad—a pilgrimage site in Moravia—at which "The Task of Conciliar Renewal" was established. This was a kind of first nationwide congress of Catholics since the Communists took power. I attended as a student delegate. Father Mandl gave a memorable speech there, in which he spoke for the first time of his prison experiences and outlined an optimistic vision of the church's renewal in a free society; he paid tribute to the legacy of Cardinal Newman, who before he made a toast to the pope used to make a toast to freedom of conscience.

A large number of bishops and leaders of monastic orders who had previously been banned from pursuing their ministry by the regime appeared at Velehrad at that time. Many of them had spent years in prison and were now permitted to officiate for the first time. I also made the acquaintance there of the legendary Benedictine abbot Anastáz Opasek, who had been dubbed the "hooligan abbot" because of his nonconformism and because he had many friends in the art world.

I recall one delightful experience. I was sitting in a room of the former Jesuit college at Velehrad with Father Mandl when a diminutive, shabbily dressed old man with a walking stick entered, carrying a battered suitcase, and asked us shyly not to concern ourselves, he simply wished to change there. He opened the suitcase and robed. Suddenly there stood before us a magnificent bishop in full pontifical splendor, like a butterfly emerging from a chrysalis; it was Bishop

Ladislav Hlad. When I subsequently asked Father Mandl whether he was intending to change into clerical robes, he replied, "It looks as if I still have a lot to teach you: the task of the present time is to liberate Christianity from clericalism, ritualism, and legalism."

Usually when I met Antonín Mandl in Prague he would be wearing his favorite outfit, one in which he would ask to be buried: a white cotton shirt and jeans. He once set off in those clothes to a meeting that was also attended by Hungarian bishops who had been ordained on the basis of a compromise with the Hungarian Communist regime resulting from the Vatican's unfortunate policy of accommodation with the Soviet bloc. "Popinjays!," Father Mandl called them. Then he said, "So I made of point of robing, so they could see what a 'very reverend' behind the Iron Curtain should look like."

█ AT THE BEGINNING OF THE SUMMER VACATION I left for an intensive English course at Bangor University in North Wales. It was my introduction to a world that totally captivated me. I had long been an Anglophile, but Britain exceeded all my expectations, so I wrote in my first letter home that I suddenly had the feeling that I had spent the previous twenty years living in a foreign country and only now was returning home. It was probably a bit impolite, but I really felt it. The drabness of brutish socialist collectivism was far away. British culture impressed me enormously. I had the feeling I had been living there my whole life.

Bangor was a little university town lying between lofty mountains and the ocean. The university was located in an ancient castle, beneath which there soared a Gothic cathedral. Not far from there I could take a ferry to Ireland. It was an international course attended by students from all over the world. They were all very interested in events in Czechoslovakia, albeit most of them tended to confuse it with Yugoslavia. People would also ask me whether we had refrigerators and telephones or whether we were ruled by a Czech or a Russian tsar. Many of the Western students had truly curious notions about the world behind the Iron Curtain. When the course was over I remained for a while longer in London, also visiting Oxford and Cambridge. In London I was able to meet a number of Czech exiles, whom I had previously known only from journals or from radio broadcasts of the BBC and Radio Free Europe. It was a magical vacation that sadly ended in tragedy. I was due to return home on August 20. Because I had visited Oxford the previous day and slightly overslept the next morning, I postponed my departure by a day—which would have been August 21. That fateful night would have an impact on the lives of two generations of Czechs and Slovaks, and for tens of thousands of people it would be a turning point in their lives. My own life probably would have taken a completely different direction if the tanks of five allied Warsaw Pact armies had not rolled into our country that night.

On the morning of August 21, my baggage was packed and I was heading home. I left my suitcases at the rail terminal and went to Mass at Westminster Cathedral before taking a last stroll through the center of London, looking forward to another visit to Britain before long. While I was waiting in line at midday for my baggage at the left luggage office, just before my train was due to leave for the port of Dover, I noticed in front of me some Swiss people agitatedly discussing something in a newspaper. I glanced over their shoulders and saw the headline in large letters: "Russian Tanks in Prague!" I was in total shock.

I returned to the Czech House in the Notting Hill district of London and found Czech students there in heated debate. We pondered what we would do next. I fervently urged us to return home to fight the invaders; others suggested I calm down because the frontiers were certainly closed and it would be impossible to get there now anyway. Some of the students immediately started considering emigration, but at that moment I ruled out that possibility for myself. So we decided to remain in London for a while. There followed several very hectic days, as we tried to obtain information and do what we could. We contacted amateur radio operators, asking them to lend airtime to the free Czech transmitters. Those broadcasts by heroic Czech journalists in Prague were quite audible in London, even the sound of gunfire in the street outside, as well as the moving singing of the national anthem, and then sudden silence. It was especially harrowing listening to it, cut off from home and with no chance of influencing events. It is at such moments that one understands the meaning of prayer. As we sat listening to those broadcasts on our transistor radios, even nonbelievers prayed with us for our homeland.

We had no idea what was happening to our relatives or whether they were even alive. About ten days later, I finally managed to telephone home and discovered that my parents were alright. They advised me to stay in England for a while longer, until it was clear how things would turn out. As she later told me, my mother was convinced that if I had been in Prague at the time of the invasion my great-grandfather's passion for mounting the barricades would certainly have taken hold of me, and my resistance would have cost me my life, as it did many of my contemporaries. For that reason she was actually glad I was far away.

A few days after the invasion we organized a demonstration in London. I drew up a petition of protest and we marched with it in a procession headed by a Czechoslovak flag to the Soviet embassy. As we marched through London, hundreds of people joined us, and everyone expressed solidarity with us. On some occasions, when we were buying food in London stores, to our surprise the shopkeeper would refuse to take payment, saying that Czech airmen had fought to protect London during World War II, so now they wanted to show their gratitude and solidarity.

My father wrote me that although I was their only son and that he and my mother were already elderly, they would fully respect my decision if I chose to remain in England, since they had always respected my freedom and only sought my welfare. It was a wonderful letter, and I still keep it within hand's reach on my desktop as a reminder that great love is always connected with sacrifice, and it gives freedom.

I then received a grant from Bangor University on condition that I pass an entrance exam. In those days it was still possible to extend the validity of the "exit permit" issued by the Czechoslovak authorities and thus legalize my residence abroad without the risk of losing for good the possibility of returning to Prague. So I took the exam, and at the beginning of October 1968 I enrolled as a regular undergraduate student at the university in Bangor with which I was already familiar.

I will never forget that early-morning train journey from London to Bangor. I observed outside the window the imposing melancholic countryside near Chester, with the sea on one side and crags on the other. All my belongings were in a small suitcase in the luggage rack above me, and my future was totally open and unknown. Suddenly, in that condition of pennilessness, uncertainty, and insecurity, I felt dizzying joy, an intense feeling of freedom, liberation, and hope, a kind of being "on the road" in Kerouac's sense. I was setting out on a journey once again, without knowing where I was heading. I remembered the prayer of the Native American warrior cited somewhere by Christopher Dawson: "Oh you who possess the skies. / I am living. I in you entrust my fate / Again alone upon the warpath." That moment was among the profoundest experiences of my life.

■ STUDENT LIFE AT A BRITISH UNIVERSITY WAS a completely new and marvelous experience for me. I found a completely different style of university work from the one that prevailed in my own country, where it consisted mainly of a teacher's monologue and where students didn't dare open their mouths. In Bangor there was impassioned debate, and the relationship between teachers and students was much more open, and closer. Every Sunday our professor would invite several students home to tea. We would sit by a blazing fire in a house full of books, sipping tea with milk, while our professor pensively smoked his pipe and talked to us. It was a breath of the university culture of Old England of which I had always dreamed. This was exactly how I had always imagined it; this was exactly the place I had always wanted to be and how I had wanted to live. I was exceedingly happy, and I never felt homesick. I also worked very hard, spending every free moment in the library, studying with all my might writings that were unknown or banned in my own country, by philosophers, theologians, sociologists, and political thinkers, all of whom convinced me that "Western values," human rights, and a free society must vanquish the barbarity from the East that had inundated my country. I thought about my favorite saint, the English Jesuit Edmund Campion, who had zealously prepared himself in the library of Prague's Clementinum college for that dangerous mission to his native land. "Centuries on, the map has simply turned the other way round," I said to myself.

It was there that I first encountered flower children, supporters of the Beatnik movement, and many other subcultures of sixties youth. I wrote about it all in letters to friends at home, and about my plans for what I would do in Prague in the future. I still counted on returning, but at the same time I wanted to stay in Britain for as long as possible.

My enthusiastic reports about student life in Britain provoked an unexpected response, however. Several days before Christmas 1968 I received a letter from a female acquaintance, to whom I had previously written enthusiastically about how the student parish in Bangor operated. She replied that she appreciated my suggestions and agreed that there was still plenty of scope for activity in Prague, but almost all the leading figures had already emigrated, and wasn't I thinking about returning? The very idea seemed utterly crazy to me, because I felt incredibly fortunate and had wonderful years of interesting university study in Britain ahead of me. With those thoughts in mind, I pushed the letter to one side on my desk. But at that very moment I also said to myself, "How can I counter a challenge like that? Does the mere fact that I enjoy it here mean that it's the right thing to do? Am I to conduct my life solely according to what I find enjoyable or according to what is truly God's will?" That thought came to me in a flash, so I canceled everything I had planned for that evening and spent the night in prayer. In the morning I decided to return.

I spent a typical English Christmas in Bristol with the family of a colleague, and for the next two days I said farewell to London with a heavy heart. On the evening of December 28, 1968, I landed at the Prague airport; it had been my first journey by airplane. To be on the safe side, I kept my options open and retained my exit permit for another month, in case I decided to go back to Britain after all. It was still possible to do so at that time, as the repressive regime had not yet fully established itself in those first months after the invasion. Many people were in a similar situation then, particularly students. They would wander around wintertime Prague wondering whether to return to the West and emigrate or to stay at home. The undoing of all the achievements of the Prague Spring was not yet in full swing, but the more realistic pessimists guessed that the Iron Curtain would soon close behind us once more, and these were the last remaining moments when we could decide under what political system we would spend the rest of our lives.

I was also of two minds. And then, like a bolt out of the blue, came the self-immolation of Jan Palach. Palach was also a student at the Arts Faculty, the same age as I was, and although I didn't know him personally, I must have encountered him sometimes in the corridors of the university.

Palach's sacrifice made me realize that there was something much more profound at stake than simply a political struggle in the Communist Party between conservatives and progressives about the kind of socialism they wanted. The real struggle was a spiritual and moral confrontation about the very moral and cultural basis of the nation. Someone had emerged who had not responded to force with force of arms but with force of character, with the sacrifice of his own life. Immolation as protest was something quite out of the ordinary in a Christian spiritual context, however, and a large number of believers condemned Palach's action as suicide. In my discussions with them I quoted the words of Chesterton, which clearly differentiate suicide and martyrdom: a suicide scorns life, while a martyr scorns death. His sacrifice was not primarily a protest against the Soviet invasion. He came to realize that solidarity in the nation and the moral strength to resist were beginning to weaken. Exhaustion was appearing, along with a readiness to compromise or even collaborate with the invaders. By his sacrifice, Palach showed that not losing our will to freedom was more important to him than his own life, that we mattered more to him than his own life. He wanted to arouse us to have greater respect for ourselves and for our freedom and dignity. I numbered Jan Palach among "my" saints, those who—whether canonized or not—all deviated slightly from the stereotypes of traditional hagiography.

I helped organize a requiem for Jan Palach at St. Thomas's Church in Malá Strana, at which the preacher was Antonín Mandl. I then carried Palach's death mask to the faculty, where I placed it in a niche above the staircase from which we had removed a bust of Lenin. I'll never forget that nocturnal walk through wintry snow-covered Prague. As I walked along the row of statues of saints on Charles Bridge, I engaged in an inner dialogue with the one whose death mask I hugged to myself beneath my winter coat. I thought of the letter that Palach left behind. In it he wrote that he belonged to a group of students who had decided to do the same deed, that they had drawn lots, and he had drawn the slip of paper with the words "Torch No. 1" written on it. I said to myself that night that Jan's action had placed us all in the position of "Torch No. 2." I asked myself what I could sacrifice, how I could respond to Jan's deed, which struck me to the very marrow.

Those reflections that night, and in the following days, gave rise to my decision not to return to Britain, not to emigrate, and to remain for good in my occupied homeland. I also promised myself never to yield to pressures to collaborate and to forgo the agreeable aspects of everyday life—not to strive to start a family and achieve material security, but instead to study in depth everything that the Communists proscribed. Although I made no explicit promise regarding the priesthood, when I am asked today to identify the first decisive step in my life in the direction of a priestly vocation, I reply that it was that "Palach night." I was drawn to the idea of sacrifice, the requirement of asceticism, and a lofty objective demanding unconditional commitment, as well as the ability to transcend and disregard everything that distracts and delays the attainment of that goal.

I'm not a born hero; my great-grandfather's genes are not the be all and end all. But whenever, in the twenty years that followed, I was tempted in the very slightest to make some moral compromise with the regime, it sufficed to remember Jan Palach, and it gave me the strength to say no. No, his death was not in vain. At the very least it established a firewall in the conscience of many people of his generation. Looking back in this postheroic epoch, my youthful idealistic enthusiasms might appear somewhat naive and ridiculous without the context of those days. But that is how I thought, and I must add that I am not ashamed of it.

I started to reflect on what form that commitment should take. Direct political resistance? I didn't feel that was a particularly promising option, or at least I didn't see myself in that role. What I yearned for was the destruction of Communism using spiritual weapons. That frosty night when I left the church after the requiem for Jan Palach, I realized that not only was it the end of the Prague Spring, and of any hopes of achieving political freedom in the short term, it was also the end of the springtime of my life and my faith. I realized that we were entering a dark and glacial night, along with the whole of society and the church. "This will not be a short night—the wolf has a craving for the lamb. Close the gate, little brother," sang our generation's bard of protest, Karel Kryl. The lengthy period from when a tree sheds its blossom to the appearance of its fruit is not so beautiful, but it is very important: this was my confessor's comment on the period of my life that I was entering.

FOUR

My Path to Priesthood

After the "unfinished Spring" our country entered a strange period of pestilence. It was neither as cruel nor as blatant as the freezing Stalinist winter of the 1950s. The neo-Stalinism of
the twenty years of "normalization" was more
like the brown slush of autumnal sleet, if I am to continue for a moment my meteorological metaphor. But whereas we lived with gagged
mouths in that "Biafra of the spirit," where many avenues in our lives
were blocked, the world outside moved on apace.

I can remember in 1969 watching on television the first manned
landing on the moon. We were overjoyed, possibly more by the political implications than by the scientific achievement as such: we were
glad that the first flag to be unfurled on the moon was the U.S. Stars
and Stripes, not the red flag of the invaders with its hammer and
sickle and its star, which by then was not a star of hope for anybody
in our country. Much later I realized that the moon landing had a
huge symbolic charge, comparable, perhaps, to Columbus's discovery
of the new continent, and that like Columbus's deed, that date can
be considered the birth of a new age. My friend Radim Palouš called

1969 the beginning of the global age. Only later did I read Teilhard's theory about the "planetary age," as well as the flood of literature about globalization and postmodernity. It was as if, in that summer of 1969, we suddenly all looked together at our earth through the eyes of the astronauts from a completely new perspective; we ceased to perceive only the individual islands of civilization as our homes and saw the planet as a whole.

That same year saw the invention of the microprocessor, which was another step toward the tremendous boom of information technology, which maybe did more than the global linkage of markets to tear down the dividing walls and turn the world into a single intricately interwoven agora, an overabundant market of goods and ideas. The nations of Central and Eastern Europe and our own country would only fully enter that hectically merging world after the fall of the Communist empire on the threshold of the 1990s.

■ THE IDEA OF A PRIESTLY VOCATION HAD naturally crossed my mind before 1968; such thoughts take hold of most converts. But because one of my confessors once broached the idea somewhat clumsily, it naturally provoked my resistance: that's not something I want. And indeed the time had not yet come.

The first clearer thoughts about priesthood came to my mind during August 1968, when we sat on the steps of the Czech exile center in London at night listening to the free radio transmissions and wondering how to respond to the rape of our country. The thoughts resurfaced with more urgency around the funeral of Jan Palach and grew stronger throughout 1969.

The day after my return from England, late in the evening of the Feast of St. Thomas Beckett, I went to Father Reinsberg for confession. After hearing my confession, he said, "I definitely don't want to manipulate you, or push you in any direction, but in your case I feel the sign of a conscientious vocation for priesthood. God is guiding you along a different path from that of your faculty colleagues.

But at present your first task is to complete your studies. You still have a long journey ahead of you, you know. It will take time! Your parents won't be happy about it, and maybe your father will cope with it better than your mother." He spoke about it as if it was a fait accompli. While he was speaking I realized that what he was saying truly represented my deepest aspirations. I felt a sense of enormous relief and clarification, as if something long hidden inside me was coming to birth. After that the longing for priesthood never left me. Admittedly I avoided it for a few more years, and its achievement was a long time coming—nearly ten years.

In those days there was only one seminary for priests in the Czech lands, and by then it was once more totally under the control of the Communist state, represented by its "secretary for church affairs" and the secret police. As it had been throughout the Communist rule—with the exception of the brief period of the Prague Spring—only candidates who had no previous academic education could enter the seminary. So that was not the path to take; I had to seek another route.

■ AFTER THE AUGUST INVASION, THE PROCESS of creating the power structures of the "normalization regime" was very slow. The first major reprisals did not take place until the end of 1969 and later. It was not until 1972 that the situation became truly oppressive and depressing. For several months after the invasion, possibly even a year, the student group Vigil held meetings in public, and there were literary evenings and discussions, until the priest at St. Thomas's Church—probably under pressure from the secret police—forbade them. Then the organizations we were involved in, like the Ecumenical Movement of the Intelligentsia and Students, were banned one by one. But we continued our work. All those activities simply regrouped somewhat and continued on an unofficial basis as circumstances permitted. During the subsequent years of harsh persecution, some of those activities ceased while others became strictly conspiratorial and clandestine.

I made my last trip to the West in summer 1969, just before the frontier was once more firmly closed and scope for travel was drastically restricted. I received an invitation to a seminar in Austria organized by British Quakers in a Catholic educational center at Grossrusbach. It was an intensive three-week seminar attended by several dozen students from all over the world. Our group, for instance, included an African from Zaire, a Catholic woman from Poland, an American who assisted Robert Kennedy's election campaign in America, a representative of the New Left from Germany, Protestants from the GDR, and a Buddhist from Japan. I also remember two Spanish worker-priests, who were the first participants with whom I saw eye to eye. Among other things, they told jokes about the dictator Franco; they were exactly the same as the ones that used to be told about the Communist president Antonín Novotný. With them I had my first experience of Mass celebrated in everyday attire, seated at an ordinary table.

Each morning there was silent meditation, and that was followed by discussions throughout the day in short, well-organized sessions on various political, social, moral, and cultural questions of current interest from an international perspective; that was the first time I encountered ecological issues, for instance. Often I would recall with a certain irony a sentence from a Turgenev novel that went something like, "How can we go for lunch when we haven't yet answered the question about the meaning of life?"

Indeed we solved none of the world's problems there, but that meeting opened up new horizons for me. It was a unique opportunity to glimpse the way of thinking and values of people of different convictions and cultures. It provided me with an experience of inestimable worth, a gift that has accompanied me throughout my life since then: It taught me to perceive the world through others' eyes. It was an enormous boost for the following twenty years of isolation. Among other things I came away convinced that in spite of ideological barriers, young people are capable of finding a common language, and understanding each other, because their fundamental concerns are similar.

I hitchhiked from Austria to Italy. It was my first visit to Rome. I found accommodation in the Czech exile pilgrimage center, Velehrad. I shared a room with a Dr. Vladimír Neuwirth, who had emigrated shortly before. He had been jailed at the beginning of the 1960s for membership in a clandestine secular institute and had only recently been released, during the Prague Spring. After the invasion he decided to emigrate and was now working at the university in Louvain. He was a cultured and truly spiritual person who fascinated me with the breadth of his education and his mature, manly piety. We visited the sights of Rome together, and he opened up for me new vistas into Catholic culture. In the end I shared my great personal secret with him, because in reality my journey had another significance. At that time I was enchanted by the Jesuits and was considering entering the Society of Jesus; my trip to Rome meant for me above all a pilgrimage to the tomb of St. Ignatius. I had come there to pray and discover whether membership in that order was right for me.

In that student fashion I traversed almost the whole of northern and central Italy, right down to the south. The most southerly point I reached was Capri, and I visited Pompeii. A few days after my return from Italy, free movement out of the country was stopped. This meant I would no longer be able to travel to the West for almost twenty years. Every application I made for an exit permit received the same stock official response: your journey is not in the interest of the State. During the next two decades, I would regularly have the following dream almost twice a week: I would be walking across a bridge over the Thames in London, or along a narrow lane in Oxford, or some part of Rome, and saying to myself, "I've dreamed of it so many times, and now it's true; they have let me travel abroad at last"—and at that moment I would wake up. When I eventually made my first trip abroad, I was in constant fear that it was just a dream.

■ WHEN, IN 1972, I SUCCESSFULLY DEFENDED my dissertation and passed oral examinations in two fields, sociology and philosophy, it might have looked like the beginning of a promising academic career; I had long dreamed of lecturing one day at the Arts Faculty, where I felt at home. But the political situation was becoming more and more oppressive, and every graduate from the faculty was faced with the important choice of which side to stand on.

For me the decisive moment came at the official doctoral graduation on July 14, 1972. On that occasion my colleagues wanted me to give the speech of thanks on behalf of the entire class, but the official at the chancellor's office insisted that it must be given by a member of the Socialist Union of Youth, who must read the prescribed text of thanks to the Communist Party, the government, and the working class for enabling them to study.

On the eve of the graduation ceremony I meditated on what might be said on such an occasion if we lived in a free country. When I arrived at the ancient university auditorium the next day, I learned that the speaker selected from the ranks of the "class-conscious students" had failed to turn up. So they asked me to read the speech, handing me a page full of sentences about the Communist Party, the government, and Marxism-Leninism. Only about three quarters of an hour remained before the ceremony was due to start. I sat below the bay window in the empty auditorium, where there was once a chapel to St. Catherine, and prayed with all my might to the Holy Spirit. I thought about the university charter of Charles IV, whose statue stood in front of me, and about the university's onetime chancellor Jan Hus. My thoughts were full of various names and faces, including that of my late colleague Jan Palach. Then I stuck the official text in my pocket, and in place of it I gave an impromptu speech at the official ceremony in which, instead of thanking the Party and the government, I expressed thanks to our teachers, including those who were no longer teaching at our faculty. I reflected on the text of our doctoral oath, which included a promise to "disseminate the light of truth": I said that this was not only a commitment to propagate true scholarly knowledge, but also to ensure that truth had an honorable place in society; we had to live truthfully and try to contribute to the creation of an atmosphere of tolerance, civic courage, and spiritual freedom. I ended my speech with a quotation from Karel Čapek: "Truth is more than power because it is everlasting." When I said it, I felt enormous relief. It was as if those words were imbibed thirstily not only by all those present but also by the very walls of the university, which was once more being humiliated and enslaved. That graduation turned into a minor demonstration. I received flowers and handshakes even from many people unknown to me who had friends and relatives among the other graduates.

There were repercussions, of course. An informer immediately left the ceremony and went to denounce it to the Soviet embassy. From there the denunciation made its way to the Central Committee of the Communist Party of Czechoslovakia and finally to the Communist Party's City Committee, a process that took about three weeks. I myself had no idea what exactly was going on. At the faculty they simply informed me that I would never be allowed to teach at university level. I had great difficulty finding a job, and eventually I was engaged as a sociologist by an industrial enterprise. There I was summoned by the head of the personnel department, who informed me that he had been assigned the task of discussing my "provocative" speech at the graduation ceremony with me and told me I was to write an explanation. So I wrote that I stood by what I had said, and I was not aware of having said anything wrong. The words "Truth is more than power" were simply another version of the motto on the official standard of the Czechoslovak president: "Truth prevails." Anyone who saw political innuendo in it should be concerned about themselves.

The comrade in charge of the personnel department put my explanation in his pocket and I never saw him again, because that very evening he suffered a stroke at a meeting and died on the spot. Maybe he was cremated with my letter in his pocket. It occurred to me that I might be of help to him at the pearly gates.

I was then summoned by the company director, a very decent man, who told me he didn't think I had done anything wrong. If anyone ever raised the matter I was to tell them that he had "sorted it out" with me. He even removed the relevant documentation from my personnel file. Nevertheless, every time I was interrogated by the secret police over the next fifteen years, they raised the matter with me.

▌A FEW YEARS LATER I TRANSFERRED TO a training institute attached to the Ministry of Industry. I had previously given several lectures at the institute as an external lecturer, and when there was a positive response to those lectures, they asked me if I would like to be a permanent lecturer in the Department of Psychology. I pointed out that I was not a member of the Party, but they assured me that a number of non-Party people worked there. It was not part of higher education, so the political qualifications were not so strict. I spent nearly ten years there, until 1984. I used to travel around giving lectures about management psychology to senior managers in the chemical industry.

In preparation for that work I attended a course in East Berlin. The psychologists there appropriated West German programs, such as managerial training, communication training, social perception, and sensitivity. These were practically unknown in my country at that time. I formed a team, and we were among the pioneers of new methods of adult education—"active social learning"—particularly the use of role play based on actual situations in the enterprise. Compared to other similar programs, including the German ones, ours also made use of psychotherapeutic methods of self-knowledge and stress management, including elements of relaxation and meditation. That later brought me closer to clinical psychology and psychotherapy. I also concerned myself with the theoretical aspects of the work, lecturing about it at conferences and publishing a few specialist papers. However, I was not permitted to publish anything at all in the fields closest to my heart: philosophy, sociology, and—later—theology.

The senior managers at major industrial concerns who attended our courses started to realize the importance of management skills, of working with people, and also the role of self-awareness and recognition of one's abilities and reserves. They included competent technocrats and managers, albeit most of them were members of the Party. However, a good number of those who attended owed their positions solely to their Party membership, and they lacked any real personal or professional qualifications. It was very difficult working with the latter, and some of them were openly reluctant to learn what they regarded as "Western" methods, considering that the main thing was to fulfill the State plan and not to worry about what people felt about their work. However, I don't think I ever encountered a sincerely convinced Communist during those ten years.

I never had a problem with the authorities. I realized that powerful people in top posts often suffer from extreme loneliness and constant overload. They would frequently share their personal and family concerns with me, so that I became their "anonymous pastor," something between a therapist and a father confessor, as I would often joke. I expect many of them in those days would have been appalled to discover that I spent all my spare time studying theology and preparing for the priesthood—or, later, that I was actually a priest.

■ FROM THE BEGINNING OF THE 1970S, my vocation for the priesthood grew even stronger. I could not take the route of the official priestly seminary or the theological faculty. Even after ordination, the work of priests was not controlled by the bishops (at the time of my graduation almost all the bishop posts that had been filled during the Prague Spring were once more vacant) but by officials of the Communist Party described as secretaries for church affairs. The latter were empowered to arbitrarily cancel priests' official authorization to pursue their ministry, or to assign them to defunct parishes in the border regions if they committed the most serious offense in the eyes of officialdom, which was contact with young people.

At the end of 1970, precisely two years after my confession to Father Reinsberg upon my return from England, I had an important conversation with a Jesuit, Father Mikulášek, about my desire to join the Society of Jesus. On that occasion he sketched out his vision of future priests: they should have a dual vocation, following a profession in secular life, and being above all a presence for nonbelievers and seekers. That greatly appealed to me; Father Reinsberg had previously lent me an inspirational book by Henri Perrin about the French worker-priest movement, and in Austria, in summer 1969, I had met two such worker-priests from Spain, as mentioned earlier.

In 1971 I fell in love with the writings of Teilhard de Chardin. As I read the texts of that amalgam of theologian, scientist, mystic, and poet, I was profoundly struck by one idea in particular: just as there were priests in working-class occupations, who sought to bridge the abyss between the church and the working class, there was also a need for priest-scientists capable of healing the rift between faith and the contemporary intellectual world. That was my path, I told myself. I yearned for priesthood, but at no moment of my life did I feel a vocation to be "the village priest"; I knew that if I ended up in a rural parish, I would be unhappy—and my flock even more so. Not that I disdained the countryside in any way, but I knew that I had no experience of that world. For my whole life, since birth, I had been closely tied to the intellectual elite of the city, so I yearned to be an apostle to the world I knew best. My ideal was the student chaplain, such as I had discovered in England. But in the Czech lands, university parishes had ceased to exist at the beginning of the 1950s. I had never really known a typical parish; the community around Father Reinsberg at the Týn Church was very distinctive. I yearned to join some order that engaged in intellectual activity.

So my first love in the church were the Jesuits, and it is a love that has never faded. In 1968 I saw a film on television about the Jesuit "reductions" in Paraguay in the seventeenth century. It fascinated me so much that time that I started to research historical materials. The "Jesuit State" in Paraguay would seem to be one of the most remarkable social experiments in the history of the church. I read Thompson's biography of St. Ignatius, as well as the saint's autobiography and letters, and heaps of other literature. I made the acquaintance of the Jesuit provincial František Šilhan (the longest-serving provincial in the history of the Society), and I naturally longed to become a Jesuit myself. I prepared for it not only by my pilgrimage to Rome but also, during the subsequent years, by means of several private exercises based on St. Ignatius's book of Spiritual Exercises.

I was somewhat confused at that time by meeting a remarkable priest, who many believed to have the gift of "cardiognosis," the ability to see into the depths of the human heart and one's destiny. I will disclose only a fraction of what he told me. He told me above all to save my strength, because the service I would show others, and for which I had been born, would probably not develop until I was much older. He predicted that I would have not only many influential friends but also many sworn enemies; that my path would not be easy, and I would undergo several hard trials. Those trials would turn out well, however, and would move me forward and deeper. He said one remarkable thing that I have recalled over and over again throughout my life: anybody who tried to harm me would eventually benefit me, in spite of their actions. He predicted that I would undergo a serious crisis around my forty-fifth year. As far as the Jesuits were concerned, he only said that whenever I was in great distress and had problems with the church, St. Ignatius would send one of his spiritual sons to render me rapid and very effective assistance. At the time I couldn't imagine how or why I would ever have problems with the church, but my intuition told me that his words were not idle.

I SPENT THE 1972–73 PERIOD ON compulsory military service. At first it was quite a pleasant time because I was doing office work and did not have much to do for most of the day. I made use of the office, where I lived a virtually monkish life. I had a carefully concealed breviary and the Spiritual Exercises of St. Ignatius and meanwhile had no need to worry about how to spend the day, or about what I should eat or wear, or all the other things that the pagans seek after, according to scripture. I decided there that I would perform the Spiritual Exercises in their traditional form and devoted the whole of Advent to them. I performed five hourlong meditations every day. In fact I meditated on sin so intensely that it made me ill, and I literally vomited. During that meditation, my entire life up until then appeared to me to be a stinking ulcer, precisely in accordance with the Baroque imagination, which characterized the original Ignatian excercises.

Part of the Ignatian Spiritual Exercises is making a "choice of status." So I meditated on my priestly vocation. On the Feast of St. Nicholas I walked around the snow-covered barracks yard and reflected on what I was called to do. On New Year's Day 1972 I said a definite yes to my yearning for priesthood. There remained only the question of how—and that was not a simple one at all at that time.

I was due to have a clandestine meeting with Father Šilhan in March of that year. It looked as if I would be accepted in the secret novitiate. Shortly before that I had requested an interview with Fr. Václav Dvořák, a priest who was then employed in a Prague antiquarian bookshop after years of imprisonment. "By chance" the meeting with Father Dvořák took place before my planned meeting with Father Šilhan. We spent about three hours walking around Libeň Island in the middle of the Vltava River. During our conversation he divulged to me that there existed a secret, strictly clandestine priestly community, which was similar to the secular institute in form. All members had secular occupations and lived in the world; their focus was not the usual pastoral activity but discreet witness among nonbelievers, a profound "sanctification of the world."

That community already had a history, dating to World War II. Its remarkable founder had to emigrate after 1948, and the community went through the hard times of the 1950s. Its spiritus agens in those days was ordained secretly in dramatic circumstances while a member of a punishment battalion in the army. During the Prague

Spring they had made contact with French worker-priests and realized that their spirituality and activity were similar. They had resisted the temptation to come out in the open, and they were now continuing their strictly clandestine activity. They met three times a year, and the purpose of their activity was not to duplicate public pastoral ministry but rather to work in depth, and each member of the community would specialize in one particular area. Their concern was to explore spiritually and theologically the relationship between a civilian occupation and the priesthood. They did not regard their situation as having been imposed by circumstances but as an opportunity for the church to acquire new experience, which would be necessary in the future, when, God willing, it would be able to operate freely. When that happened, the church should not simply return mechanically to where it was before 1948 but put to good use everything the Lord had guided them to during these years. After all, crisis, persecution, and a cross are a normal state of affairs for the church. Indeed it is *kairos*, the time of visitation. That concept of priesthood is not a part-time job; it pervades one's entire life, including one's civilian occupation. It was a question of fully living that experience while thoroughly reflecting on it theologically. The time had now come to think through the concept of the church for the future, maintaining contact with the culture of one's own country and with world Catholicism, so that the Czech church did not end up isolated or drowned in provincialism.

It all resonated profoundly with what I had long been seeking intuitively. Even so I left open the possibility of joining the Jesuit order. I returned to the barracks and took out my breviary to pray the Te Deum in thanks. At that moment the door opened, and the officer in command of the barracks entered. He announced that I had been posted out of Prague and must pack my things by the morning. At six o'clock the next morning a number of us set out on our journey on a bus with its windows painted over. On the way we got to know each other better and discovered that all of us who were being transferred at short notice had spent some time in the West, so we were probably regarded as politically unreliable and therefore had to leave Prague. I spent the final months of my military service—after being shifted from one place to another several times—in the Bohemian Forest, guarding military equipment. Once again I had plenty of time for prayer and reflection. Had my transfer from Prague after that talk with the Father Dvořák been a message from God?

When I returned from military service I told Father Dvořák I had decided to join that community. He found a priest who would take care of me and be my spiritual guide and tutor for the overall preparation. On October 1, 1973, I had my first meeting with him, and from that moment we worked together intensively for ten years.

At the time that man was a researcher at Charles University with degrees from two of its faculties; none of his colleagues suspected that he had been secretly ordained a priest abroad several years earlier. He was a striking person, very intelligent and well educated, whose background, like mine, was the Prague bourgeois intelligentsia. During those long years of preparation for the priesthood, I experienced some wonderful moments with my tutor, several vacations together, possibly hundreds of hours of spiritual conversation, and deep liturgy in the most modest surroundings. Among other things, I greatly enjoyed his cultivated taste and his sense of beauty. At the same time, however, he was someone with a complex character, who suffered from severe depression. I now see that during those long years of close contact, what was happening in our relationship was what psychoanalysts call transference and countertransference: we would see mirrored in the other the traits of our own character that each of us found hard to come to terms with. That would greatly complicate our relationship, particularly in later years, when I was already a priest and felt the need to go my own way.

When he realized that I must take a path that would be very different from his own, I could see a sadness in his eyes that mirrored all sorts of feelings, including understandable fears for me. Whenever we meet today, we don't understand each other. But maybe our relationship will be healed one day—either in this world or the next.

I sometimes wonder how I will cope if my students part company with me and take the opposite course to the one I consciously or subconsciously expected of them. All I can do is go on being aware that love is total respect for the freedom of others and that is precisely what distinguishes real love from self-love.

■ IN THE 1970S AND 1980S, WHEN HIGHER education was once more under the ideological dictatorship of the Communist Party, clandestine underground philosophical and theological seminars were held in private apartments in Prague and Brno. One such seminar took place every Friday evening for over seven years, and I regard it as one of the best intellectual initiatives in Prague at that time, one that possibly gave me more than university. In those days, the art of reading and interpreting philosophical texts was neglected at university. When one masters the hermeneutical approach, texts come alive in much the same way as when one starts to learn Hebrew or Greek, and a page of text that was previously just an art object starts to make sense.

We first read Max Scheler, and then for several years we would return repeatedly to Nietzsche's text *Thus Spoke Zarathustra*. Professor Jan Patočka visited the seminar several times, and on one occasion he gave a splendid lecture about Faust and about Europe and its heirs. From that environment there emerged one current of Prague philosophical thinking and an orientation that foreshadowed Charter 77, bringing together many people who played a key role both in the dissident movement and in politics after November 1989. Almost all the participants in that seminar became signatories of Charter 77 and were its foremost activists. The Charter spelled the end of that seminar, however, as each of its participants who signed it was constantly tailed by the secret police after February 1977.

I first learned about the preparations for the political initiative of the founding group of "Chartists" on August 21, 1976. At that moment I was attending a kind of dissident retreat at Houska Castle, where the Protestant pastor Svatopluk Karásek was employed as a custodian after he lost his permit to exercise his ministry. During a discussion one evening, the philosopher Jiří Němec informed a few of us that he and Václav Havel were drafting a manifesto that could be the starting point for an opposition political party or a human rights movement. At Christmas 1976 we already knew the complete text of the manifesto, and some had signed it. At the beginning of January 1977, when the text was submitted to the authorities in dramatic circumstances and published in the West, I received an early-morning visit from my friend Ivan Medek (President Havel's future chancellor), who warned me that a campaign of secret police harassment was under way, and we agreed on a method for keeping in touch.

This was a dramatic period for me. I felt a moral duty to sign the Charter, but my superiors in the clandestine community of priests were opposed to this at a time when my preparation for the priesthood was reaching its climax. They anticipated a harsh response to the Charter on the part of the regime and told me that I must choose. If I were to attract the attention of the secret police I would put at risk the entire clandestine structure of this part of the underground church. It would mean I would have to leave those circles. I spent several sleepless nights trying to decide what to do and spoke about it with a number of Chartists. They were also of the view that I should find other ways to show my solidarity with the signatories than by publicly appending my signature. I therefore decided to take a more active part in distributing the documents of the Charter, as well as its regular newsletter, and later the newsletter of the Committee for the Defense of the Unjustly Prosecuted.

Our community of priests—unlike some other deliberately apolitical groups of Catholics—sympathized unequivocally with the Chartists and was aware of the importance of political and cultural dissent. And for that reason, the superiors in the community eventually agreed—not entirely without difficulty or reservations—that I should continue, even as a secretly ordained priest, to take an active part in a number of underground philosophical seminars. Thanks to its relations with the dissidents, this group had certain contacts with the broader cultural dissent and could thus achieve one of its objectives: not to allow the church to lose contact with the best and most vigorous elements of contemporary Czech culture and of philosophical thinking, in particular. Later, in the 1980s, that complicated my relations with that community of priests somewhat, because I was interrogated by the secret police more frequently, which increased the risk of exposing the clandestine network.

For a number of years, one of those philosophical seminars would meet every Monday evening in the atmospheric apartment of Radim Palouš (appointed chancellor of Charles University after 1989) on Kampa Island beneath Charles Bridge in Prague. We dealt with various issues there but also political philosophy in the works of Hannah Arendt, Paul Ricoeur, and Erik Voegelin. On occasion, those seminars—which had to vary their venues, of course—hosted lectures by distinguished English, American, French, and German philosophers who traveled to Prague incognito as tourists. They included Charles Taylor, Jacques Derrida, and Paul Ricoeur. Sometimes the secret police received information about those clandestine trips, and the Western guests were interrogated and expelled from the country. We published a number of compilations in samizdat under the title "New Paths of Thinking." Later we collaborated regularly with the international journal *Il Nuovo Areopago*, which was published in Italy and had been founded on the initiative of Pope John Paul II as a platform for philosophical and theological dialogue between the West and the countries of Central and Eastern Europe. Our essays were published there, often under pseudonyms.

The activity of the Monday seminar included a regular three-week summer conference at the country cottage of Václav Havel at Hrádeček in eastern Bohemia. It was a time of lively discussion in a marvelous atmosphere of friendship and humor, which was not even marred by the presence of the "lunokhod," the nickname given to the mobile secret police observation post, which monitored the participants but did not intervene. Havel spoke little, tending instead to listen and ask questions; and he was also a marvelous cook. Later, when I read his speeches as president and the lectures he gave abroad, I would note with pleasure many echoes of the discussions we had at Hrádeček, during which his political philosophy crystallized.

That seminar survived until the end of 1989, but then the regular meetings stopped because most of its participants assumed important functions in the state or university. We still get together sometimes, however, and Václav Havel would occasionally attend our meetings when he was president. I remember shortly after the Velvet Revolution arriving at the seminar and seeing on the steps of the venue a conspicuously inconspicuous individual, and immediately past associations leapt to mind: Havel had arrived, and here was his "shadow." It was indeed the case: he was shadowed by a plain-clothes policeman but for rather different reasons now that he was president. Since it was just after the change of regime, it is not inconceivable that they were the same agents who tailed him when he was a dissident.

■ WHEN I HAD COMPLETED ROUGHLY FIVE years of spiritual training and theological study, my superiors came to the opinion after a series of interviews and meetings that the time had come for me to be ordained. In our community, however, it was taken for granted that a priest's spiritual training and self-education was a lifelong task and a natural dimension of his life. In Erfurt, at the beginning of June 1977, I was secretly ordained a deacon. The ordination took place in the private chapel of Bishop Aufderbeck. It was there that I first made the acquaintance of the then auxiliary bishop of Erfurt, Dr. Joachim Meisner. On the day of my ordination, while still a layperson, I joined the crowds of believers at a major celebration in the cathedral, which was also attended by Cardinal Bengsch of Berlin, the heads of the different orders, and other bishops, so I had the chance to see a "normal" church for the first time in a long while. The church in the GDR was marginalized, but life within it was relatively free—compared to us, at least.

In summer 1978 I undertook spiritual exercises in Slovakia on my own in preparation for priesthood. I embarked on them with my mind fully made up, but on the last day but one of the exercises I was gripped by a fear I had never known before: doubt and mental agony.

All of a sudden I was scared at the thought that I would soon be a priest. I had an acute longing not to lead such a demanding and unconventional life. I felt a yearning to have a wife and children like every "normal" man of my age, in short, to be like the rest, not to swim against the tide, to pursue my career and have free time when I wasn't working, not to have to live in constant uneasiness at the thought of disclosure and police persecution. Maybe that is why, many years later, I understood so well the message of the controversial film *The Last Temptation of Christ*. I also came to realize that the priesthood is not simply the splendid fulfillment of a noble personal ideal but a service requiring sacrifice and self-denial, and in the face of my weakness I doubted whether I would be capable of it for my entire life. On that occasion I made one symbolic act of sacrifice and self-denial, but it only served to increase my uncertainty. I discovered how little I was capable of real sacrifice; it was a moment of intense pain. I was afraid of the life I was preparing for. I yearned body and soul for a woman. I spent a sleepless night tossing and turning, and in the morning I rose with the conviction that my entire life so far had been a mistake and a pathological perversion. Instead of an elated *yes* I was filled with a painfully defiant *no*. I saw my future as a dark looming pit. I have to admit that toward the end of those exercises the thought of suicide even occurred to me. Throughout the return journey—because the period of my exercises had expired, and I had to return from my solitude—I had to grip the seat tightly, as I was strongly inclined to hurl myself out of the speeding express train: my entire life seemed to me like a locked railway train hurtling in the wrong direction. I took out my pocket edition of the Kralice translation of the New Testament and Psalms, which I had carried with me

since my military service, and I started to read one psalm after another until by the end of that journey I had read through the entire
Book of Psalms. "Clouds and darkness are round about him. . . . As for
me I am a worm and no man: a very scorn of men, and the out-cast of
the people. . . . Turn thee unto me, and have mercy upon me; for I am
desolate, and in misery." And still now, whenever I read those words
in the Breviary, I recall that moment. I arrived in Prague, got off the
train, the storm abated, and my heart yielded up a calm and clear yes.
I could now say with sincerity the closing prayer of the exercise of
St. Ignatius: Take, Lord, and receive. . . .

I knew that no one would show me in advance the path I was
embarking on; no one would guarantee it would be easy; it was necessary to set out and to question the Way itself, to commit myself to
it with confidence. When I told my confessor all about it the next
day, all he said was, "If you hadn't been through that trial during your
exercises, I could never have agreed to your ordination; now I can
agree to it with a clear conscience: go in peace."

After that everything was prepared for my secret ordination to
the priesthood, and I was only waiting for the clandestine message
to come from Germany when we received the news of the death of
Pope Paul VI and shortly afterward that of his successor, John Paul I.
We thought that this might mean the secret ordinations would be
held up until the new pope was installed and it would depend on the
stance he would take regarding the underground church in the Eastern bloc. Nevertheless, in spite of those events, a coded message was
received from Bishop Meisner, through whom our community maintained contact with Rome, saying I was to come.

Just before my departure, I went to my confessor to make a
whole-life confession. Then we prepared on a small table everything
necessary for the Mass and switched on the radio for a moment as
the conclave happened to be in progress at the Vatican. The general
opinion in the afternoon news was that the election of the new pope
would take several more days. However, from Vatican Radio there
came an excited announcement, interrupting the usual program and

switching over to St. Peter's Square from which the words, "Annuntio vobis gaudium magnum! Habemus papam!"—I announce to you news of great joy! We have a pope! The Most Reverend Karol Cardinal Wojtyla!—were broadcast to the world. A pope from the East! I was thunderstruck. There were no words to express our joy. As soon as the cardinal's words ended, we commenced the Mass—maybe the first Mass in the world in the reign of the new pope.

Then I immediately went to see a friend of mine who had recently been secretly ordained in Kraków for the Premonstratensian Canonry, possibly by Cardinal Wojtyla himself, or by one of his auxiliary bishops; the rule of underground activity is that one should never know more than is absolutely necessary. That particular friend had told me hundreds of stories about the courageous and highly nonconformist bishop of Kraków, who, like us—Patočka's pupils—was an exponent of phenomenology. My friend had not yet heard the fantastic news and reacted in a surprising manner: "I always used to bring Cardinal Wojtyla a bottle of home-distilled apple brandy as a gift from Moravia. I was due to make a trip to Kraków next month and I have the brandy ready for him in the cupboard. I shouldn't think we'd manage to smuggle it into the Vatican, so we'll drink it together now to his health. We're intoxicated with joy anyway, so a bottle of brandy won't do us any more harm." And so we did. As I left I had a yen to write a story in the style of Jan Neruda titled, "How I Drank the Pope's Brandy."

The very next day was fixed for my departure. The journey to one's ordination is taken up with much prayer, and there is much to reflect on. Just before the crowded train reached Erfurt, a sixteen-year-old German girl sat down beside me. She was reading a book with such intense excitement and uttering audible sighs from time to time that I couldn't resist taking a peek over her shoulder. It was some sex guide for girls, and the chapter she was tackling was titled "The French Kiss." She must have been on her way to a date and was eaten up with impatience at the thought of putting her newfound knowledge into practice. I realized that in the same town and at about the same time I would be committing myself to lifelong sexual abstention, and I couldn't help smiling at that coincidence and at the rich variety of human paths.

In Erfurt a red banner was strung out along the entire length of the station, with a quotation from Lenin: "Sparks create a flame." So do ours, I said to myself, but ours will blaze much longer than yours. And I thanked Vladimir Ilyich Lenin for providing an entirely fitting motto for my entry into a town where, in just a few hours' time, I was to become a priest, or to put it in Old Testament terms, a burnt offering for the Lord. I thought again about the day Jan Palach died and my meditation that day about what I would do if I had a slip of paper in my pocket with the words "Torch No. 2." I was thirty years old. Something had died within me, and something new was to be born.

▌ BEFORE THE ACTUAL ORDINATION CEREMONY, I spent three hours in private prayer in the chapel of the Ursuline Sisters Am Anger. I was aware of the significance of the moment when I would accept the "irrevocable sign" of Christ's priesthood. What was going to happen could not unhappen. I was fully aware of my freedom: were I now to say no, my life would clearly unfold quite differently. I now held my entire future in my hands. And at that moment it came home to me as never before that by freely choosing the only option, and burning all my other bridges, I wasn't destroying my freedom but realizing it. Yes, Abraham trusted the Lord and set off on a journey without knowing where he was bound. Why be afraid? After all, didn't the one who is the Way love me, and wasn't he wiser and more powerful than me, who foolishly wanted to run my life from the periphery of my little ego, when he was the real center of my life and of all life. Could I say anything other and better than the word I would shortly say to the ordaining bishop: "Adsum"—Here I am? I let go of the reins and released the cares from my heart, and I embarked on the journey.

I was driven to the bishop's house, covered by a coat, in the backseat of a car. Although the Catholic church in the GDR had greater freedom, we could not be sure whether the entrance to the bishop's residence was monitored by an East German secret police camera. The theme of the bishop's homily consisted of three words of the liturgy: *respice, suscipe, accipe*—look upon, receive, accept. It was Saturday, October 21, 1978. After five in the evening I was ordained a priest by Bishop Aufderbeck in the private chapel of his residence in the shadow of Erfurt Cathedral.

I COULDN'T GET TO SLEEP THAT NIGHT. Very early the next morning I celebrated my first Mass in the same small chapel of the nuns where I had meditated the previous afternoon before my ordination. My concelebrants in the empty chapel were Bishop Meisner as consecrating bishop and Fr. Václav Dvořák. I offered up that Mass above all to the newly elected pope. Our intention was to finish the Mass before the nuns arrived for Morning Prayer, but we overran, and by the end the chapel was full of nuns, who must have understood what was going on when they saw a young bearded priest celebrating Mass in the company of a bishop and an older, gray-haired priest. One of the sisters approached the bishop and asked whether their community could sing the Te Deum. And so the Mass concluded with the singing of the assembled nuns, some of whom were elderly, but they also included some quite young novices. It was a pleasure for me, because I had always felt a close affinity with members of women's orders, whom I truly perceived as my sisters.

After the Mass, the bishop and I went to watch the live broadcast of the pope's enthronement on West German television and heard his first homily on St. Peter's Square, which culminated with the words, "Do not be afraid!" It was obvious to us that the first Slav pope would have a great effect on the life of the Czech church also, and possibly the future of Europe as a whole. I realized that I must have been the first priest to have been ordained during his pontificate and wondered whether I would ever have the opportunity to meet him in person and share that fact with him. I sensed in my heart that I would, but more than eleven years would pass before it happened.

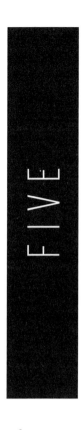

FIVE

A Priest of the Underground Church

It was obvious to me that ordination as a clandestine priest involved serious risks. When I was taking leave of Bishop Meisner I told him I didn't know what to expect back in Czechoslovakia and whether we would ever see each other again. He replied, "Yes, one must anticipate every eventuality." He said it so calmly that his words would bring me comfort for years afterward. Yes, I would repeat to myself, one must indeed anticipate every eventuality.

It is very difficult in hindsight to tell what were one's subconscious longings and intimations and what were rational considerations, but it strikes me that I never expected to live to see freedom for the church. I thought it was much more likely that sooner or later the police would find me out, and I would be gotten rid of in one way or another. I just hoped that it wouldn't happen too soon. For one thing, I was not a born hero hankering after the martyr's palm, and for another, I wanted the chance to serve people as a priest for a while after having prepared for it for so long. My friend Jaroslav Kašparů once brought me the news that one of the clandestinely ordained bishops in Moravia had been found dead in a pool of blood; the case still remains unsolved, and it would seem that he was murdered by agents of the KGB because he had contacts with the underground church in Russia. He asked me if I was afraid for my life. "I am," I replied frankly, "but what the hell?" I am convinced that not being afraid isn't the most important thing (it can also indicate apathy or not being well informed); the key thing is not to let fear dictate our actions. Fear (like pain) can be a useful sign of impending danger, but we must not let it rule our lives.

The community of priests that I belonged to operated cautiously, covertly, and on the basis of strict secrecy, and this proved to be a prudent strategy. We would all meet as a group three times a year, but otherwise we only met in twos. Most of the time we celebrated Mass alone very early in the morning, and on Saturdays special occasions with friends. I celebrated my "first Mass" in the Czech lands with my brother priests on the Feast of Christ the King at a country cottage not far from Prague. After that I celebrated Mass fairly regularly in the home of my friends, the Kováříks, a couple whom I had been with in autumn 1968 during our brief exile in Britain. The windows of their apartment looked out over the old Jewish cemetery in the heart of Old Prague, and during Mass I would often think of the chosen people of Israel, God's first love, and ask forgiveness for all the suffering we Christians had caused the Jews, both in the Prague ghetto and elsewhere in the world. I also liked to celebrate Mass in summer with friends in the open air, at early morning in the forests or in the mountains.

We operated according to the principle that we could divulge our priesthood to others only if three conditions were fulfilled—and always under an oath of total secrecy. They had to be people we knew very well, they had to be capable of keeping a secret even in extremis, and they had to require our service as priests for some reason. But as a matter of principle, it was forbidden in our circle to inform our own parents, because apparently in the past carelessness had resulted in a breach of security when someone from the family circle had let the cat out of the bag. This could, of course, jeopardize the entire group, and betray the whole network of the hidden church, which had contacts abroad. Such carelessness could have dire consequences, not only for the clandestinely ordained priest, but also for other people. Priests risked several years' imprisonment for the "crime of impeding the state supervision of churches and religious societies"—which in our day usually carried a two-year sentence—but they could also be charged with "collaboration with foreign enemies" and goodness knows what else. However, there was no longer the risk of a death sentence or imprisonment for life for "spying for the Vatican," as there had been in the 1950s.

So I couldn't even tell my mother, with whom I lived until her death in 1986, that I was a priest. However, I am sure that a mother's heart can sense many things. Although we couldn't speak about a lot of things specifically, it was obvious toward the end of her life that she knew somehow what my situation was. She respected my secret, however, and I was glad she didn't know absolutely everything, because it would have been hard for her to live with the knowledge that I could be sent to prison any day. Although she did not profess membership in the church during her adult life, I don't think she ever abandoned faith as such in her heart. A few years before she died, Father Reinsberg, who was fond of both my parents, reconciled her formally with God and the church. From then on, during her lengthy time in the hospital, I was able to bring holy communion to her.

It rather distressed my mother that I had no family of my own or close blood relatives. Although she knew I could make my way in the world, she also knew I wasn't a practical person and had various other vulnerabilities. It was a great relief to my mother just before her death when the family of Dr. Scarlett Vasiluková-Rešlová, who was part of my closest spiritual family and selflessly helped me take care of her, fully "adopted" me and forever after was my calm human support.

My mother died peacefully in my arms, reconciled with God and people, on May 1, the Feast of St. Joseph the Worker, to whom every day for years she said the prayer she had prayed since child-hood: "Preserve me from sin and grant me a happy death." Previously I was unable to imagine what a "happy death" was, and I had feared the day of my mother's death since I was a child. But when I held my mother's hand, said a few words of farewell, and gave her holy communion, she immediately closed her eyes, and I felt her passage into eternity as a gift, and I knew her prayer had been heard.

■ THE "UNDERGROUND CHURCH" AND "illegal church structures" were actually what the secret police called us. We never regarded ourselves as some special church "alongside" or even "against" the church that officially functioned in Czechoslovakia.

Every baptized person is part of the church. I have always attached importance to Karl Rahner's assertion that the church is the sign of the unity of humankind, and those who are not formally members of it belong to it in a certain way by the very fact of being human, and particularly by virtue of their yearning for meaning, truth, and good. We realized that under a Communist regime, the church could not publicly perform much of what is a natural and inseparable part of its life. We wanted to prevent the church from being reduced to the bare minimum of activity permitted by the atheist regime, which was essentially just the liturgy, and the repair of church buildings, a situation to which many members of the laity and even the clergy were beginning to become accustomed. In the ranks of the officially active clergy we carefully distinguished between many self-sacrificing priests whom we deeply respected and with whom we co-operated where possible and the officials of the regime-sponsored Association of Catholic Clergy—Pacem in Terris, who could be seen embracing the Communist bigwigs in front of the TV cameras; we could only pray for the latter. But both the "official" church and the "unofficial" structures were multifaceted and extremely variegated. I never thought of the Czech church in those days as monochromatic;

those of us who were clandestine priests never thought ourselves better than those priests who continued to serve in parishes and often
had to compromise with the regime. As it was later proved, there were
heroes and traitors—but above all weak and erring individuals—on
both sides.

Our circle did its best not to dissipate our efforts unnecessarily.
On principle, therefore, we did not perform activities that people
had public access to in church, as we did not want to draw them away
misguidedly into "underground" activity, thereby risking too great a
split in the church. We concentrated on what was officially forbidden: spiritual exercises, study groups, and attempts at a kind of cate-
gorical pastoral activity, particularly in areas familiar to us and which
were strictly prohibited by the Communists, such as work with students and young intellectuals. In the latter activity we intentionally
collaborated with some "officially" permitted clergy.

I later told Father Reinsberg that I was a priest. He replied that
he had already been sure of it for a long time. That marked the start
of a new form of cooperation between us. Sometimes when he was
approached by students who had grown up without any religious
education, he would tell them that he did not have time to deal with
contemporary theology but he had a psychologist friend who was
very interested in theology and could introduce them to the mystery
of faith in a way that was in tune with their thinking and education
and could answer their questions. Over the years I prepared a number of people in that way for baptism and first communion, without
telling them I was a priest; they subsequently received those sacraments in church, mostly from Father Reinsberg. On occasion, such
as when a student's public baptism could mean his or her expulsion
from university, or if it might jeopardize Father Reinsberg's official
permit, the baptism would take place in the Týn Church in the evening behind closed doors.

Later still, I chiefly prepared candidates for the priesthood, assisting their studies and spiritual training and giving them exercises

prior to their ordination. In some cases I was witness to their secret ordination, mostly in Berlin, in the private chapel of Cardinal Meisner, or at night in the crypt in St. Hedwig's Cathedral, which was connected to the bishop's residence by an underground passage.

THESE DAYS THE ISSUE OF CELIBACY IS bound to crop up sooner or later in conversations about the Catholic priesthood. I was already in my thirties when I was ordained and made my promise of celibacy. I have never broken that promise. However, I must add that at certain moments of my life, sexual abstinence came at the cost of great inner struggle; I am not entirely sure that God intended me to invest so much energy in that direction. I am now convinced that the time is approaching when the Latin branch of the Catholic Church will return to the practice of the first millennium—still maintained in the Catholic Church of the Eastern Rite—that alongside celibate priests there will also be ordained married priests. For a long time I defended celibacy by reference to myself. If I had had responsibility for a family, I don't think I would have risked undertaking a clandestine role during the time the church was persecuted, and even now, when my working day starts early in the morning and finishes long after midnight, I find it hard to see how, in addition, I would cope with the role of husband and father. I know from many of my friends among the Protestant clergy the tensions that exist between the demands of pastoral service and those of family and that these sometimes lead to marital and family breakdown.

Nevertheless, I have always considered it my duty to warn candidates for priesthood and monastic life not to be lulled into a false sense of security by the fact that they have little interest in erotic or sexual activity at a time when they are most involved in spiritual exercises with their peers. Young people are capable of such enthusiasm for a religious ideal that they often spontaneously, and with little effort, sublimate their sexuality and come to the naive conclusion that it will always be like that. It often happens that around the age of thirty maturity arrives naturally, along with greater harmonization of the personality, which previously developed in a very one-sided way. Only then does the yearning for a woman well up like an unexpected underground spring, and it tends to have a powerful sexual charge. And because such people are often unprepared and unexperienced, it can catch them unawares, and they will have an uphill task during their fourth decade of life. If they have been taught by bad spiritual literature and neurotic confessors to reject sexuality as such and vilify it, and if they have a subconscious horror of it, the outlook for them is either neurosis or a dramatic and often traumatic reversal in their career.

Even though I knew that blood—and not ink or holy water—coursed through my veins and that I was fundamentally a very passionate person, I wouldn't say I had any great problems in that respect in my early youth. My passion tended to spill over into spiritual and intellectual activity, leaving only enough for a few platonic love affairs in the "mundane" world. They were fairly calm experiences, and I viewed them as a natural expression of the fact that I was a normal person capable of falling in love, someone of flesh and blood, not wood. That was always the assessment of my wise confessors, even in the period when I was contemplating holy orders.

I had the great advantage of having studied philosophy, but I have to admit that I myself had to cope with tension and problems, particularly during my thirties, in the period after ordination. I would strongly caution against playing down these serious human problems by misguided reckless reliance on "supernatural means." St. Thomas Aquinas taught wholesomely that "grace does not destroy nature, but perfects it," and in this connection in particular, misbegotten disregard of nature (including psychological knowledge and competent psychotherapeutic assistance in crises) can gravely backfire. I have sometimes experienced some very awkward "anti-natural" behavior from the victims of those enthusiasts of the supernatural.

There is a tendency to look for some romance in a priest's past. To satisfy such curiosity, I'll mention something that certainly had a touch of the romantic novel about it. At the beginning of the 1970s, when I was first thinking about the priesthood, I had a platonic attachment to a very beautiful and interesting young woman. It was a romantic relationship and for my part strongly influenced by my reading of the priest-poet Jakub Deml, particularly his collection *Miriam*; in my letters to her I always addressed her as "little sister." That relationship meant a great deal to me, and only now can I appreciate how she probably experienced it: on the one hand, simply loving me, and, on the other, knowing that I was contemplating the priesthood, which meant a great deal to her as a believer, particularly in light of the situation of the church at that time. I remember a date we had on March 15, 1972, on Charles Bridge. She told me that Fr. Antonín Mandl had died that day, and she added that although it was not easy for her to say it, she was convinced that I should take his place and become a priest. Twenty years later to the day, I told that story to the students at St. Salvator Church. If on that spring evening I had been enabled to see into the future and see myself celebrating Mass at the same hour, twenty years later, in the church just a short distance away, where Father Mandl also served, would I have believed it?

My yearning for the priesthood did indeed become a firm decision, and she and I parted company. I didn't see her for several years, but I knew that she remained single, although she was nearly thirty. I couldn't help wondering, therefore, whether my involvement with her wasn't ill fated. In my whole-life confession prior to ordination I mentioned that separation years before and voiced my concern that I might have inadvertently marred another person's future and happiness. Around midnight a few days after I returned from Germany following my ordination, I opened my mailbox and discovered her wedding announcement inside. During the first Mass I celebrated back home in Prague, I included a prayer for the happiness of their marriage.

We met by chance years later, and she told me that her husband was at home in bed dying from cancer. In that situation I revealed to her that I was a priest. I subsequently visited her home several times and said masses there. I will never forget a Mass on the first Sunday of Advent. Her husband actually got out of bed and played the harmonium, even though he could no longer hear because of a brain tumor; I wrote the homily down for him. It was a meditation on the words of the psalm: "I was glad when they said to me, 'Let us go to the house of the Lord!'" Apparently Pope John XXIII had replied with that verse when the doctors told him of his impending death. It was obvious to the three of us that the husband was standing on the threshold of the Lord's house, and indeed, just a few hours after that Mass he died peacefully. Whenever I celebrate Mass on the first Sunday of Advent, and read that verse, I remember him and our story.

■ SOON AFTER ORDINATION, I WAS ASSIGNED — along with Petr Pit'ha, another secretly ordained priest — the task of revising the basic documents of our community, including key texts about the spirituality of our mission. After that I was elected by our community as spiritual director for the priests of that sector, and my appointment was confirmed by our superiors.

An important tenet of our association was that the linking of priesthood and a civilian occupation, as well as living in secular surroundings, was not regarded as a temporary stopgap situation imposed by political conditions but as a significant approach that would be necessary, particularly in the future, even when the church would be accorded complete freedom. And if we live to see that day, we used to say, we will definitely not all disperse into local parishes, even if we won't be obliged to conceal our priesthood.

In that respect we were very different from underground groups that regarded this form of priesthood as "a reserve" for when the situation deteriorated and there would be dramatic persecution of the church like the former genocide of Catholics in Mexico, Albania, or Romania. Our estimation of future political developments was not as pessimistic as among those associated with Bishops Davídek and Blaha. We hoped for a gradually improved scope for activity.

Of course we did not dream of some future "Christian society," but we assumed that following a possible erosion of the totalitarian regime, society would be considerably dechristianized, and for such secular conditions there would be a need for priests with great experience of secular life.

Nor did we regard the purpose of our priesthood as a frantic pursuit of quantity—celebrating as many masses as we could, baptizing as many people as we could, or ordaining as many priests as we could, and definitely not trying to patch up the disintegrating network of parish-based pastoral activity. We strove to understand what God was telling us by permitting this state of the church. Was he inviting us to multiply our pastoral activities or instead to meditate honestly on the "signs of the times" and reappraise many things on which the church had become fixated in the recent past? We considered the classic territorial network of parishes outmoded. Our maxim was, "Quality takes precedence over quantity." We wanted to go deeper rather than wider; reflection was not a luxury but work that would pay off. It wasn't possible to pour new wine into old wineskins: we would have to explore and experiment with new paths and new forms.

In a similar vein, Josef Zvěřina wrote a text titled *A Third Way*, in which he sought to defend this form of priesthood linked with civilian occupation as a legitimate model alongside those of parish priests and priests in monastic orders. We gave thought to a theology and spirituality for this path of ministry. In the spiritual exercises that I gave our priests prior to ordination, and later in the course of their ministry, I would stress that priesthood was not just a social role that could be characterized by the customary external signs, but a lifetime vocation and way of life. So it was necessary to take that ontological core and develop very creative and bold new forms, a new style of living, praying, and working. A priest without a parish, a church, a clerical collar, or a rubber stamp was obliged to reflect constantly, and ever more deeply, on what constituted the true essence of priesthood; he must seek it deeper. The fact that even now I am loath to go around in a clerical collar and conform to the traditional image of a "reverend gentleman" is not out of some facile attempt to be assimilated with the world, or to endear myself to nonbelievers, but instead to pose afresh, for myself and others, the question about the true meaning of priesthood. We did not regard ourselves as part-time priests who looked forward to the end of our working hours in order to devote ourselves fully for a while to our "real" work as priests: celebrating Mass somewhere or teaching the catechism.

Since we considered our civilian profession an inseparable part of our priestly vocation *to sanctify the world*, we did not seek low-skilled work, which would be relatively less time-consuming and occupy our minds less, but—where possible—demanding and responsible occupations, enabling long-term working partnerships with thinking and educated people. We did not look on such partnerships as mission opportunities, aimed solely at maximizing the number of conversions, but as real opportunities for dialogue, solidarity, and finding out what people who were distant from the church really thought. We tried to respect them and to seek what we had in common.

We were therefore inspired by Rahner's idea of "anonymous Christians" and looked for points of contact between a "universal priesthood of all believers" (Zvěřina preferred the term "shared priesthood") of all the baptized and the "ministerial priesthood," without seeking to entirely eliminate or relativize the difference between them. It was those elements of Rahner's thinking that we tried to incorporate into the community's original constitution, and its spiritual guidelines, which were formulated sometime in the 1950s and which, like the concepts of Felix Davídek, were clearly inspired by Teilhard's theology of Christian existence as participation in the "Christification of the cosmos," the "culmination of Creation," and the coming to maturity of the human race.

That concept has theological, spiritual, and practical pitfalls, of course. In the polemic with the so-called silent church, some of our bishops today talk about the temptation to disparage the distinctiveness of the laity and about a kind of sophisticated clericalism, and even in those days, some Western theologians we met secretly (particularly during regular vacations in Hungary) criticized us for what they saw as a slightly romantic mystique of priesthood. Such objections cannot be merely swept aside. And yet I believe that the underlying vision that guided us in those days was right and is still inspirational; it is very unfortunate that what was clearly the most valuable achievement of the period of persecution was so casually forgotten and abandoned by many people after 1989.

The developments in the 1990s—particularly my move from the Theological to the Arts Faculty—led me, in a circuitous fashion, to acknowledge once more that the linkage of priesthood and a civilian profession was a charism to which I should remain true.

THE UNDERGROUND CHURCH ESSENTIALLY comprised three groups. The "unofficial structures" covered those who had been publicly ordained but whom the state had subsequently banned from pursuing public ministry, so that they were obliged to work in civilian—often unskilled—jobs, such as night porters, lavatory cleaners, or boiler operators. They pursued their pastoral activity only clandestinely. They included, for instance, my friend Miloslav Vlk, future archbishop of Prague and cardinal, who was employed as a window cleaner because his state permit had been revoked. We would often meet each other in the street when I was on my way to work at the clinic, and he would be carrying a pail in one hand and a brush for washing store windows in the other.

But the actual core of the underground church was made up of those who had never received a state permit because they had been ordained secretly, either abroad or in Czechoslovakia. We did not all know each other by any means. It was not a coordinated network with a single organizing structure but rather a number of groups, which worked autonomously, and whose members knew only a few people outside their own particular group. We were not curious about the details of each other's lives because we knew that at future interrogations it would be impossible to beat out of us information we didn't have. Apart from our own circle, I only knew a few others who were ordained abroad, either in the GDR or Poland, or exceptionally—around 1968—in the West. They were mostly members of religious orders, chiefly Salesians, Franciscans, Dominicans, and Premonstratensians, or people from quasi-monastical communities recognized by Rome, like our own. Monastic life, particularly that of men's orders, was virtually eliminated and forced into illegality by the Communist regime in the course of a single April night in 1950. That night, all the monasteries and convents were invaded by the police. The members of orders were transported to a number of locations from which many were transferred to forced labor units or punishment detachments of the army, and some were put on trial and sentenced to lengthy penal servitude in prison or in the uranium mines.

Members of orders who survived that period, or who joined orders clandestinely, spent decades protesting that genocide by means of their underground activity, and they heroically kept alive one of the fundamental dimensions of the life of the church. And even some priests who graduated from seminary and operated officially as parish priests secretly took monastic vows. This gave rise to many ideas and practical experience, which I believe could lead to a greater aggiornamento of the orders in the conditions of secular society; I think it is a sin that that hard-won experience is ignored nowadays.

Among the underground priests there were also those who had been ordained by Czech or Slovak bishops who themselves had been secretly ordained. The genesis of that branch of the clandestine church dated to before the Communist putsch. Unlike many Western politicians, who were lulled into a false sense of security by the wartime anti-Hitler alliance with Stalin, Pope Pius XII harbored no illusions that Soviet Communism could ever change. As soon as Stalin discovered that large sections of the Soviet population—particularly in the Ukraine—were unwilling to sacrifice their lives to maintain Soviet rule and that they even welcomed German troops as possible liberators, he changed his tactics and his attitude to the church—for a time. The war against Hitler ceased to be publicized as defense of the Communist empire but as a "Great Patriotic War," and Orthodox priests started to be seen heading Red Army units with icons and banners bearing images of the Mother of God and Christ the Savior. Combined with the dread of the violence wrought by Hitlerite troops—and SS divisions in particular—on the conquered territories, this marked a turning point in the war, and it led to the defeat of Hitler's eastern campaign. Once the war was over, however, Stalin's brief love affair with the Orthodox Church came to an end, and there was a return to the previous model: the church was totally in thrall to the state, and its top representatives became collaborators or actual agents of the secret police; religion was once more forced out of public life, and those priests and believers who failed to conform were persecuted once more. Pius XII anticipated Communism's expansion to the other countries of Eastern and Central Europe and therefore adopted a number of preparatory measures for a period of persecution. These measures included the instruction to each of the bishops in Czechoslovakia to ordain an auxiliary bishop to serve in the event of their being imprisoned, sent to a concentration camp, or executed. It now appears that Pius XII expected that the period of repression would be exceptionally harsh (which is why he encouraged priests to accept martyrdom) but of short duration. He did not believe that the victory of Communism would be long-lasting or indeed permanent, which is also why he opposed any compromise with the Communists. Those who were willing to come to terms with the Communist regime in any way were liable to ecclesiastical sanctions; there was the threat of excommunication for reading the Communist press. That was the spirit of the pastoral letter circulated by Prague archbishop Josef Beran, protesting the first measures against the church and religious freedom by the Communist government. Any priest who read that letter from the pulpit was blacklisted by the regime.

Some of the measures taken by the Vatican just prior to the 1950s were unsuccessful, however. The names of secretly ordained bishops were soon discovered. It is said that some worthy monsignor in the Vatican, under the impression that the purple buttons on his cassock and the physical proximity of the tomb of the apostolic princes were sufficient guarantee of intelligent decision making, allowed their names to be printed in the official documents of the Holy See, where they were read with interest by Soviet agents. Those who were secretly ordained were rounded up and imprisoned, often before the sitting bishops were forced out of their residences and ceased to perform their duties.

Likewise, the Vatican's assessment of the viability of the Communist regimes turned out to be wrong. Later, during the pontificates of John XXIII and particularly of Paul VI, the Vatican authorities concluded that it was necessary to reassess the hardline approach to the Communist regimes, which had not achieved the anticipated results, and that a new strategy should be formulated chiefly in coordination with those who had most experience of the actual situation in those countries, in other words, the representatives of churches under Communist rule. However, those who were able to speak officially on behalf of Czechoslovak Catholics, namely, the vicars capitular, who acted as would-be administrators of dioceses from the long-abandoned episcopal residences, were puppets of the Communist regime and mouthpieces of their propaganda. The priests who supported the regime-sponsored "peace movement of Catholic clergy" were obedient tools of the "pax sovietica." Seemingly influenced by the global movement toward détente in the 1960s and the anticipated gradual liberalization of the Soviet bloc, the Holy See replaced its hardline Cold War tactics with a much more accommodating Ostpolitik, conceived and led for many years by Cardinal Cassaroli. In some countries, however—particularly Hungary—that policy of compromise and "small steps" caused the church long-term damage by undermining its moral credibility. Fortunately, the Czechoslovak Communist regime, almost throughout its existence—apart from a brief period during the Prague Spring—was so intransigent in its hostility toward the church that not even Cassaroli's more amenable approach led to any compromises that might have made things slightly easier for the church but would have gravely compromised it in moral terms.

Let us return, however, to the origins of the clandestine church in the 1950s. It seems that before they were arrested, some of the secretly ordained bishops of the "first wave" managed to ordain bishops to replace them. But by then the situation was such that the normal procedures for appointing bishops could not be followed, and there was no time or opportunity to ordain bishops on the basis of papal appointment. However, in this matter canon law is inflexible: a bishop who ordains another bishop without papal appointment and also the bishop who accepts ordination in this way face the church's severest penalty: excommunication. Was there perhaps some possible dispensation for such extreme situations? Was it possible to assume that such procedures undertaken in good faith, and on the basis of heroic sacrifice and a sense of responsibility for the church, would be subsequently brought into line with canon law? Here we enter the labyrinth of conjecture regarding matters that still remain a conundrum, and painfully unresolved, not only in Bohemia, Moravia, and Slovakia but also in China and in other places where the church has found itself in extreme situations.

That was the beginning of the genealogy of one part of the clandestine church, which would later achieve notoriety, particularly because of the activity of the Moravian clandestine bishop Felix Davídek. I never met Davídek, although from the end of the 1960s I heard a lot about him, particularly from priests who were in prison with him. I got the impression that he was an exceptional individual who was on the borderline between genius and insanity. Davídek undoubtedly had many remarkable intuitions, as well as enormous courage, but his assessment of the situation was not always realistic, and he lacked the patience of far-sightedness. A number of not entirely level-headed or reliable people clearly became involved in his grandiose structures. Moreover, "information noise" probably disrupted the clandestine negotiations with Rome, as a result of which Bishop Davídek and his followers—in good faith, I am sure—considerably exceeded their authority. That was one of the stumbling blocks in the negotiations between his followers and the hierarchy after 1989. My guess is that the confusion was caused chiefly by the clandestinely ordained Bishop Hnilica, a Slovak Jesuit, who spent many years in exile in the West. I met with Hnilica several times around 1989, and I gained the impression that he was an extremely unreliable person, who was unable to distinguish between reality and his fantasies and wishes. This was a typical illness that threatened people who spent years in extreme conditions of clandestinity and persecution. It was above all Hnilica's reports that presumably convinced Davídek that the pope was informed about his experiments and that he approved of them.

With his original, albeit confused, Theilhard-inspired theology, Felix Davídek influenced a lot of people. He personally, or through the intermediary of his collaborators, ordained many priests, who included and still include people of great worth, both among celibate and married priests. From my own experience of a number of clandestinely ordained married priests, I know that they never called into doubt the vow of celibacy for priests of the Western Rite, and they accepted ordination in the conviction that Davídek and his people had Rome's permission, in our exceptional situation, to ordain Roman Catholics in the Eastern Rite, in which, throughout its history, it has been possible for married men to be ordained priest. Those married priests whom I knew were not dissidents or progressives in the church—some of them had very traditional theological views, just like some married priests, former Anglican priests—whom I later met in Britain. Some Western campaigners associated with the Wir sind Kirche movement subsequently took a great interest in Davídek's married priests, and they were particularly impressed by the fact that Davídek ordained at least two women as Catholic priests. He justified it on the grounds of his expectation that in the 1970s the Catholic Church would be persecuted as it had been in the 1950s and that women Christians would find themselves in prison or concentration camps, where there would be a need for the services of a priest. That mistaken assessment of the situation was evidence, however, of the fact that Davídek was gradually losing the faculty of sound judgment. That was one of the reasons divisions and splits started to occur among the priests and bishops in his Koinotes community. Davídek himself did not live to see the events of 1989.

■ ALTHOUGH STALINIST TERROR DID NOT return after the suppression of the Prague Spring, we still lived in a police state. Even in the late 1980s, harassment of the church and persecution of underground activities continued. From time to time, the secret police would remind us of their presence by an unannounced visit to one's apartment and absurd checking of identity documents. It was meant as a deterrent: Watch your step; we know about you! At other times, on the contrary, they did not interfere for a long time and carefully concealed their surveillance, in preparation for the moment when they would have enough documentation for arrest and indictment.

From time to time the news would reach me that inquiries had been made about me during the interrogations of others, starting with the first imprisonment of Ladislav Hejdánek. That was long before my ordination. Later, the police became increasingly interested in me. As soon as my name was mentioned during an interrogation of someone else, I would have to break off contact with other members of our circle, in accordance with agreed tactics, so as not to endanger the entire group. I would then spend several nights hiding samizdat materials somewhere safe and burning any notes.

Once the secret police made a surprise visit in fairly dramatic circumstances, when I was visiting my friend Martin Palouš (after 1989 our ambassador to the United States and later at the UN in New York) at the boiler room where he worked. We used to hold philosophical seminars there, and on that particular day, we had celebrated a Mass there. It was St. Andrew's Day in November 1977, and by then I took part in the Mass as a deacon. While clearing the table after the Mass, our colleague Zdeněk Neubauer jokingly commented that, just as we were told not to believe that the first Christians spent most of their time in catacombs, when the history of the underground church in Czechoslovakia came to be written one day, historians would be obliged to add that those people did not spend all their time in cellars.

At that very moment, there was banging at the door, and we heard the announcement from the other side: "Security check of the boiler room!" The security referred to was State Security, in other words, a raid by a group of secret policemen. In hindsight, I realize that at such moments one is endowed with an exceptional ability to react at lightning speed. We instantly hid any evidence of the Mass we had celebrated, as well as all samizdat materials associated with Charter 77. We were taken to the secret police headquarters on Bartolomějská Street and interrogated all night. We repeated the story we had previously agreed on about celebrating St. Andrew's Day and refused to answer any other questions, so in the morning they released us for lack of proof (luckily they did not carry out a thorough search of the boiler room).

I was brought in for questioning several times afterward. However, the questioning mostly had no direct connection to my activity as an underground priest (I have reason to believe that the police never did discover I had been ordained, although they suspected it, of course) but instead concerned my contacts with the cultural underground, the political dissidents, and the Catholic samizdat network. During interrogation, I was first subjected to threats, but then I was promised that I could immediately start to teach at university and travel abroad if I signed a document saying I would collaborate with the secret police. The classical model of interrogations was a combination of good cop/bad cop. The bad cop would yell and make threats, then go away for an hour and leave the person being interrogated alone with the good cop, who was understanding and full of promises. In the beginning a lot of people at that moment would agree to cooperate. Every interrogation was good training in self-knowledge. Their questions were like X-rays, trying to uncover people's weak points and identify things for which they had an inordinate longing or what was their greatest fear.

Thank God I always said a clear no to all threats and inducements, and it turned out to be a better solution than attempting to use other strategies with the police, as some tried to do. When the secret police archives were opened after 1989, I read in the police files that I behaved "arrogantly and refused to cooperate" and that I "made a show of intellectual superiority."

My interrogators once told me that in spite of all their efforts they had not managed to find anything in my past with which to blackmail me, but they were already working on some forged materials that could be used to compromise me morally. They used various methods of psychological pressure on me, but I was not subjected to beating or physical violence, unlike Václav Malý, the future auxiliary bishop in Prague. I may be mistaken, but sometimes I had the impression that some of the more intelligent interrogators actually respected me. During those years, what interested them were my relationships with dissidents in the field of culture, as well as with philosophical circles and samizdat, and in particular with Václav Havel and his brother Ivan. At the end of one of those interrogations they said to me, "Don't think we don't know about your important position in the Jesuit order." I replied with a smile that I admired the police, who know more about me than I know myself. So I realized that they did not know so much about me after all and that in many cases they were just bluffing.

Our personal attitude to our interrogators was a psychological and spiritual problem. It may sound like something out of a book of devotion, but, following the advice of priests who spent many years in prison, I often prayed for my interrogators. Once during an interrogation I imagined what it would be like if the regime changed and this secret police interrogator came running to me to protect him from an enraged mob. I asked myself whether my love for my enemies was genuine enough that I would do it even at risk of my own life. And that time my answer was yes.

That imagined situation had a comical sequel when the regime did change after 1989. I happened to be standing at an intersection when a luxury automobile stopped next to me. The driver wound down the window and greeted me cheerfully. Only when he declared, "I am following you again, Dr. Halík," did I recognize my interrogator, now the commercial representative of some Western company. Seeing the look of surprise on my face, he added that he had seen me on TV and was impressed with how well I had spoken and that he had it in mind to come to listen to one of my sermons sometime. He drove off in high spirits, leaving me, on foot and in the rain, to wonder whether he had no clear memory of those earlier days or no conscience or whether he was simply arrogant; whether it was his fault or the fault of our Velvet Revolution for being too soft; or whether I had imagined it all. I was not so much annoyed as profoundly ashamed on his behalf (or on behalf of someone, or something); it was one of the few moments in my life when I felt like getting drunk.

■ DUE TO PRESSURE FROM THE SECRET POLICE I later lost my job at the Institute of the Ministry of Industry. The director more or less openly told me that the police were putting pressure on him, and he would find it impossible to keep me on the staff. So I preferred to offer my resignation. At that time a job became vacant at the treatment clinic for alcoholics at the university hospital of St. Apollinaris— just a few steps from the maternity hospital where I was born. I expect the secret police thought my work with alcoholics and drug addicts was not harmful to the regime, so I managed to remain there until the end of 1989. I was engaged as a psychotherapist after obtaining a certificate in clinical psychology. This opened a new and very rewarding chapter in my life and once more confirmed that those who sought to harm me actually benefited me.

There was an extremely wide range of patients, from typical drunks and young junkies to overworked doctors and many artists, not to mention washed-up officials of the Communist Party and former intelligence officers, who had become victims of their own profession. They included not just "déclassé elements," habitual criminals, and small-time crooks but also extremely sensitive individuals who had fallen prey to alcohol at objectively difficult moments of their lives. Alongside psychopaths and people with personality disorders, there were people who had held important jobs, but their drug addiction had gone unnoticed. Work at the Apollinaris clinic was demanding and interesting, and I treated several hundred people whose lives had been affected by addiction to alcohol or other substances. I was able to work and live with each of my patients for several months, from morning to late afternoon; the basis of treatment was a therapeutic community and group therapy.

This was a new human experience for me. For the first time, in fact, I stepped outside the world of intellectuals and had to learn to communicate intelligibly with people who were often very unsophisticated—which I did not find at all easy. I never looked down on people without education, or of lower social status, but because of the surroundings in which I grew up and worked, I had simply not come into contact with them. And so I was obliged to make up for that lack of experience, like when one starts in a new profession.

The first time I made a tour of the facility—starting with nighttime duty in the "sobering up" unit—I recalled the words of Dostoyevsky from *Crime and Punishment*: "I bowed down to all the suffering of humanity." I realized I was in the right place: a priest should serve the poor, and these patients seemed to me truly the poorest of our times. Alcoholics and drug addicts gradually lose everything: health, money, family, career, reputation, and self-respect. Had I not undergone that experience during those years, my priesthood might have remained slightly ineffectual, and would certainly have lacked an essential dimension.

These people need human acceptance above all but not acceptance that is sentimental. Love and human solidarity must also be shown by insisting on order, and it is necessary to have the courage to engage in conflicts and to withstand from patients every kind of projection. Every time it is necessary to go through the entire drama of the therapist-patient relationship, including what psychiatrists call negative projection. Psychotherapy is hard and very demanding work that calls for extreme patience and resilience in the face of disappointment, particularly when it comes to psychotherapy of addicts, in which lying and relapses are common expressions of the disease. Even in such circumstances, one cannot write off a patient.

I was helped to understand the cause of addiction by the title of a book by a psychotherapist who had studied with the founder of "logotherapy," Viktor Frankl: *Every Addiction Hides a Longing*. It is necessary to identify that longing and find a better way to satisfy it than the treacherous shortcut of drugs. Among the social causes of addiction is the limited scope for celebration in secular society. People need "holy days" and celebration; but in a society in which there is such little space for the "holy," holy days and the culture of celebration are in decline. I expect my country is not the only one where "Let's go celebrate" is becoming synonymous with "Let's get drunk."

Drug addiction—like any addiction—has a religious dimension. In fact, it is idolatry, an enslaving fixation on an idol. That is why one must help the addict find another route to inner freedom. There is no single model for treatment of addiction, neither medical, nor social, nor simply moral. An alcoholic is not "just a sinner" or "just a sick unfortunate," nor is he or she "just a victim of social conditions." Addiction tends to have all those aspects, as well as others. In my practice I was also aware of the profound analogy between sin and sickness and the link between individual sin and "structural sin," the social and super-individual aspect of evil. One cannot simply morally condemn and admonish addicts, but neither can one divest them of all responsibility by emphasizing that it is "only" a disease. If we exclude, albeit with good therapeutic intentions, any degree of actual blame, then we exclude the element of responsibility, and in fact we are denying the freedom of the individual, and we see addicts simply as the play of biological and social conditionalities.

I pondered a great deal on those damaged destinies and studied them. I did not try to evangelize patients. Indeed I regard such abuse of the therapist's power over the patient as not only a contravention of medical ethics but also counterproductive from the view of pastoral care. The theologian Bonhoeffer rightly criticized his colleagues who felt a need to corner people with two blows (you are sinful! you will die!) in order to prepare them for their subsequent ministry. I don't have much trust in prison or hospital conversions out of fear or distress. I think that people must first be brought from fear into freedom; God deserves a *free* yes.

Nevertheless, I became aware that when addiction therapy (and psychotherapy in general) goes deeper, it also affects people's spiritual dimension. God has his own narrative with each human being. He is at work in the heart of every human being, even of every inveterate atheist. Sometimes I could feel God at work in the destinies of my patients. I know that some of them later took the step of baptism, or their religious life was revived, and I don't think it was by any means due to me. God once more manifested his power anonymously in the lives of others, such as by restoring their appetite for work and love.

It is interesting how religious themes emerged in the dreams and drawings of atheists. I became convinced that this dimension is essential to human beings. People are incurably religious, even though today they often displace religion, and it becomes taboo, similar to Dr. Freud's Victorian patients' suppression of their sexuality and aggression. "Who today still suppresses their sexuality or aggression?," I would ask my psychoanalyst friends. Classic Freudian theory is now an anachronism, and a case of bringing owls to Athens. It is possible that today Freud himself might focus instead on removing obstacles in the path of suppressed and displaced religiosity and spiritual values in general.

Every Thursday, a cultural program was organized in the patients' club, which provided an opportunity for people to ask me about these matters as well. My own programs before Christmas and Easter became a tradition. I would familiarize the participants—patients and their families but also the doctors and nurses present—with the gospel narratives, by means of music and a commentary on customs and traditions. Once, one of the patients stood up and asked me in front of everyone whether I was a believer. To ask such a question in those days in front of the entire community of patients, colleagues, and nurses was regarded as obvious provocation, with dangerous political implications, and everyone waited with bated breath to see how Dr. Halík would worm his way out of it. "Yes," I replied. From then on, I gained respect among the patients and staff, even among nonbelievers, who were in the majority. One must be ready to respond but not to agitate.

My workplace at the clinic was a tiny narrow room, and I vividly remember the conversations with patients that took place there. Sometimes I slept there overnight, and at sunrise after night duty in the sobering-up unit I would celebrate Mass on my own with the door locked. I experienced there what I had read about in Teilhard de Chardin's *Mass on the World*, in which he speaks about how he places all human yearning and suffering in the chalice and becomes aware of the cosmic dimension of worship. In that way I was able to place on the paten the destinies of the people I encountered there. I discovered a new dimension of the Mass.

During my time at that clinic, which was part of the university hospital, I gave courses for medical students, and I prepared lectures for them on addiction and on psychotherapy in general. At that period, students of medicine learned practically nothing about the psychological, philosophical, and ethical aspects of their discipline, particularly with respect to patient-doctor relations. By then I had been cooperating closely with Dr. Scarlett Vasiluková-Rešlová. Scarlett had spent many years studying cancer. While in the United States, she helped discover a platinum-based treatment of tumors; she was also concerned with medical ethics and lifestyle questions. What I knew from the standpoint of psychology and philosophy she complemented with qualified perspectives on the scientific context of those questions, particularly with respect to psychoneuroimmunology. We discussed all of that a great deal, and eventually we drafted together a teaching program for medical students and doctors dealing with patient-doctor relationships and relationships within a clinical team.

We lectured on these matters to medical students for a number of years in the framework of a "scientific student circle" and then to doctors in association with the Institute for Further Education of Doctors and Pharmacists, in the form of active social teaching. It was interesting and useful work. Now that new discoveries in medical research offer humankind previously undreamed of possibilities, I consider it doubly important that medicine—and it already concerns the teaching of medical students and the ongoing education of doctors—should not remain simply a "natural science" discipline; systematic efforts should be made to foster the philosophical—and above all, ethical—aspects of medicine.

After a while, my work at the alcoholism treatment center permitted me to undertake a number of interesting official trips. The first of them was to Russia at the beginning of the Gorbachov era. My task was to bring back the Soviet comrades' experiences with Gorbachov's alcohol ban, which was aimed at enforcing abstinence in society.

Although at that time Soviet propaganda continued to insist that the great land of the Soviets was practically unaffected by the problem of alcoholism, which was a typical aspect of "corrupt capitalist society," semiofficially there was recognition that the opposite was true. Alcoholism was rife in the Soviet empire from top to bottom, probably more than in any other country on earth. In the Russian countryside it was women who were to be seen toiling away with pickaxes and shovels; the men were lying around drunk from early morning. It was rumored that the Soviet leadership's sudden readiness to sign disarmament agreements and peace treaties with the Americans was not so much due to the Russians' love of peace as to the fact that in many barracks of the glorious Red Army it was hard to find a soldier sober enough at nine o'clock in the morning to tell the difference between a machine gun and a toothbrush.

I spent most of my time in Moscow, but I made secret trips to the celebrated Orthodox monastery at Zagorsk. Foreigners were not allowed to move about freely in Russia. Tourist routes full of Potemkin villages were prepared for them, and their guides had special instructions. But by that time the country was in such a state of devastation that the terrible truth was all too evident beneath the ideologically gilded lies.

The atmosphere of Russian society was appalling. I had never before encountered such coarse and uncivil behavior as the tasteless underground cathedrals of the Moscow metro. I found the gray, lifeless faces of the crowds that streamed along the Moscow streets really depressing. Sometimes the sight of ragged old ladies tore at my heart strings—to have spent almost seventy years of their lives in that hell! I smuggled a Russian Bible into Moscow and made contact with a group of purported Christians whose addresses had been supplied by friends in Prague, but my conversation with them was no less depressing than the overall panorama of Moscow society. Their heads were filled with a strange mixture of religion and occultism akin to the theosophy of Madame Blavatsky.

I had expected perestroika to engender an atmosphere in Moscow reminiscent of the Prague Spring. It's true that I did see in the cinema Tenghiz Abuladze's remarkable Georgian trilogy, which included the long-shelved film *Repentance*, which rightly went on to win prizes. But apart from that, there was no enthusiasm, no breeze of freedom on the streets, just the infected breath of a society that had died spiritually long ago and now lacked the strength to mask the process of disintegration. I went around the art galleries and the Kremlin, visited the tomb of the philosopher Soloviev, and meditated over the monuments to Russian culture. I knew that "another Russia" must exist somewhere—the legacy of Dostoyevsky's psychological depth, the engaging beauty of the Russian icons, and the dynamic of Russian classical music—but I did not encounter it, either in the Soviet metropolis that time or anywhere else later. Looking at the painting of Peter the Great shaving the beards of the obstinate Boyars, I forgave the spirit of Enlightenment and rationalism, which many Catholics like to disdain. Lo—the horror of a society that did not undergo the Enlightenment, and all attempts at implanting Enlightenment values into it met with failure.

I have always tried not to allow my aversion to the Soviet regime to affect my attitude to the Russian people and its culture. However, seventy years of Communism on top of centuries of autocracy succeeded in deadening that society spiritually and corrupting it morally on a huge scale. I was always extremely sorry for the brave and isolated "Westernizers," who, in the past, tried to introduce European values into Russian society. The drug of the pan-Slavic myth, which was peddled by the Slavophiles and which so perfectly suited the ideological needs of Russian imperialism, both in tsarist times and during the Bolshevik regime, was always stronger. Even in Czech history, many nineteenth-century patriots fell prey to that ideological drug, and our nation paid dearly for it. There were only a few of them—such as the journalist and politician Karel Havlíček Borovský—who had the courage to visit Russia, and their encounter with reality cured them for good of those illusions about "light from the East."

I loved Dostoyevsky and Bulgakov, and I read Merezhovsky, Berdyaev, Shestov, and many other Russian authors. I don't think there was another human being—perhaps with the exception of Nietzsche—who gazed at the dark side of life with such courage and was capable of describing the hidden and murky corners of the human soul in such a penetrating way as Dostoyevsky. I long considered Alexander Solzhenitsyn one of the great men of the twentieth century. However, after I returned from Moscow I no longer considered Solzhenitsyn one of my favorite authors. I continue to value his courage, his resilience, and his novels, particularly the magnificent frescoes of *The Gulag Archipelago*, which capture the anatomy of the most monstrous regime in human history. But when it comes to his political philosophy, and particularly as expressed in his speech of acceptance of the Templeton Prize, I regard him as a false prophet. His critique of the West, founded on Russian messianism, testifies to his profound misunderstanding of modern culture, which had no impact on Russia, not to its advantage, but to its detriment. I will continue to repeat with reverence the foresighted answer that Solzhenitsyn once gave to the question, what will come after Communism?

A long, long path of recovery. I don't think that path will take the direction that Solzhenitsyn expected, however. I don't expect that the light of salvation that will renew the world will come from Holy Russia. On the contrary, I fear that Russia will go on being tossed to and fro between dictatorship and chaos, because it lacks the cultural and moral preconditions for building a democratic society. I also fear that John Paul II's ideal of the unity of Europe from the Atlantic to the Urals, which played a positive role in the destruction of the Communist empire, is nevertheless just a beautiful dream, which will not be fulfilled in the foreseeable future.

I frequently recalled the words of the great Russian theologian Sergei Bulgakov, who wrote in his masterful analysis of Dostoyevsky's *Brothers Karamazov*:

> How is it that the sickness of conscience is our national trait to such a degree? The answer to this question must be obvious to everyone. It is because between the ideal and reality, and between the requirements of reason and conscience on the one hand, and life on the other, there yawns such an enormous abyss. There is such an enormous discrepancy, and that is the cause of our illness. In its very essence the ideal does not correspond to reality and denies it, but the degree of that discrepancy can vary and in Russia the difference amounts to several centuries.

I fear that those words still hold true. Russia has still not expelled the demons from its soul, and the world ought not to underestimate this.

■ I RETURNED ONCE MORE TO RUSSIA in January 2000 to give a lecture on religion and international politics at the Fulbright Foundation in the center of Moscow. But that was only the pretext for my trip; what I wanted to see above all was what had changed there during the fifteen years since my previous visit.

January is an ideal month to travel to Russia. The Moscow streets are covered in snow, and frost stings your face. From the airport we drove down a long, wide boulevard leading to Red Square. I was surprised that the square was surrounded by newly rebuilt churches once demolished on Stalin's orders so that columns of tanks could make a triumphal entry in parades. In the distance, where I could still remember there was once a swimming pool in the center of the city, there now soared the majestic cathedral of Christ the Savior. It was restored in record time on the orders of Moscow's ambitious mayor Luzhkov. In front of the entrance to Red Square an enormous political demonstration was taking place. A speaker was berating someone and shaking his fist, and the crowd followed suit: it reminded me of something from a film about the October Revolution. The interior of the wonderful Univermag opposite the Kremlin, once the main department store in the whole country, where I could still remember endless lines of fractious people in front of half-empty shelves and arrogant female store clerks, was now reminiscent of a Western supermarket. This temple to consumerism of the New Russia, together with the Orthodox cathedral and the holy necropolis of Communism, formed the symbolic foreground of the government buildings.

Lots of Christian wayside chapels had sprung up, but there were memorials to Communism almost every step of the way. The red stars had disappeared from most of the Stalin-era skyscrapers, so that these buildings now recalled parts of 1920s New York. It is worth spending a whole day in the New Tretyakov Gallery, with its interesting counterposition of Russian and French early modern art; one can observe there the gradual decline of art from a remarkable sensitivity for social themes to the frightful, gigantic propaganda paintings of Stalinism. It was fascinating to go from a display of contemporary art to the section of the gallery with icons, before which a young woman was telling Bible stories to her students in a touching manner.

Moscow had visibly changed since the fall of the Soviet Union. But even on my second trip, I sought in vain—in the stores, in the metro, and in fleeting eye contact on the street—what always enchanted me during my first trips to the West: politeness; natural gentility; amiable, easygoing, obliging behavior in normal everyday communication; the mutual respect of free people.

Will the spirit of heaviness ever disappear from Russia? Will the Western esprit ever blow this way bringing political liberty? Maybe the dust from the ruins of the dehumanizing Communist empire still weighs heavily on people's souls. The shameless cultural barbarism of the upstarts of the new economic elite is no different from the coarse arrogance of the Bolshevik apparatchiks, while the poverty of ordinary people is not hidden away as it was years ago. What I admired was the courage of journalists and the openness of certain TV reports that criticized the cruelty of Russian soldiers in Chechnya, for instance; from time to time that public service cost some of them their lives.

There is a place in the middle of Red Square that I found particularly alluring: the Lenin Mausoleum, one of the main cult sites of the previous regime, where silent crowds came to pay homage in endless rows, which people of my generation were familiar with from photographs and films. Who knows whether on a future visit, if I ever return, this place will still be here or whether it will be transformed into an American-style attraction like Disneyland? On the third day of my stay in Moscow, I did visit that weird cavelike tomb of red and black marble. I didn't have to wait long in line, but the body search before entering was very thorough. Everything, including the holy icons of the revolution and the wax-pale body in the crystal coffin, seemed surprisingly small to me. All around stood soldiers who rudely admonished you if you tried to whisper something or walked too slowly. That morning I had found the passage in the New Testament about Christ's tomb, and here it struck me that there could be no greater contrasts in the entire universe: Christ's tomb was simple and *empty*; the mausoleum is opulent, and it is dominated "for eternity" by an embalmed corpse.

The tragicomic aspect of the fate of this materialist caricature of eternity is confirmed by a rather morbid anecdote that I was told by someone at the Czech embassy in Moscow. There is a massive building not far from our embassy that used to be carefully guarded. It has a somewhat mysterious name that indicates that it was once a kind of biological research institute of the Academy of Sciences. In fact it is the headquarters of an institution whose sole task for decades was to ensure that the holy relics of the Great Leader of the proletariat should always appear immaculate. Apparently they also look after another corpse, that of a man who died at the same time as Lenin, and they first experimented on him to determine how to improve the best-guarded corpse on the planet. But because care of the holy icon of the revolution is not very profitable at a time of exuberantly blossoming market capitalism. The institute, with all its academics, makes some extra money by building—for dollars—splendid private mausoleums on the estates of the "new Russians"—the Mafiosi and nouveaux riches, who are more abundant in today's Russia than they were in the Chicago underworld of the 1930s. Lenin would probably turn in his crystal coffin if he knew how the carefully selected guardians of his mortal remains now kowtow to the truly odd taste of the pioneers of victorious Russian capitalism.

After everything I saw and heard in Moscow, I was almost sorry for the "eternally living Lenin." Now that the entire context of fear of the Mighty was gone, the abandoned corpse, which had outlived the era of its veneration, seemed somehow woefully naked and lonely, like the pillaged tombs of the Egyptian pharaohs. The man who had woven a new variation on the world-dominating dream of Russia as a "third Rome, after which there will be no other," the man to whose visions millions of people were sacrificed in the hell of the concentration camps, the man whose promises of heaven on earth once hoodwinked a great number of European intellectuals, now lay here like a yellowing worthless banknote, without the gold of hope to back it. Once in a Russian church at the foot of the Mount of Olives in Jerusalem, I saw a painting in which Mary Magdalene, with an egg in her hand, is explaining to Pontius Pilate the mystery of the resurrection. Here there was just an empty shell. Desolation. Time decaying in a blind alley of history. There was no space here for resurrection.

■ FOR YEARS, AT LEAST TWICE A WEEK, I dreamed that I had been allowed to travel to the West, and I would be walking along a street in London or in Rome around St Peter's Basilica. I would say to myself in that dream, "I've dreamed of it so many times, and now it's real." At that point I would always wake up. When at last I was allowed out, I seemed to me like a dream, and I would say to myself, "This time I won't be fooled." The police under the Communist regime used to have sadistic inclinations, and sometimes they would allow people to complete all the formalities before turning them back at the frontier.

During the period of Gorbachov's perestroika, a private trip to the West was out of the question for me, but to my surprise I managed to receive permission in 1988 to make an official trip to neutral Switzerland. Former fellow students from university days, who emigrated after 1968, obtained an invitation for me to attend a congress of the Daseinanalytical Psychotherapeutical Association in Zurich. I gave a lecture there and obtained membership in the association. I combined that lecture with a three-week stay in Switzerland and made full use of my time. I now look back on it with a smile and amazement, recalling everything I managed to achieve during that first breath of freedom in the West.

I first stepped onto free soil in Munich, where I had an hour between trains, and I went for a short walk in the city center. I knew that somewhere in Munich was buried the Jesuit Rupert Mayer, a courageous opponent of the Nazis, who was later beatified. I wanted to ask whether his grave was somewhere nearby. I saw a house that looked a bit like a church, and I went inside to ask the way. Instead I found myself in front of the tomb of Rupert Mayer. So I committed the whole of my journey to his care, and that was the start of a succession of little miracles.

At the congress I met colleagues whom I had not seen for twenty years, and we were able to share our adventures, which complemented each other perfectly, like two versions of the Czechs' fate at that time. Even our dreams complemented each other: they used to dream of returning to the Czech lands and then being unable to come back. It was a typical émigré's dream.

While I was in Switzerland, two events occurred that had an impact on developments in the Catholic Church, and not only in Switzerland. Monsignor Haas was appointed coadjutor bishop of Chur. He was known to be an extreme conservative, and his appointment threatened tension in the Swiss church. I was able to follow closely the heated controversy in the press and understand how polarized the church there was. Then came the news that the traditionalist archbishop Marcel Lefebvre had decided to consecrate four new bishops without permission from the Vatican, which meant he would be excommunicated, and that there would be an open schism.

I heard a lot about Econ, Lefebvre's traditionalist seminary, which was the headquarters of the opponents of the Second Vatican Council in the Catholic Church, and where the consecration was to take place. I said to myself that I ought to take a closer look at the setting, and on my first free day I took a train, although I only had a vague idea of Econ's location. In the train I fell into conversation with a young priest in a soutane. He turned out to be a supporter of the Lefebvrists from the United States who was traveling to the controversial consecration. He offered to take me there. On the way, he told me his life story. As a result I was also able to get a view of the traditionalist movement from the other side. According to that priest's account, the movement was a counterculture in opposition to America's church, which was too left-wing and too socially and "horizontally" oriented and which had allowed itself to be enslaved by the spirit of the times with irresponsible liberalist recklessness. It had lost the sacral dimension and was being transformed into a media business, uncritically accepting the political slogans of the Left, including those of the gay and feminist movements, and step by step it was selling out the Catholic identity. The traditionalist movement, on the other hand, was preserving oases of traditional family values. He cited large harmonious families, in which children obeyed their parents impeccably, in which they all prayed the rosary, and mothers gave preference to bringing up their children over a professional career. The thin man in the long clerical gown undoubtedly believed everything he said, and he certainly meant it in good faith. It raised many questions in my mind. Was American society and the church, which was integrated into it, really in such a state of decay? Was traditionalism capable of preserving the idyllic state of premodern society—and if so, at what cost?

I walked around the seminary at Econ and even saw the staging prepared for the bishops' consecration. I spoke to a number of people, and I prayed for a long time in the chapel there to know the truth and to maintain understanding for both sides. Traditionalist abbots and nuns in preconciliar habits converged on the seminary. At first sight, some of them were odd characters. I had the impression of watching a scene from a historical film; sometimes it even reminded me of a clinic for neurological disorders. There was something sectarian and forced about the overall atmosphere. It truly was not a healthy spiritual environment. I told myself that this really was not the way forward.

Another of my trips took me to the Czech-born Professor Christoph Schönborn in Freiburg, who was dean of the local theological faculty. Our conversation touched on many issues to do with developments in theology and the church, and it went on until dawn. I then carried back to my room a mountain of books that he gave me. When I expressed sadness at the tension in the Swiss church, Schönborn reassured me. He seemed to me to represent a cultured "center-right" position, to which I felt the greatest affinity. With Schönborn's recommendation, I wanted to make a visit to the great Swiss theologian, whom I had always admired, the aged Hans Urs von Balthasar, called by some the most educated man of the twentieth century. Once he had endured injustice and misunderstanding in the church, but now he had been appointed cardinal by John Paul II and was about to leave for Rome. I was therefore astounded to read the following day that Urs von Balthasar had died suddenly on the eve of his departure for Rome.

I didn't only associate with Catholics in Switzerland, however, but also met some Tibetan Buddhists. Friends invited me to a meeting with the Dalai Lama, who was staying in Zurich at that time on a visit to Tibetan émigrés. I knew that an invitation was extremely rare, but I went with a certain reluctance, nevertheless. I asked myself what I was actually seeking there. I entered a large hall, in which several hundred Tibetans were seated on the floor. At the side there were several Americans with shaved heads and wearing saffron-colored robes. When I sat down, one of the Tibetan children rushed up to me and sat on my lap. The Tibetans nearby took this as a sign and started to give me big smiles and bow to me, accepting me among them and offering me food.

I listened to the Dalai Lama with no great enthusiasm, because I had the feeling that I had heard it all many times already and read about it. It was an almost catechistically simple exposition of the basic truths of Buddhism. But as I was leaving that place, I suddenly experienced a powerful touch of goodness, light, and power, which I carried with me with for several days during meditation and prayer. I felt as if I had entered the force field of something profound and peaceful, comparable to what I had experienced on several occasions during spiritual exercises or at the culmination of the Easter liturgy. In the document *Nostra aetate* of the Second Vatican Council I had read that the Spirit of God operates even in non-Christian religions, that it "bloweth where it listeth," as it said in the gospel, but only now was it confirmed by my own inner experience. Something powerful and good certainly did radiate from the Dalai Lama. I didn't become a Buddhist, but the evangelicals who protest against the Dalai Lama's visits to my country will never have my support.

In subsequent years I met the Dalai Lama on repeated occasions in different parts of the world, including Prague, and had several opportunities to speak with him in person. Once we meditated together in our Church of St. Salvator. Maybe I can say we have become personal friends. I always found him very likable, but he no longer made such a powerful impression on me as at that first encounter. I have met only three other people in my life from whom I have experienced similar "radiation": Professor Patočka, John Paul II, and Roger Schutz, founder of the Taizé community.

During my stay in Switzerland, I visited a number of places that made a profound impression on me. I found my way to a famous Trappist monastery in the mountains and also took a look at the places where Friedrich Nietzsche lived when he was writing his *Zarathustra*. I spent beautiful moments in the alpine hermitage where Nicholas of Flüe—"Brother Klaus"—Switzerland's patron saint, was living after he heard God's call and abandoned his secular career and family life. The final hours of my time in Switzerland brought me a remarkable gift. On my return journey, I stopped at a place that I thought might be near the Bollingen Tower, the legendary house of C. G. Jung, which he built with his own hands and where he wrote his most significant works. I wanted to catch a glimpse of it from a distance at least, having been told that Jung's relatives, who now live there, did not permit visits to the house itself.

I searched for a long time and was about to give up when I approached a boy who was sitting on the shore of a lake. I really did not hold out much hope that he would be able to tell me where Jung used to live. But it turned out that the boy was more than familiar with the house: he was one of Jung's grandsons and lived there. Because no adults were at home, he let me go inside—probably against his parents' wishes—and I was able to able to view places that are hallowed by every follower of Jung. Those familiar with Jung's essay about communication with the dead will not be surprised that I accepted with gratitude this "accident" as a gift from the "sage of Bollingen Tower." After so many years of "starvation," this first trip to the West was truly a cup filled to overflowing!

The Decade of Spiritual Renewal

The Charter 77 movement, the election of a Polish pope, the emergence of the Solidarity trade union movement in Poland, and the change of direction in Western foreign policy—Jimmy Carter's emphasis on human rights and Ronald Reagan's explicit declaration that the Communist system was the Evil Empire—Margaret Thatcher's determination, and finally Mikhail Gorbachov and his perestroika—all indicated that the Soviet empire was starting to be shaken to its foundations. The Czechoslovak Communist regime still showed no signs of reform, however; on the contrary, it monitored the unofficial activities of political, cultural, and religious dissent with increasing nervousness.

In opposition circles there was an increase in samizdat activity and clandestine lectures, some given by visiting Western intellectuals, and people were thinking more and more about the future. Sometime around 1983, Father Mádr contacted me and asked me to edit an underground magazine for Christian-oriented psychologists, psychiatrists, and psychotherapists. We decided to use the Greek letter "psi" as its title.

Later, Mádr involved me in his other plans and activities. As I said earlier, we practically saw nothing of each other after 1968, although he remained remarkably well informed about me; he was convinced I was a priest and a Jesuit. After mutually clarifying matters, he revealed to me that he was setting up an advisory center, which would prepare a new direction within the church in response to newly emerging needs. It was intended to be a sort of brain trust for the aging Cardinal Tomášek, whom he said we ought not to write off in spite of his age and cautiousness; after all, on several occasions, he had shown himself ready to use quiet diplomacy to defend persecuted priests. If the cardinal had appropriate support from reliable and competent colleagues he could have the courage to go even further. The group should include representatives of the main male orders working clandestinely, as well as a few key priests representing individual dioceses (thus constituting an important point of contact between the "aboveground" and "underground" church structures), together with some open-minded theologians like Josef Zvěřina, the editors of the most influential samizdat periodicals, and representatives of church movements and other active Catholic circles. Its first job would be to map out the overall situation, overcome fragmentation, and, in the absence of a bishop's conference, direct the life of the church. It should, in Mádr's words, "analyze the present situation with a sort of episcopal overview and with an eye to the future."

I carefully discussed his offer with my superiors in the community of underground priests. It was obvious to me that the creation of such a center was needed, even imperative; it was also in line with the tasks that our community had set itself, namely, to provide scope for conceptual thinking about the future. Nevertheless it was also clear that it involved enormous risks. If I were to join that circle I would transgress our fundamental principle of strict secrecy and endanger not only myself but also the other clandestinely ordained priests and candidates for the priesthood that I was working with. Initially Mádr rejected a compromise proposal that I would be only a sort of liaison officer between him and those circles. (For years I served in that capacity between our community and Cardinal Meisner, whom I regularly met with during my trips to Berlin in connection with my professional activity. Meisner was the only East German bishop to travel regularly between West and East Germany—he was bishop of both parts of Berlin—and the link between our circle and the Vatican). There were many reasons Mádr wanted me to be a permanent member of his group, including this contact with Cardinal Meisner and Rome. In the end we decided that I would be released from the community in order to devote myself to that activity with all the risks it entailed; I would keep our community of underground priests informed by just three clandestine meetings per year.

Over time several working groups were set up. The most important of these was nicknamed "Senior" to distinguish it from a study seminar of young theologians. Senior would become the nerve center of church revival prior to 1989. It was attended by, among others, both future Czech cardinals, Miloslav Vlk (in those days a window cleaner) and Dominik Duka (employed at the Škoda engineering works in Plzeň). The meetings were held in various apartments, and after the opening prayer we would always start with an overview: a summary of reports about the situation, followed by discussion and the delegation of tasks. Later an inner troika was created, consisting of Zvěřina, Mádr, and me, to maintain close contact with Cardinal Tomášek, and it mostly fell to me or Mádr to draft the texts of the cardinal's open letters to the government, as well as various sermons.

In addition to this group of priests, there was later created a sort of "second chamber," consisting mainly of laypeople. That group even tackled political issues. We realized that the national pilgrimage to Velehrad in 1985, which had grown into a demonstration for religious freedom, was the moment when the Catholic minority had regained its courage. The yearning for religious freedom started to be linked with the nation's political awakening and with a movement that might be capable of undermining the totalitarian regime.

In 1986, the Polish magazine *Tygodnik powszechny* published an article by the philosopher Stefan Swiezawsky titled "Jan Hus—Heretic or Forerunner of the Second Vatican Council?" Since this was a text by a former close associate and friend of Pope John Paul II, we saw it as a sign of a possible reevaluation of the legacy of Jan Hus on the part of the Catholic Church. I was very enthusiastic about it and returned to my study of Hus after many years. I wrote a reflection that first appeared in the samizdat edition *Teologické texty* and then in the exile magazine *Studie* published in Rome. I expressed the view that if the Catholic Church was to play an integrating role in the renewal of Czech society, it must break free of narrow clerical confines and participate in healing the scars of the past, and be true, in some way, to the great archetypes of the Czech nation, of which Hus was undoubtedly one. "Hus is also ours," I wrote, "not as a banner, . . . but as our debt and cross."

I proposed that a new examination of the "Hus case" should carefully distinguish between the person of Hus, Hus's works, and Hus as a screen onto which various eras project their own ideals. Every interpretation of the past was done from a certain angle of "pre-understanding," and we had to reflect on our current standpoint, which was different, for instance, from our standpoint during the First Republic. In conclusion I presented, as a "dream," a vision of a Slav pope arriving in Prague and taking part in an ecumenical meeting of Czech Catholics and Protestants, at which he would pray for the healing of the scars of the Czech past and would even speak positively of Hus. My article gave rise to some controversy, and one Moravian Catholic roundly mocked my mad dream. It came to pass, however, in April 1990.

■ OTO MÁDR WAS ABLE TO THINK PRECISELY and strategically. He could realistically appraise a situation and people's capacities. He would meticulously analyze texts he received for samizdat publication and always identified their weak points. One of the weaknesses of samizdat publication was that it was not subjected to sufficient criticism. Everyone was so glad that something like samizdat existed that they overlooked mistakes, because they were aware of the difficult conditions in which those texts were created and distributed. But Mádr was demanding, obdurate, and a perfectionist. I recall that I once brought a samizdat article to his apartment. He welcomed me as always with a green eyeshade on his forehead. We talked about important matters in the bathroom with the water running to make it more difficult for the secret police to listen in to our conversation. When we were sitting at his desk he would pass me messages on a small chalkboard, which he would then immediately erase. On that occasion, he took a long time reading my text, and then commented, "According to the new spelling rules this should be spelled with a *z*, not an *s*; there's a comma missing here," and so on. I protested that I had brought the article to him as theologian, not copy editor. He simply cleared his throat and said, "You people wouldn't dare bring copy to a Communist newspaper in that state. But anything is good enough for the Lord, is that it?" I felt like making some caustic remark and leaving for good. Instead I walked up and down his study a couple of times and counted to ten. Then I decided to stay.

The next time I brought him an article, he told me it was good, but I ought to bear in mind that it might be read by some ordinary traditional parish priest in a Moravian village. Would he understand it? Might it contain something that would offend him unnecessarily? A week later I brought him a revised version. This time he suggested I should imagine a "Protestant brother" reading my article. Was my text ecumenically balanced enough? The following week he asked me whether I had taken into account that it might be read by some sincere atheist. Might he not think that the article belittles his view of the world? In that way I was obliged to read my text again and again with different eyes and revise it. But I gradually learned to read my texts more critically, and from different points of view, and to present my views more understandably for different readers. I am now very grateful to him for that training.

The day arrived when the police decided to carry out a major sweep of Catholic samizdat, and they arrested a number of people.

Many of us were anxious and in shock. We waited to see what would happen next. The next day Mádr turned up in high spirits. He said, "We're in the front line, so there are bound to be losses. We keep going. The main thing is to let them understand they haven't scared us off. Are you prepared to take on something else? We will pray for the people who are in prison. It's not as bad as all that, and they will draw benefit from it, so it won't be wasted." When I recalled that this was being said by someone who had been imprisoned awaiting a death sentence and was then given a life sentence, after which he spent many years in prison, it was obvious to me that the world looked very different from his perspective. His courage and under-standing were a great help and encouragement.

Oto Mádr worked fearlessly and with total commitment, above all, so that the Czech church and its theology should not lose its im-portant links with theological thinking in the West, so that the Com-munists should not succeed in isolating it totally from the global church, which could result in its being bogged down in provincialism and becoming paralyzed. It was chiefly thanks to Mádr that during the worst years of "normalization" under President Gustav Husák, a series of lectures by leading Western theologians was organized in private apartments in Prague and outside the capital. It was an al-most unbelievable achievement involving enormous risk and com-mitment. The lecturers arrived in the country as tourists for a few days and moved from place to place in secret, which was often quite an adventure. They included Walter Kasper, Christoph Schönborn, Hans Küng, J. B. Metz, Hans Waldenfels, Günter Virt, and the Parisian Jesuit Paul Valadier, among many others. I recall that in the discus-sion following Metz's lecture, "God after Auschwitz," I voiced the hope that this theology, which was an expression of restraint in reac-tion to the theodicy of the Enlightenment, would be supplemented by a "post-Gulag theology," which would propose a reevaluation of captivation with Marxism and the ideology of the Western Left. I had come to realize the extent to which West German theologians drew inspiration from the situation of the churches in Latin America while having not the slightest idea about what was happening just a few kilometers beyond their eastern frontier. But who could create an alternative liberation theology and reflect theologically on our experience without being drawn into the ideology of the American Religious Right, or another form of the opposite extreme?

■ I WENT TO ST. VITUS CATHEDRAL on New Year's Eve of 1984, as I did on every eve of the new year, in order to end the year before the Lord and ask for blessing on the year to come. The sacristans already knew me, and after the Mass ended and the doors were closed, they allowed me to stay for several hours to pray before they cleared the cathedral. I found it hard to concentrate that evening, and then suddenly I fell deeply into prayer, like a stone into a deep well. And from that depth there emerged ideas that had never occurred to me before: the millennium of the death of St. Vojtěch—known more widely by the name St. Adalbert—was approaching, and it was necessary that not only the church but also the entire nation should prepare themselves for that moment. There was need for systematic preparation, like the Great Novena of the Christianization of Poland, for which Cardinal Wyszyński prayed during his house arrest. It was necessary to appeal to all people of goodwill and invite them; it was necessary to heal and transform hearts and minds, because a new time was coming.

I had never thought about it before, but when I left the darkness of the cathedral, numb with cold, that idea already burned clearly inside me. When I got home I checked the actual date of St. Adalbert's death and discovered that there still remained a few years for preparation—and then the Great Novena could begin. The first person I shared my germ of an idea with was my confessor at that time, Petr Pit'ha, and behold, independently of me, he had been giving thought to similar things and by and large our ideas fitted together like two halves of a broken ring.

And thus the Decade of Spiritual Renewal came into existence. This initiative was intended not only as preparation for the millennium of St. Adalbert, but the approaching millennium. It was to be a kind of laboratory of a new lifestyle for the third millennium. The plan was to have joint spiritual exercises and reflection on tradition but above all to discover afresh values that could help form the basis of the society of the future. We felt that great changes in society were imminent, and we did not want them to consist simply of some Gorbachovian perestroika. We knew that if there was to be a truly radical renewal of society—one that went to the root—then it was necessary to go beyond mere external change—the transformation of political and economic structures—and envision a revolution of hearts and minds, or rather, cultivation of the overall moral atmosphere of society.

The Decade of Spiritual Renewal project was based on a theme for each of the years, which would be a positive expression of one of the Ten Commandments, for example, "You shall not kill"—"serving life"; "You shall not steal"—"work and social responsibility"; "You shall not commit adultery"—"family life." The theme chosen for each of the years was intended not only to focus on the renewal of a particular area of the life of the church and society but also to address a specific segment of society according to the patron saint for that year: the St. Agnes year would be devoted to service to life, workers in the health service; the year of education, teachers; the year of St. John of Nepomuk, lawyers; the year of St. Procopius, members of religious orders, and so on.

The basic theme of each year was symbolized by a Czech saint, so that it would not be abstract but given a face and thereby rooted in national tradition. And in view of the fact that in those days the religious orders in Czechoslovakia operated in total clandestinity, we wanted to commemorate a specific religious order in each of the years: St. Agnes, the Franciscans; St. Adalbert, the Benedictines; St. Zdislav, the Dominicans.

In each of the years we also wanted to focus on specific regions and dioceses linked with a particular patron saint. Pilgrimage started to become more important again as it had in certain earlier periods of Czech history; there started to be demonstrations in favor of religious freedom, as well as opportunities for new forms of pastoral activity. Although the Mass was the only permitted form of religious activity for the Catholic church in those days, during the first pilgrimages of the Decade, still under totalitaritarian conditions, lectures started to take place, as well as discussions, Eucharistic adoration, and concerts and theatrical presentations by young people. From the point of view of the state police, this was a mass contravention of "state control of the churches," but the regime no longer had the power to completely stop it.

The Decade was intended to link the underground and aboveground structures of the church and also involve ecumenical activity, in the broadest sense of the word. We wanted to unite Christians of the various churches as well as offer something to the burgeoning number of sympathizers who, for the time being, observed the life of the church with a certain detachment.

The entire program commemorated the figure of St. Adalbert as the symbol of our Europeanness. Adalbert may rightly be considered the first European of Czech blood and the first Czech with a European outlook and of European significance. Nevertheless, his native Bohemia lacked understanding for his reforming zeal and rejected it, as a result of which that great bishop was forced—like so many Czechs in subsequent eras, including his latter-day successor Cardinal Beran—to leave his homeland for foreign lands. That theme is still topical and prompts reflection on Czech history.

Like many proposals of reform in the Czech lands (such as Masaryk's political program), the Decade was inspired by a specific philosophy of Czech history: we stressed that the common thread running through Czech history was the striving for moral renewal, which returns repeatedly after periods of decay. Adalbert was linked with one of the great reform movements in the church of his day, the Cluniac reforms. Since then, reformist ideas have always found fertile soil in the Czech lands in certain periods of history. Since the fate of Adalbert embodied that tragic counterpoint (prophetic figures never had it easy in our country) our aim was to avoid holding the Adalbert commemorations in 1997 as a superficial triumphalist adulation of a local hero. Instead we regarded the millennium, and preparations for it, as an opportunity for metanoia—conversion, repentance, and the nation's reconciliation with the saint it rejected and with everything the figure of Adalbert represented. Incidentally, that is what the Czechs ceremoniously vowed to do at Adalbert's tomb in Gniezno almost one thousand years ago, when they went to bring the saint's remains home.

Since I always regarded the idea of the Decade as divine inspiration and never as my own work, perhaps I may be permitted to say that I still regard this project as one of the most promising spiritual initiatives of our generation. When, several years later, the gates of freedom opened, most of society was taken aback by the new situation. Many social groups hastily cobbled together ill-prepared policies and projects, and many supporters of the old regime simply switched allegiance. Years after the change of regime, politicians continued to complain about a lack of vision. Yet the Catholic Church had in its hands a project that was an opportunity to offer society not only a vision but also a concrete program that could confront the most urgent issues of the period. The church truly had a great historical opportunity at that time, and there were great expectations of it. Besides, who else was better equipped to connect with society than the Catholic Church, which, thanks to Cardinal Tomášek's "new course," became more popular than at any other time in modern Czech history? The church started to enjoy great moral authority and credibility among broad swaths of society.

We realized, however, that the motto "We are many and have suffered much" would not serve us for very long, and the church would have to find something that would appeal to society, a new idea to give encouragement on the path ahead. Yet in the statements of purpose that accompanied the initiative, we constantly emphasized that the church neither wished nor was able to act as the nation's savior and that an attempt by the church to make itself the sole promoter of society's moral renewal would be both naive and arrogant. We stated plainly that the church could only contribute to the renewal of society if it consistently and humbly worked at its own renewal and if it was capable of admitting its historical faults and present weaknesses, and in these coming decades took the path of renewal, repentance, and recovery. The Decade of Spiritual Renewal was not intended as an expression of Catholic messianism but of the church's readiness to cooperate as a partner in the renewal of society with all those who felt a responsibility for the moral state of society.

But it was clear to us that this idea would not promote unity and become generally acceptable unless it came from the lips of the Czech primate and received papal blessing. And before we could submit this matter to the highest church authorities, it must not be simply the work of two clandestinely ordained priests but had to achieve a certain consensus in the country. This could only be achieved if people in key posts in the church could say that they were not only aware of the project, but had had an opportunity to be involved in it, to express their opinion before it was finalized, and did not have the feeling of being caught unawares "from above." But how was this all to be achieved without the omnipresent secret police finding out about it and eliminating its organizers in some way or putting pressure on the cardinal not to link his name with anything of this kind?

This laborious and difficult task required prayer above all. From 1985 to 1992, the Decade was the number one priority in my life. I invested myself in it heart and soul, and it was in my thoughts day and night. The idea infused and powered all my activity and consumed me like a passion or a fever: I was convinced that with this mission God had fixed the direction and purpose of my life for a long time to come. I was happy like someone who had managed to forget about himself almost entirely because of something that transcended him.

First of all, I managed to win Oto Mádr and Josef Zvěřina to the cause, together with an entire team, in which superiors of religious orders and priests with great moral authority from each of the dioceses were represented. Next we had to win over two of the most influential spiritual movements in the Czech church at that time: the Focalare and the charismatics. I spoke with several representatives of political dissent about the civic ramifications of the project. In order to gauge how the intelligentsia outside of church circles might react, I decided to talk to Václav Havel with whom I had had a close friendship from the beginning of the 1980s. Havel had heard me lecture on several occasions at seminars in private homes, and he invited me to contribute to a representative compilation of Czech thinking, which was published in samizdat, and also abroad, to mark his fiftieth birthday. Even though Havel's time was fully taken up with dissident activities, he carefully studied not only the draft of the Decade's plan but also my study on Jan Hus, in which I first hinted at the philosophical context of the project, and he made useful comments.

An important but also very difficult aspect of the project was how to lend it an ecumenical character. I recall a clandestine nighttime meeting with quite a large group of Protestant theologians, pastors, and lay activists, mostly from dissident circles within the church, at a Protestant parish office in northern Bohemia. In the course of the many hours of discussion, it turned out that the Protestants found the emphasis on the Czech patron saints unacceptable, because the cult of saints (and particularly those who were given prominence by the Counter-Reformation) offended them, and some of them clearly feared it might be a sophisticated version of the recatholization of the Czech nation. We were obliged, first of all, to speak in great depth about our notions of ecumenism and about the possibility of transcending denominational stereotypes and conceiving together a philosophy of Czech history that would overcome the existing "schizophrenia of traditions." We wanted to concede a just place in history to all great Christian figures, including those who, in the course of centuries, had been burdened with the ballast of later ideological projections.

The outcome of those discussions was the subsequent Easter message of Cardinal Tomášek, which invited Christians of the reformed churches to espouse the idea of the Decade in the spirit of their own traditions: the Catholic church was putting forward this idea as inspiration based on the Ten Commandments. Although the Catholic church, for the benefit of its own believers, and in the spirit of its own traditions, cited witnesses to the faith whom it regarded as saints, in order to illustrate the different aspects of the Commandments, it did not seek to impose that dimension of the Decade on anyone. He would welcome it if Protestant Christians were to present to the nation witnesses to their own tradition, such as Comenius and Hus, and reflect on the possibility of reaching agreement with the Catholic church about honoring great figures of their shared past before the church divided, such as Wenceslas, Adalbert, Ludmila, Procopius, or Agnes. At the same time, he knew and respected the fact that style of honoring witnesses to the faith differed theologically in the two traditions.

That Easter message opened a new door to deeper ecumenical dialogue. I realized that we had allowed ourselves to be lulled into false optimism by the positive experiences of spontaneous ecumenism from the period when we confronted repression at the hands of the same adversary and how much work remained to turn that shallow "negative ecumenism"—the product of external circumstances—into "positive ecumenism," by means of honest theological reflection, and bring about a process of genuine reconciliation and healing of relations.

We felt it was very important to obtain the support of the Holy See for the project. But how were we to do this when most of the bishops' seats were vacant and contact with Rome was extremely difficult?

Before I describe the lengthy process of negotiation with Cardinal Tomášek, I will mention a story, which, again, were it not for witnesses and even photographic documentation, might seem like a fairy tale. Without experiencing the situation of Czech Catholics in those days, it is hard to appreciate how enormous was our respect and love for the person of John Paul II. Shortly after his election, the Polish pope was asked by journalists about his policy toward the church in the Communist bloc. He replied that it would "not be naive," whereby he sent beyond the Iron Curtain an enormous signal of hope. And his subsequent actions did much to keep those hopes alive. Thanks to him cracks started to appear throughout the Eastern bloc. The moral atmosphere of his visit to his Polish homeland gave rise to the Solidarność movement. Thanks to the pope's moral authority, his idea of a "common European home," which Gorbachov would borrow for his rhetoric, and his vision of "a Europe from the Atlantic to the Urals," "breathing with both lungs," started to be incorporated into international politics. "The silent church is silent no longer, it speaks through the mouth of its pope," John Paul II declared in response to a Czech banner in the crowd during his first visit to Poland. Through his influence, he breathed unanticipated courage and strength into the cautious and aging Tomášek. Unlike the sensationalist press, we did not regard the Polish pope as a "superstar"; for us he was something more: a star of hope. But how were we to reach him, seeing that it is not easy or straightforward even for cardinals and heads of state to mount the staircase beyond the Bronze Gate? Then it turned out that the Bronze Gate could be opened by prayer.

In 1986, my friend Scarlett Vasiluková first traveled to the West as a tourist. She and her husband took part in an architects' excursion to Italy, and the program included a brief tour of Rome. "What's the official way to address the Holy Father?," she asked me jokingly just before her flight. Scarlett looked on the tourist excursion as a pilgrimage. Instead of a full-day tour of Rome, she decided to spend the time at prayer in St. Peter's Basilica. But after a while the stewards asked her to leave the Chapel of the Blessed Sacrament, because an important ceremony was due to take place there: the pope himself was to come and ordain a bishop. But shortly afterward, she returned to the basilica and approached a group of priests—they turned out to be Poles, as the bishop to be ordained was Polish—and she asked them in English whether they would take her to the pope. When they heard she was Czech, they actually pushed through with her to the very front row among the bishop's family, and when the ordination was over, they accompanied her to a small private audience with the Holy Father. Surprised by the presence of a woman among the bishops, priests, and the family of the bishop, he spent more time with her then the customary short moment for formal presentation and the kissing of his hand. Scarlett made use of the time to tell him at lightning speed about the planned decade of preparation for the millennium of the patron saint of both Czechs and Poles and about the idea of national renewal aimed at all people of goodwill in our homeland. The pope gave the idea his blessing, and he blessed Scarlett and her family, pressing two rosaries into her hands. Scarlett claims that when she handed me one of the two rosaries on her return, she saw me moved to tears for the first and last time in the many years of our cooperation.

■ TWO YEARS LATER, JUST PRIOR TO the memorable Feast of St. Agnes in St. Vitus Cathedral, I learned on the Tuesday before the Sunday ceremony that the following day, Wednesday, March 2, which was celebrated in those days as Agnes's Day, Cardinal Meisner was due to fly to Rome. It occurred to me that public papal audiences take place on Wednesdays, and I decided to act. I took a day's leave from the clinic and traveled to Berlin by the night train, arriving there at 5:30 in the morning. Forty minutes later I concelebrated Mass with the Berlin cardinal in his private chapel, after which, as was customary, I joined him for a working breakfast. The cardinal tended to choose a different room than the refectory, which he assumed was bugged by the Stasi, the East German secret police. I handed him a text, which mentioned Agnes of Bohemia, the Year of Agnes, and the Czech Decade, which I had waited until that morning to write so as to avoid the risk of its being discovered at the border. The cardinal flew to Rome an hour later, and while still at the airport in West Berlin he telephoned a request to the Vatican that the Holy Father should include in his address a sentence that he would hand to him at the audience just before he spoke. I traveled back to Prague, and that evening with some friends, just before 8:00, we recorded the Vatican broadcast in Czech with that sentence from the pope's address, which was immediately included graphically in a poster inviting people to Sunday's ceremony. That too is how we worked, and the hand of the Lord was with us. It was truly an adventure of small miracles.

■ BUT SUPPORT FOR THE DECADE DEPENDED crucially on Cardinal Tomášek. In order to recount my relationship with this man, it is necessary to go back many years. My first meeting with Bishop Tomášek was in spring 1967. It was a year after my conversion, and I was only too glad to accept the invitation of a certain theologian to pay a visit to the bishop with a number of friends, because the bishop apparently liked to hear the views of young people. At the time I didn't know much about the role of a bishop in the church, so I borrowed from the university library a social catechism for priests dating from between the world wars, from which I learned inter alia how a canon is to behave at a public bath and discovered that one greets a bishop by kissing his hand in a kneeling position and addressing him as "Your Excellency" or "Your Grace." Thus instructed, I set off for the Archbishop's Palace.

It turned out that the author of the social catechism had failed to predict the Second Vatican Council. The bishop shook us by the hand and asked us to address him as "Father Bishop." I found it extremely perplexing that the Prague hierarch had the manner of a Moravian rustic. He talked to us in a strong Moravian accent and fired at us short catechism-like axioms as if we were schoolboys, and the entire conversation was rather sluggish. On the way to the palace, one of the group had told me that the Church of St. Salvator in the Old Town of Prague was once a university church, so I asked the bishop whether that tradition might not be revived. The bishop coughed and switched on the transistor radio on his desk, filling the room with the sound of a hit song by the singer Waldemar Matuška, and his action struck me as rather odd. My companion, an ecumenically minded recent convert, suggested that the church in question could be renamed the Church of the Three Johns: John the Evangelist, John Hus, and John of Nepomuk. At the time I didn't know much about ecumenism or to what extent Bishop Tomášek was ecumenically minded, but it did strike me as rather bold, and I feared that the bishop might either throw us out or suffer a stroke. But nothing of the sort happened; the bishop smiled politely and just took notes. He encouraged us to pray the rosary and to attend confession regularly. He asked us whether we had bags with us and discreetly slipped into them rosaries and a copy of the spiritual diary of Pope John XXIII. Then he switched off the radio, and we went home.

Only much later did I understand the function of the radio on his desk. Bishop Tomášek lived totally surrounded by listening devices. The transistor probably served more of a psychological function rather than as an effective jamming device. Nevertheless, I was touched to find, twenty years later, when I was tackling with the same man, at the same desk, momentous issues that would go down in the history of the Czech church and society, that the same transistor radio that had accompanied our naive youthful talk in 1967 was still playing on his desk. When, at that same desk in January 1990, I received from Cardinal Tomášek a certificate to say that I was now spiritual administrator of the university Church of St. Salvator, the transistor radio was still there but was now switched off. I was convinced that if we switched it on, we would hear the same song by Waldemar Matuška as that time, but I was not brave enough to ask the cardinal's permission.

For some time after that brief meeting in 1967, I used to attend the Sunday morning Mass at the cathedral, and I would be asked by one of the canons to accompany the bishop from the cathedral to the Archbishop's Palace, so that he didn't have to walk through Prague Castle on his own. This happened several times, and on those occasions Bishop Tomášek would always ask me questions and express interest in student life. Then, during the period of the Prague Spring,

I was in contact with him as a representative of the Vigilia students' association. When I graduated I sent him the announcement, and I was surprised to receive a personal letter in response, in which he wrote: "Since I have made your personal acquaintance, permit me to express my wishes for your future. You have discovered early on that if there is nowadays an activity that is beneficial for the good of the world, then it is spiritual work. But in these times this requires a deep philosophical foundation. This you have acquired, so now you must analyze your vocation from the standpoint of God and join the ranks of experts as one of Christ's apostles. I don't know what paths your activity will follow, but may it always be that of a faithful follower of Christ who manages his talents well."

In subsequent years, we saw little of each other. As a clandestinely ordained priest I observed the instruction to draw attention to myself as little as possible. However, in the mid-1980s, when the preparatory work on the Decade of Spiritual Renewal was complete, I accepted the task of informing the cardinal about the plan and winning his support, which was absolutely vital for its success. I was full of misgivings when I went to see him. Would the eighty-seven-year-old primate recognize me after all these years, and would he trust me?

Our first meeting was not very reassuring. I walked through the immense empty rooms of the Archbishop's Palace, which put me in mind of Kafka's castle or scenes from Buñuel's films, and arrived at his office, where I found the old man, who looked very lonely and depressed. The only spark of hope was that he immediately recognized me, and he behaved toward me without the tiniest shadow of distrust. However, his only response to it all was to repeat over and over again that he was totally alone. Several times he asked about the situation "outside," by which he meant Czech society but also the church. It struck me that he was under a sort of house arrest in his palace; maybe it was a moment of fatigue, when he really did feel that way. There was the same desk with the transistor radio. The cardinal listened to what I had to say, nodding and taking notes.

"Ten years," he sighed. "I won't live to see it." He accepted the draft pastoral letter announcing the Decade but went on repeating that he was completely on his own. "We won't leave you on your own," I promised him. "At the very least we can support your hands, like they supported the aging Moses's hands in battle. As you know from scripture: When Moses lowered his hands the Amalekites were winning, when he held up his hands, Israel was victorious. And we now face a battle over fundamental values. This Decade, Your Eminence, your hands will be raised above the nation, a sign of communication with God, a sign of hope." He switched off the radio and accompanied me with shuffling feet downstairs to the door, where he blessed me. The pastoral letter was not issued, however.

I recounted this to Mádr and Zvěřina. They assured me that they had been endeavoring for some time to overcome the cardinal's isolation and were assisted in this by the cardinal's excellent secretary, Father Vyhlídka. In moments of exhaustion, however, the cardinal apparently felt he was completely alone. I decided to rely on persistence and started to make repeated visits to him. I redrafted the pastoral letter again and again and strove to adapt myself to his style. Since each of the drafts had to be screened by the censor at the State Bureau for Church Affairs, it was necessary to be cautious. But none of them was successful.

And then one summer day I arrived at the Archbishop's Palace and the doorkeeper informed me that the cardinal could receive no one that day because Cardinal Gantin was on a visit, and the two of them were at that moment in the cathedral. Then the door suddenly opened, and Cardinal Tomášek came in. Yet again I started to talk to him about the Decade and handed him my latest draft of a pastoral letter. I felt like an obtrusive insurance salesman and said to myself, "This is my last attempt." As usual the cardinal read the text carefully, but this time he complimented me on it: "That's the way pastoral letters should be drafted, by people in the field, not as an armchair decision! But why ten years at the outset? Wouldn't the first one—the Agnes year, suffice? And then wait and see?" I reminded him of his own words from a sermon about the priestly vocation that he had that preached a long time ago: Young people need demanding goals; minor and easy targets aren't attractive. "That's true. You've got a good memory," he said. "And also," I added, "the reader needs to know at the outset whether it will be a short story or the first chapter of a lengthy novel." "That's also true," he agreed. Then he blessed me and gave me a rosary as he had years before.

On the day of the Assumption of Mary, a pastoral letter was issued that included the first mention of the Decade, and on September 8—the Nativity of Mary—the entire program was included in the circular of the archbishopric. It is curious how decisive steps in the Decade happened on Marian feast days. Then in November I brought the cardinal a text that ceremonially proclaimed the Decade of Spiritual Renewal. He thoroughly reworked it, but the opening sentence—the one that I cared about most—remained. It read: "Stand up and raise your heads!" The Decade was no longer a dream; it had become reality. It was proclaimed on the first Sunday of Advent of 1987. That same day the Moravian activist Augustin Navratil launched his "31-point petition" for religious freedom. In just a few months it had been signed by over half a million people, making it the most successful petition ever in the Communist bloc.

AT THAT TIME NOT EVEN CARDINAL TOMÁŠEK knew I was a priest. This bothered me, because I was a frequent guest of the cardinal in years 1985–89, whether in the matter of the Decade or the Senior working group. It was I who brought him most of the drafts of the pastoral letter, of an open letter to the government, and of important sermons. Some of the texts I drafted myself, others I worked on with Mádr or with a group. I must add that the opinion of the secret police that the cardinal was a senile puppet in the hands of several representatives of the underground church was totally untrue. Naturally, a man of the cardinal's age and status did not draft all texts himself, but Cardinal Tomášek read through everything and considered it carefully, seeking others' advice and also making amendments to texts. He consciously bore the entire responsibility. I admired his courage and the humility with which he confided not only in the distinguished theologians Zvěřina and Mádr, his experienced colleagues from the period of the Prague Spring, but also in me, fifty years his junior, who, moreover, he believed to be a layman.

I asked Cardinal Meisner, to whom I owed obedience in those days (our community had "exemption" in a certain sense and did not come under the authority of the local bishop but that of the ordinary bishop who linked us with Rome, who in those days was the bishop of Berlin), whether I could tell Cardinal Tomášek I was a priest. He instructed me to maintain secrecy about my ordination, even with the cardinal, as long as I could. I expect in Berlin they did not have much faith in the powers of a transistor radio to block the listening devices. In fall 1988, I came to the conclusion that I could keep it secret no longer. When the cardinal once more spoke highly of the competency of his laity when reading a text I had brought him, I wrote on a small piece of paper the words, "Your Eminence, for over ten years now I have been a priest clandestinely ordained abroad," and let him read it before I immediately destroyed it. The cardinal beamed and said, "I thought as much!" Then he stood up and came over to embrace me. We never mentioned it again until November 1989.

In a short space of time I submitted a number of draft texts connected with the Decade to the cardinal for his consideration and approval. In spring 1988 it was the Ecumenical Message to representatives of churches and all people of goodwill in our country, which was intended to explain the ecumenical character of our project and promote support for the Decade from outside the Catholic Church. The cardinal accepted that text without demur, even though it was a very serious step in the ecumenical process, which was officially more or less frozen because of Communist disapproval. It included the following sentences: "When we consider our past we all have cause to ask for forgiveness and God's mercy. The Catholic Church does not conceal its share of the blame for painful aspects of our history (about which Cardinal Beran, for example, spoke in connection with the immolation of Master Jan Hus or the violent recatholization of Bohemia after the Battle of White Mountain). Our wish is that the Decade project should help us avoid carrying discord of the past into the next millennium."

The ecumenical response to the Decade was fairly fragmentary and remained so. No doubt this was partly due to the fact that many officials of the non-Catholic churches at that time were either directly embroiled with the regime or extremely cautious lest too close links with Cardinal Tomášek and the Catholic Church would put their churches in even greater disfavor with the authorities.

At the end of 1988, I came up with the idea of inviting bishops linked by veneration of St. Adalbert (including the bishop of Rome) to an annual "bridge of prayer for European unification and the moral and spiritual renewal of the European nations, for understanding, and for the respect of all human rights" and proposed establishing an international circle of St. Adalbert. At that time I even dreamed of the cardinal requesting the pope to proclaim St. Adalbert the patron saint of central Europe and sought advice from the publishers of the samizdat underground journal *Střední Evropa* (Central Europe). My friends thought the idea was excessive, so I abandoned it. But the European Bridge of Prayer was realized.

On an official trip to Kraków at the end of 1988 (which I made use of for lengthy and fruitful discussions about the Decade with Cardinal Macharski, as well as with people associated with the magazines *Znak* and *Tygodnik Powszechny* and the local Dominicans) I heard the news about the catastrophic earthquake in Armenia. A few days later I proposed to Cardinal Tomášek that believers be invited to set up Christian aid committees in all parishes, initially to assist the afflicted in Soviet Armenia (the Communist regime could hardly forbid that) but also with a longer-term aim, of course, namely, to assist the lonely and afflicted in our own country. The objective was clear: to use this achievement of the Year of Agnes, which was devoted to service, and focused on those people assisting the afflicted, to break the monopoly of the state in the field of social work and lay the institutional foundations of a network of charitable work by the church. The cardinal fully agreed, and the idea caught on in a number of places. These were the foundations on which the nascent *Katolická charita* was able to build after the fall of the Communist regime.

■ DURING THE SECOND HALF OF THE 1980s, it became the custom for various foreign bishops to make trips to Prague to lend moral support to the Prague cardinal. Likewise, foreign politicians on official visits would include an audience in the Archbishop's Palace on their agenda. The regime was understandably concerned about its reputation abroad, so it was obliged to tolerate it grudgingly. This led to the growing political and diplomatic importance of the cardinal's person and office. During those years the cardinal would quite often invite me to those visits—thanks largely to his secretary, Monsignor Vyhlídka—and I would accompany them around Prague, officially as a volunteer guide to the churches and historical monuments. It was a welcome opportunity to escape premises that were wiretapped and to inform the bishops truthfully about the situation of our church. I also used the occasion to ask about the situation in the West and their experience. They knew from the cardinal (and later from their brother bishops and some people in Rome) that I could be trusted absolutely, so they were as frank and open with me as I was with them.

This did not entirely escape the attention of the secret police, of course. In the secret police archives, which are now open to the public, there is a police report in which I am described as a particularly dangerous individual who helps prepare the cardinal's texts and associates under the cardinal's protection with top-level members of the Western hierarchy. "We have so far been unable to subdue his activity," the report ends. That was around the beginning of 1989, when major changes were already in the air and when the secret police tended to monitor dissident activity rather than eliminate it. It would seem that by then political struggles were under way in the top echelons of the Communist Party, particularly in the secret police. It is possible that some of them were already thinking of an escape route, while others were in favor of a hard-line approach. Rumor had it that experts from the Soviet KGB were coming to Prague, and they were selecting an alternative list of "cadres" from among certain economists—including those who were not members of the Communist Party or had been expelled after 1968—who could eventually replace the existing compromised leadership of the Party and the state. It's interesting that many of the names that were whispered about in those days really did emerge after the fall of the Communist regime in key posts in the new political parties, as well as in very important posts in the leadership of the state.

▌ AROUND THE BEGINNING OF APRIL 1989, the archbishop of Paris, Cardinal Lustiger, arrived in Prague. I knew him to be one of the outstanding figures of contemporary European Catholicism and someone very close to the pope. We met secretly late one evening in the Malà Strana quarter and spent several hours walking up and down the castle steps and then through the winding lanes. We were followed from a distance by the cardinal's secretary, who made sure we were not followed or monitored by the police. We talked about the situation, as well as about the underground church, the Decade of Spiritual Renewal, and the influence of Gorbachov's perestroika on the regime's policy on the churches. Noticing that the cardinal had an uncommon interest in our situation and that his ability to understand it was incomparably greater than the majority of the Western hierarchs, and also sensing an obvious spark of personal affinity between us, I was emboldened to share with him all my ideas about mutual relationships in Central Europe, including the idea of an intermediate church structure for the area of Central and Eastern Europe. His very animated reaction took me by surprise: "You must meet the Holy Father in person and explain it all to him." I replied with a smile, "I'm sure that's no problem for you, Your Eminence, but I am an unknown Prague psychologist and clandestinely ordained priest, and for exactly twenty years now, the regime has not permitted me a single private trip to the West." He said that we must pray for it and also think up a plan. I replied that there was possibly one glimmer of hope: the regime had slightly liberalized foreign travel, and during the previous year I had managed to travel abroad, albeit only on official trips. So I would apply for a private visa; there would be a youth pilgrimage to Compostella in the summer. "There are you," he replied, "the pope will be there, and so will I. Come and see me, and I'll take you to the pope. These matters are truly of the greatest importance and your meeting is part of God's plan, of that I'm convinced."

That unusual meeting had an even more remarkable sequel. To my great surprise, the authorities gave me permission to travel to Spain. We journeyed along the traditional routes from Paris to Compostella, with stops at places like Paray-le-Monial and Le Puy-en-Velay and a succession of splendid old monasteries lining the centuries-old European pilgrimage road. We visited Lourdes and Loyola, the birthplace of St. Ignatius, as well as the small Romanesque church in the Spanish mountains where the Holy Grail is hidden, according to legend, and several large cathedrals in Spain. On the way, I met a number of interesting people, for example, the well-known Parisian priest Guy Gilbert, who worked with drug addicts. Like a true Frenchman, he did not know a single word of a foreign language, so in the bullring at Pamplona we attempted a very comical conversation in Latin, which ended, nevertheless, with a mutual blessing and embrace; in that we understood each other.

The last lap was more demanding than the entire exhausting journey that preceded it, and the conditions were truly spartan. The final night we slept thirsty, hungry, dirty, and exhausted on the bare earth near the stadium, where the pope was due to celebrate Mass the next morning. Everything was covered in dust. When I woke up in the morning I discovered, first, that I had been sleeping in the open in the dust with my feet in a puddle—which was in itself an uncustomary awakening for an unathletic forty-year-old—and, second, that standing over me was the archbishop of Paris. Both situations were fairly outlandish in themselves, but in combination the effect was so bizarre that I closed my eyes again and thought I was dreaming. But it was no dream. Cardinal Lustiger had set off for a walk that morning, and in that field of about a million recumbent people, who had journeyed here for the World Youth Day gathering with the pope, we actually met. He instantly recognized me, although I was covered in dust, and in jeans, and he said, "You see, it all worked out. Come and see me after the pope's Mass, and somehow I'll arrange for you to meet him." At that point the miracle would seem to have come to an end, because after the Mass it was impossible to force my way through the police cordon and the million-strong crowd before the pope flew off in his helicopter.

That afternoon I met with Dom Helder Camara and had a further meeting with Cardinal Lustiger. I apologized for not turning up after the Mass, to which he calmly replied that we would have to find another opportunity. It occurred to me that it might be possible on the occasion of the beatification of St. Agnes of Bohemia in November in Rome, so long as the regime allowed me to travel. Cardinal Lustiger told me to leave details about myself and the Decade project with the Jesuit Petr Kolář in Paris on my way home, and he would sort out a meeting in Rome in advance. If I managed to get to Rome I was to approach the pope's secretary with a request for a personal audience, mentioning the cardinal. During the return journey—on August 21, 1989—we heard about demonstrations in Prague. There was something in the air, and we prayed very hard.

SEVEN

The Revolution
of St. Agnes

The national pilgrimage to Prague's St. Vitus Cathedral to mark the Feast of St. Agnes in spring 1988 was a kind of public overture to the Decade of Spiritual Renewal, since the first year of the decade was the Year of Blessed Agnes of Bohemia, intended to prepare society for her anticipated beatification. I wrote the text of the novena for that feast day, and Father Vágner prayed it courageously, and with dignity, at the Church of St. Salvator. For nine successive evenings, groups of mostly young people gathered there for shared meditation accompanied by Taizé singing. One evening, Václav Havel also attended. Of course we noticed the presence of secret police agents, and it became evident that the Sunday celebration might face some difficulties.

When, two days prior to the celebration, I brought the cardinal the draft of the homily he had asked me to prepare, together with the pope's words from the Wednesday audience in Rome, I was met in the anteroom by the vicar general Monsignor Lebeda, who would subsequently be appointed auxiliary bishop of Prague by the grace of the Communist regime. Monsignor Lebeda had just returned duly unnerved from the Ministry of the Interior, to which he had been summoned. He urged me to persuade the cardinal to drop the idea of the pilgrimage. "It will be a political demonstration! Agnes would not have agreed to that; she liked peace and quiet!," he yelled at me. Lebeda was an odd person. That unhappy man had a particular fondness for the quiet of the graveyard. He mostly spent his spare time walking in cemeteries, and in his poems and interminable sermons he would often speak about his conversations with the dead; years before, I found a grave that he had already prepared for himself with a decorative inscription, and I suppose he used go there and mourn over himself. The regime seemed to prefer such melancholic types in the upper echelons of the church.

The cardinal showed me a threatening letter he had received, signed by "Satanists": "We convey to you a message from the darkest of darkness, from the Lord of Evil and Terrors . . . by whose will we live, destroy and murder. . . . [Y]ou are inviting flocks of your sheep to that celebration at Vitus. . . . [W]e hope you won't be too surprised when it explodes," and so on. I told him I thought it was a provocation by the secret police, who were trying to find a pretext to ban the celebration Mass and in the process had unwittingly provided a fairly apt description of themselves. He laughed and maintained his resolve.

Nevertheless, the Communist police state had indeed prepared some devilish maneuvers to demonstrate its power. Police units were drafted to Prague from all over the country; the People's Militia (the Party's paramilitary corps set up after World War II along the lines of the Nazi Stormtroopers) were mobilized, along with factory organizations of the Communist Party, to delay trains and buses bringing pilgrims to Prague. Leading dissidents were arrested and held in "preventive detention," trams were diverted from the area of the castle, and the nearest subway stations were closed. Areas were cordoned off, and medical personnel in Prague hospitals were placed on emergency duty to deal with eventual injuries. The regime was obviously seized with fear. Yet again it became clear to me that those who fear need others to fear them, but in their fits of paranoia they can be

Halík's baptism in 1948; Halík is in the arms of his uncle Josef

Halík with his parents and grandmother Filipina in 1958

Great-grandfather Jan Halík with his wife, Dorota, and their ten children

Mother, Marie Halíková, in Chod folk costume in a portrait photograph from the 1930s

Graduation at Halík's gymnasium in Prague, 1966

As a server with Fathers Reinsberg and Mandl at St. Gall's Church in 1972

Requiem for Jan Palach in St. Thomas's Church in January 1969

Speech during
doctoral graduation
at Charles University
in 1972

With Scarlett Vasiluková-Rešlová and Zdeněk Neubauer in 1983

With Václav Havel at a seminar in the home of Radim Palouš, around 1989

With Cardinal Meisner in 1990

At Red Square in Moscow in January 2000

Scarlett Vasiluková-Rešlová at the Vatican in 1986

With Cardinal Tomášek in 1990

With John Paul II during an audience after the canonization of St. Agnes of Bohemia at the Vatican in November 1989

Halík presides
at his belated
first Mass in
the Týn Church
in 1990

A speech to pilgrims during the summer visit of Pope John Paul II in April 1990

Mass with Petr Vacík, SJ, in the Israeli desert in 2012

Speech at a Warsaw synagogue where Halík was awarded the title "Man of Reconciliation 2010"

With Archbishops Graubner and Vlk at the Sea of Galilee in Israel in 1992

In friendly conversation with Václav Havel in the mid-1990s

With Michael Novak
and Peter L. Berger
in Washington, DC,
in 1995

On the road in India, 1995

With the patriarch of the Buddhist School on Mount Koya in Japan, 1998

On Mount Sinai in Egypt, 1998

With Pope Emeritus Benedict at a symposium at the Vatican, August 2015

Receiving an honorary doctorate of divinity at Oxford University, June 2016

The procession of honorary doctorates at Oxford University

With Pope Francis at the Vatican in 2014

Hermitage on
Nelson Island

On Nelson Island in Antarctica in 2002

truly dangerous. I felt most uneasy when I entered the cathedral and saw a large number of "inconspicuous gentlemen," who, as we later heard, were equipped with rosaries and coins for the collection and had even undergone liturgical training ("The greeting is 'Peace be with you!' not 'Greetings, Comrade!'"). However, the Mass proceeded in such a dignified fashion that during the Hymn of St. Wenceslas maybe even Satan's helpers felt something beneath the vaulted ceiling of St. Vitus Cathedral that Party training courses did not offer.

Nevertheless, when, three weeks later, several thousand believers gathered in Bratislava on Good Friday to pray for religious freedom, the police brutally dispersed them with truncheons, dogs, and water cannons. And there was also bloodshed.

■ FOR US 1989 BEGAN WITH Jan Palach Week—mass demonstrations in Prague on the twentieth anniversary of Palach's death, during which Václav Havel was arrested—and was followed by heightened political tension. None of us suspected how the year would end.

The cardinal became more radical in his relations with the government. In January he wrote an open letter to the government protesting the brutal treatment of demonstrators by the police during Jan Palach Week. Then in April, to mark St. Adalbert's Day, he issued an appeal to all Catholic believers and wrote a letter to the prime minister. Cardinal Tomášek called on believers to actively defend their rights; he urged the government to change its attitude and start to respect human and civil rights and to engage at last in a dialogue with citizens and the opposition. The cardinal offered himself or his colleagues as mediators in such a dialogue.

At that time I decided to make a public appearance. In May 1989, a pilgrimage was organized to commemorate Clement Hofbauer, the saint connected with the second year of the Decade of Spiritual Renewal, and on this occasion Brno Cathedral was chosen. It was clear to us that such a large gathering must not be simply the expression of the growing confidence and numbers of determined believers, but the church had to offer above all the power of inspiring ideas. After careful reflection, prayer, and consultation with friends, I decided to step out of anonymity in spite of all the risks. Before the main religious service began, as part of the program of spiritual renewal, I spoke for about an hour to the pilgrims from every part of the country who filled the cathedral, focusing on the meaning and objective of the Decade and the imminent canonization of Agnes of Bohemia.

I described Clement Hofbauer as a man who fought for the freedom of the church in the face of bureaucratic harassment from the absolutist state, who strove so that the church should not lose its active connection with the world of the spirit, or with leading thinkers and artists, or with the world of the poor and wronged. I built my entire address around Hofbauer's words, "preaching a new gospel." I said:

> Many have now concentrated on defending the rights of believers. Suffice it to say that it is necessary to seek a worthy place for the church in this society, so that its hands are free to serve all, and fully develop its witness. And who should work for this, if not the believers themselves, and their pastors? But we must not strive for that alone; it is a means, not the final end. We will soon cross a new threshold. We will enter a new phase in which the main emphasis will be not on our rights but on our responsibility—our shared responsibility for the life of the nation and society. . . . What is the essential expression of maturity, if not the capacity to assume responsibility—not only for ourselves, but also for others, and for the community? . . . We don't want to be concerned only about ourselves, or about our own survival and security. We don't want simply to care about our own back yard. We are assuming afresh, and with determination, the fundamental mission of the church: to proclaim the gospel to all creation, to heal all sickness in people, and to be the salt of the earth. The gospel must be proclaimed and borne witness to in an entirely new way. This does not mean,

of course, that it is our wish to assume sole responsibility for the nation's renewal. We want to assist the common good in the spirit of dialogue, broad ecumenical openness, and civic cooperation with all people of goodwill.

I presented in detail the entire program of the Decade and the content of each of the years and explained the significance of St. Adalbert.

In all the vicissitudes of life and faced with the many opportunities, let us be extremely watchful, lest—in the words of scripture—our hearts grow fat and harden. The church must not become a ghetto closed in on itself. It must not lose its active connection with the ordinary lives of people around us, and with their problems and hardship, a connection that has deepened so much in recent years. Let us beware of self-satisfaction, and not return to old ways. In particular, let us avoid all triumphalism, ostentation, pomp and externality— the pomp that repelled so many people! Our nation is particularly sensitive in this respect. The way to its heart is neither in hobnailed boots, nor in golden slippers, but "barefoot." This nation has never been impressed by might or luxury. All those who have wanted to win its favor while seeking privileges for themselves have always lost its trust. Let us also in the future safeguard the spirit of humility and modesty in the life of the church like a crown jewel and something of great promise!

I said that the present awakening of the church and the conversion of young people were the fruit of suffering, and I thanked the persecuted: "It is a law confirmed by twenty centuries of Christianity, that suffering and persecution invariably cleanse and strengthen the church. Many of these people still live amongst us today. I would like, on behalf of myself, of my generation, of those who are younger, and of those who are yet to come, to express warm thanks and gratitude to them. Christians in the first centuries used to kiss the hands of those who wore shackles for the sake of Christ. When we celebrate the saints of past centuries, let us not forget the great disciples who still live amongst us!"

I also addressed myself to the priests who had come to Brno Cathedral from all corners of the country.

> We are grateful to our priests for their service in difficult conditions. But here, too, there are many things that we cannot go on forever blaming on external difficulties. . . . Who will take our priests down from the scaffolding, to which they often escape to avoid their fundamental tasks, and bring them to the sanctuary, and to the center of the community of believers? Who will show them that they owe a much greater responsibility to us, the living temple of God, than to church buildings? Who will transform the many solitary and isolated priests into a fraternal community of colleagues? Who will teach them to listen to and speak with those to whom they were sent? Who will take care of the greater education of our priests? Who will overcome the mentality of simply keeping things going in the church, and arouse within it the missionary spirit of its founders and creators?

I voiced the vision that in spite of all the difficulties we would soon have bishops and the hope that they would be men "who will understand with their hearts what the Spirit is telling the church, who will love the church, and also understand the times and the world we live in, men who will have a broad outlook and be deeply anchored in the Lord, who will lead us along the path of renewal."

I spoke from the depth of my heart and to the best of my knowledge and belief. As I once did in my graduation speech, I forbade myself to think of the consequences my words might have for me. I was convinced that the message now had to be said out loud. That speech was soon reproduced in samizdat magazines, and it was disseminated throughout the country as tape recordings. I was told by many people that this finally made them realize that life with the church was not simply a matter of personal piety, regular attendance at church services, and striving to live a well-ordered private life but that the church and each of its members had real responsibility for society as a whole. The die was cast.

■ AT THAT TIME I SENSED I WAS UNDER intensive police surveillance, but I experienced only one obvious case of intimidation. On the occasion of the second culminating pilgrimage that year— the pilgrimage in June for John Nepomucene Neumann, onetime bishop of Philadelphia, at Prachatice—the local priest showed up five minutes before I was due to give my previously announced address and told me he had been ordered by the police to prevent me by all possible means from speaking in public, which he did.

Nevertheless, I still have a fond memory of that pilgrimage. After the dramatic circumstances of the Agnes pilgrimage, I proposed to Cardinal Tomášek that he invite to each of the major pilgrimages of the Decade a leading representative of the church from the West as an official guest. Since the regime was concerned to maintain a certain degree of decorum vis-à-vis the outside world, this would also serve as a kind of protective shield. The Brno pilgrimage was attended by Cardinal Groer from Vienna; the Prachatice pilgrimage was attended by Archbishop Bevilacqua, Neumann's successor to the Philadelphia see.

Archbishop Bevilacqua arrived well in advance. We met in a small café in Prague and spent three days walking around town, during which time we became very close. He was very interested in the life of the church in our country, particularly the life of the underground church. He answered very frankly my questions about the situation of the church in the West. He also had several meetings with young people in their apartments, and they were enchanted with his spontaneity, openness, and humor. Even I was shocked when we encountered some pious young girls on the street who wanted to kiss his episcopal ring, and he reacted by saying, "Not here, kiss me on my cheek. We have a campaign in America: Today kiss your dog. And today I declare, Today kiss your bishop!" Later, in, Prachatice, he went to the local pub in full regalia for a beer and had a very lively conversation with the terrified locals. He listened with American magnanimity to my ideas and plans and gave me much useful advice from his rich fund of experience, which is still a living inspiration for me. When he left Prague he went straight to the pope, and he was willing to take with him my letter concerning the Decade of Spiritual Renewal. Years later I met with Cardinal Bevilacqua in America, and we spent a splendid evening together in the garden of his residence. He gave me a very cordial welcome, and it was clear that he had found his encounter with Prague inspirational, and he could recall it in astonishing detail.

WHEN THE DEFINITIVE DATE FOR the canonization of Agnes of Bohemia was fixed, and it was decided that it would take place in Rome—although the Czech Catholics had been hoping that the pope would come to Prague to canonize her—everyone waited to see what attitude the regime would adopt. Someone cleverly warned the Communist authorities that if they failed to permit believers from Czechoslovakia to take part en masse, the entire event would be under the control of Czechoslovak émigrés, which would create an enormous international scandal for the regime. The authorities really did make concessions and decided to allow thousands of believers to travel to Rome, even including those who had been prevented from traveling to the West for years. Nevertheless, a number of the best-known dissidents, whose passports had previously been taken away, including Josef Zvěřina, were refused permission to travel even on that occasion.

I waited in suspense, and to my surprise I received permission. Cardinal Tomášek requested me to leave for Rome in advance and devise, at the Czech section of Radio Vatican, spiritual preparation that would be broadcast to Czechoslovakia every evening for nine days before the canonization, which the hundreds of pilgrims could also listen to during their journey.

My entire stay in Rome seemed like a dream to me. It was almost twenty years since I was last there, and I met with many people whom I had previously known only from books or exile journals, in particular, Monsignor Škarvada, the bishop for Czechs in exile. My accommodation was in the generalate of the Jesuits not far from the Vatican, and I spent a lot of time on the terrace at the top of that enormous building, where I prayed and prepared meditations for the radio and observed the unique panorama of the Eternal City at sunrise and sunset. Apart from working at the radio, I would spend my days as a pilgrim visiting the churches of Rome, and in prayers of intercession to the saints I would confide to them my great wish: to meet the pope.

As advised by Cardinal Lustiger, I sent a letter to Monsignor Dziwisz, secretary of the Holy Father, via Bishop Škarvada, requesting an audience and setting out the matters I would like to submit to the pope. I waited in suspense, wondering if I would receive a reply. On the Saturday evening I was in the chapel in the basilica where the pope prays the rosary with believers, a prayer that is broadcast to the whole world by Radio Vatican. Just when the pope was passing with his colleagues, I approached his secretary, who asked me my name, and it was obvious from his reaction that he had read my letter. He gave me a conspiratorial wink and led me through the cordon of Swiss guards into the adjacent room, where I had met the pope in person the first time. I only managed to say a few words to him about the Decade of Spiritual Renewal and tell him we were looking forward to his visiting us one day. I had the feeling that that was that and was rather disappointed. I talked to Bishop Škarvada about the meeting, and he told me, "Hold on, I don't think that's the end of it."

Two days later, I received a letter from the pope's secretary that the Holy Father had invited Bishop Škarvada and me to a private dinner on November 7. I spent the afternoon of that day in the basilica of St. Bartholomew on the Island, which contains the relics of St. Adalbert. During the midday break I celebrated Mass in private for the Decade and for a blessing for the meeting with the pope. When, that evening, Bishop Škarvada and I drove through the gates of the Vatican and passed one line of Swiss guards after another, I started to become slightly weak at the knees. At that moment Bishop Škarvada said, "I bet you never thought we lads from Prague would be going together for dinner with the pope one day!" When he said, "we lads from Prague," all the tension fell away from me, and at that moment I fell in love with Bishop Škarvada for life.

We passed by guards in old-fashioned uniforms and then walked up a wide staircase to a place where the chamberlain asked us to wait for a moment. Then the pope's private secretary, Monsignor Dziwisz, came to welcome us and lead us to the papal apartment. The Holy Father entered and led us first—as he would do on all subsequent meetings—to his chapel, where he knelt with us before the tabernacle for a long time in silent prayer. That was the most powerful moment. I saw the pope submerge himself in prayer like a stone falling into a deep well, and he seemed to be drawing us into those depths with him. I said to myself, "So it is from here that the entire church is run," and I thought of various situations in the history of the world and of the church that the pope and his predecessors brought to the Lord in prayer and sought instruction for their decisions.

Then the pope invited us to his dining room, where the four of us ate for about an hour and half as if in a family circle. I told him about the underground church and the situation in our country. I could tell that the pope was very well informed.

At the very outset the pope asked what language we would use. In broken Polish I suggested that we could converse in German or English, to which the pope responded, "But you speak Polish very well!" I countered that this was not Polish but "panslavonic Esperanto." The pope patted me on the shoulder and said, "Fine, we'll speak in panslavonic Esperanto then." So we spoke in this strange universal Slavonic dialect and understood each other very well.

It was curious to see how totally coordinated the pope and his secretary were, so that they almost formed a single person. Most of the time, the pope listened attentively, and often it was his secretary who asked questions and reacted. When I spoke of the need to integrate the work of the church in the countries of Central and Eastern Europe, the conversation naturally turned to politics also; it was the eve of the fall of the Berlin Wall, and the television already had coverage of the demonstrations in East Germany, which were growing in strength. "This is the end of Communism," the pope declared with certainty, "and not just in East Germany. Get ready: you too will soon be free!" I permitted myself to say that papal infallibility did not extend to such things and voiced the skeptical view that there might be a few years of Gorbachov-style perestroika. The pope mentioned that he had recently spoken with Gorbachov on this very spot. But he repeated once more that Communism would soon collapse, and our church should prepare itself for that moment.

Then he asked me about my personal plans. I shared with him something I had been thinking about in the recent months, namely, entering the almost moribund Order of the Knights of the Cross with a Red Star—the only religious order of Czech origin and the only male order founded by a woman, Agnes of Bohemia—and, in conjunction with Agnes's canonization, inject a new spirit into it. I thought that since it was established to offer medical care, the order might turn its attention to issues of medical ethics and evangelization in the world of medicine, promoting particular reverence for the Czech saints. In this way it could become a kind of spiritual driving force of the Decade of Spiritual Renewal. When I suggested that the order could have a close relationship with the archbishop of Prague, similar to the Jesuits' ties of loyalty to the papacy, John Paul laughed. "The Jesuits? That used to be the case, Father, four centuries ago!" Then he reacted to my idea of joining an order by shaking his head: "Your order, Father, will be the church!"

We went back to the pope's private chapel for a short period of prayer, when I took the liberty of asking the Holy Father to say a prayer of intercession that I might one day be allowed to serve the church publicly. Then came the moment to take our leave.

■ THE DAY BEFORE THE CANONIZATION, I walked around Rome with a priest friend, who had also helped with the Decade of Spiritual Renewal. I spent about two hours discussing with him my visions of what direction the church in our country should take if the Communist regime should happen to fall. Afterward we prayed in silence for a long time in a church. As we left the church my friend said to me, "I've been praying that you would become a bishop one day." I replied truthfully, "I was praying that you would become a bishop." It seems that I was more pious than he, because my prayer was granted soon after the fall of the Communist regime, whereas God mercifully decided not to grant my friend's prayer.

The canonization took place on Sunday, November 12, in St. Peter's Basilica, and the next day eleven thousand Czech and Slovak pilgrims had an audience with the pope. It had been agreed that I would say a few words of greeting to the pilgrims just prior to the pope's entry into the Paul VI Audience Hall. I remember walking around Rome the previous evening wondering whether I should finally emerge from clandestinity and speak publicly as a priest. I asked Bishop Škarvada about it the next morning, and he went with me to the State Secretariat. Archbishop Colasuonno and Monsignor Bukowski, who in latter years had been dealing with the Czechoslovak government on behalf of the Vatican and were familiar with our situation, were of the opinion that I should remain incognito.

In my speech to the pilgrims I mentioned a Czech legend that when Agnes of Bohemia was canonized all would be at be well in the Czech lands. "We can already feel the approach of better times like a breath of spring already touching our hearts," I declared, and the pilgrims responded with a storm of applause. I managed to catch sight of representatives of the Czechoslovak State Bureau for Church Affairs in the front row, their faces contorted with hatred.

■ On November 18, 1989, I was in Ostia with Karel Skalický, émigré Czech professor at the Pontifical Lateran University, who told me that according to world press reports and Italian television, a large student demonstration had been brutally suppressed by the police the previous day, November 17. Further information gradually reached us. Early in the morning of November 20, I was co-celebrant at a Mass at the altar of St. Wenceslas in St. Peter's Basilica in the Vatican, at which hour the church was still empty. Something important was clearly happening in my homeland. So I consigned the fate of our nation to God in that Mass at the Czech altar at the heart of the Roman Catholic Church.

That evening I flew home to Prague with Cardinal Tomášek, and as it was a Czechoslovak airplane, there were copies of the regime's daily newspaper, *Rudé právo*, containing the news that a student had possibly been killed in the demonstration and reporting appeals for a general strike. Cardinal Tomášek came across to me from his seat on the other side of the aisle and showed me the newspaper, saying, "What do you think of that? What do you think of that?" At the Prague airport the cardinal was welcomed by the Italian ambassador with the words, "Eminence, there is a revolution here."

■ Some of my friends were already waiting for me at the airport, and they immediately took me to their home and told me that demonstrations against the regime were growing stronger by the day. When I arrived home two students came to see me around midnight, and we drafted a declaration by Catholics about the situation. The next day I started to receive invitations from the striking students to speak to them. As part of their occupation strike the students organized a series of lectures under the heading "What They Didn't Teach You at School," and invited various speakers who were previously banned from teaching at the university to give lectures on hitherto taboo topics. I gave several talks on religion, the church, and the Decade of Spiritual Renewal and took part in discussions.

I was surprised to find that in almost all of the faculties during the strike a room had been allocated for prayer and meditation, in which many students prayed day and night. In those days providing that opportunity was taken for granted by everyone—in a society which had been fashioned for the previous forty years by the State's atheist ideology. Those rooms were visited not only by students from families of believers and those who had converted to Christianity in recent years—unity among believers from the various churches was an accepted fact—but there were also many who had discovered God in the course of those dramatic days. Some of those "November 17 converts" were baptized by me in subsequent years, while for others it was a simply an episode in their life story. I realized that at moments when everything was at stake, when young hearts above all are awash with powerful experiences and feelings—happiness at their lives' new perspectives, hopes, but also anxiety that the Velvet Revolution could still be violated by the terror of the shaken regime—people start spontaneously to express those powerful emotions in prayer. At such moments, secular language and secular means of expression turn out to be too dry. Even those who previously regarded such behavior as totally alien and foolish find the courage to pray.

There were remarkable moments when many things happened that would have been unthinkable just days before. At that time Prague had two heroes: Václav Havel and the priest Václav Malý. Neither of them was particularly well known outside Prague and dissident circles, except for the occasional mention in vitriolic articles in the Communist press. Havel became the leader of the Civic Forum, and Malý assumed the crucial role of moderator at the mass demonstrations. I discovered another dimension of his personal charisma but also the charisma of the priesthood as such. His moral strength, his calm, and his sense of humor enabled him to cope with the moods of the crowd. Had there been a demagogue in his place, whipped-up emotions could have transformed the crowds of hundreds of thousands into a destructive force. Father Malý managed to stimulate something that surfaces only at dramatic moments of Czech history: the capacity for effective solidarity, mutual kindly concern, creative reactions, and, above all, splendid humor. Political scientists and social psychologists ought to study those unique situations when the crowds entered into dialogue with Václav Malý, standing at the microphone on the balcony in the middle of a jam-packed Wenceslas Square, and responded to him literally as one man.

It was a revolution marked by wit, laughter, and singing. The people lynched nobody but instead jangled their house keys to ring the knell of the regime. No violence, no calls for vengeance, no searching for scapegoats; instead a fiesta, a joyful popular carnival. The icy November days were transformed into a spring of great hopes. Nevertheless, some of us who stood there in the crowds on Wenceslas Square could not suppress one painful regret: there were parents, relatives, and friends who had not lived to see it, all those who, in those dark days of the fifties, reassured themselves every year that "it won't last to Christmas!" In those frosty November days we were warmed by the thought that the coming Christmas would possibly be the first truly free Christmas of our lives.

Oto Mádr put together for Cardinal Tomášek a radical proclamation regarding the events and submitted it to him for approval and signature immediately after his arrival from Rome. But then a news item was published in *Rudé právo* saying that the text had been forged by the enemies of socialism and that the cardinal distanced himself from it. The cardinal even received a visit from the secretary of the Communist Party for Prague, Miroslav Štěpán, and there was TV footage of the meeting. Štěpán crowned it by declaring in the media that the cardinal knew nothing of the proclamation. As a result people were disillusioned, and there was public confusion. So I quickly went to inform the cardinal about the seriousness of the situation and warn him that his appearance on television with Štěpán could mean an enormous loss of prestige. We decided that the cardinal would clarify the entire matter after the Saturday Mass in the cathedral, which was one of thanksgiving for the canonization of St. Agnes. He said to me in the determined tones of a commander, "Prepare a text. And make it fierce."

It was the first live broadcast of a Czech religious service in the history of Czechoslovak television. The cathedral was full to overflowing, and millions of viewers were glued to their TV screens. Just before the Mass was broadcast, the television screened footage from the previous night's meeting of the Central Committee of the Communist Party, at which the Communists decided to offer the nation certain reforms—at "five minutes past midnight." But nobody was interested in that anymore. For the first time in forty years, it was suddenly quite immaterial who headed the Communist Party. The president of the Republic, Gustav Husák, seemed to have disappeared from the scene. He reappeared when it was all over, for a brief moment in public, when he shook hands with the new government, and then abdicated without a word. The live broadcast of a dignified Mass from the cathedral coming soon after Communist ideological blather showed the total contrast between the two worlds. The mind of the nation was in the cathedral at that moment, and Communism collapsed like a house of cards. The nation returned once more to the historical stage above the tombs of its saints and kings.

At the conclusion of the Mass, the cardinal spoke the historical words, "I wrote a message for you and I stand by every single word in it. In this important hour of the struggle for truth and justice in this country, I, and the entire Catholic Church, stand on the side of the nation! None of us should stand aside when a better future for our nation is at stake. I ask you in these days to combine courage with wisdom, and reject the path of violence. Oh God, free us by the truth and renew the face of our homeland, the entire land, the entire world!" At that moment I had the dizzy feeling that the centuries-old barrier between the church and the nation had fallen, as if our still unhealed historical wounds had suddenly healed, and that we would all cross the new threshold together.

The throng spilled out of the cathedral onto Letná Plain to join the greatest demonstration in the history of Prague—half a million people at the very least. The crowds welcomed Václav Havel and booed Adamec, the prime minister, off the platform. There was considerable tension in the air when one of the policemen from the task force that had suppressed the student demonstration mounted the speaker's podium. His first words were met with growling from the crowd, and I feared that the spirit of vengeance might be unleashed and the man would be torn limb from limb. The young policeman apologized with a faltering voice, and Václav Malý appealed to the crowd for reconciliation and forgiveness. He invited them to join in the Lord's Prayer with their gaze on the cathedral and special emphasis on the words, "forgive us our trespasses, as we forgive those who trespass against us." I could see many people in the crowd searching their memory for the words of the Lord's Prayer, which they possibly once knew.

It was no longer a political struggle but something much more significant: spiritual healing. The situation suddenly turned into a sacred moment with a therapeutic dimension. Afterward I heard many people criticize Václav Malý for that appeal: believers who maintained that prayer belongs in church and not at a political demonstration; nonbelievers who saw in it an attempt to exploit a dramatic moment for ideological ends. It is my conviction, however, that Father Malý was truly an instrument in God's hand and that something stupendous happened there. Just as the events of 1968—the Prague Spring and the August invasion—acquired a spiritual and moral dimension for me with Palach's sacrifice, so also the Velvet Revolution of November 1989 became a turning point for me at the moment of that prayer on Letná Plain. I will leave it to historians to argue about which moment in those developments marked the end of the totalitarian regime; as far as I am concerned, it happened when that symbolic gesture cut through Communism's deepest root, namely, hatred.

EIGHT

Exodus

"When the Lord restored the fortunes of Zion, then were we like those who dream. Then was our mouth filled with laughter and our tongue with songs of joy. . . . The Lord has indeed done great things for us, and therefore we rejoiced" (Psalm 126). In the period immediately following November 1989, this psalm was indeed often in our minds and on our lips.

I lived through that period as if in a feverish dream. Everything merged together in quick succession. Even with the benefit of lengthy hindsight I find it hard to untangle the memories and experiences of those days. My thoughts continued to be dominated by the idea of the Decade of Spiritual Renewal, while I was kept busy with service in the shadow of Cardinal Tomášek. When, during those revolutionary days, some people close to Václav Havel asked me whether I would like to become minister of culture in the nascent future government, I refused. I had not yet realized how familiar my name had already become since my speeches in Brno and Rome. In light of the pope's reaction, I had given up the idea of entering the Order of the Knights of the Cross with the Red Star, so I continued to carry out my work at the clinic while also being involved in surrounding events, of course. I simply had no time to think about my own future.

Then I received the news that the students at the Catholic theological faculty in Litoměřice were also on strike. They were demanding the resignation of teaching staff who had compromised with the Communist regime, and among the names the students wanted to see appointed in their place was my own. They wanted the teaching of Marxist "social science" to be replaced by courses in psychology and sociology. So I wrote an official letter to Cardinal Tomášek about the circumstances of my ordination, and about my qualifications, and told him that I was ready to give up my secular employment forthwith and enter the service of the church full-time. I wrote that I was willing to fulfill the wishes of the students at the theological faculty that I should teach there and also that I had long yearned to fulfill our dream from 1968 of establishing a student chaplaincy in Prague. I added that I placed all these matters entirely in his hands, of course, and that I was willing to take up priestly duties anywhere he, as my bishop, might send me, even as a chaplain in a remote parish in the frontier areas—and I meant it sincerely.

At a Christmas party at the Apollinaris clinic, I announced to all my colleagues and patients that I had been a priest for the previous eleven years and that I was now leaving the clinic in order to devote myself to work in the church full-time. Our leave taking was not easy, as I had cordial relationships with most of my colleagues and patients. Interestingly, they all took the news that I was a priest with understanding and approval. Many of them, including nonbelievers, said they had suspected "something of the sort" about me.

I received a similar reaction from almost all of my many acquaintances, whom I was able to inform fully only now. Believers and nonbelievers expressed the wish that I would be able to fully accomplish what I had freely decided to do years ago. I didn't have much time to explain to them that even the hidden path I had followed as a priest had been a thoroughly priestly experience. These were hectic revolutionary times. Even I didn't think too much about whether the charism and spirituality of my priestly vocation might not be violated by the transition to public ministry. I simply made myself available and was ready to accept the bishop's decision obediently and as a matter of course. And I have no regrets. God himself made sure afterward that I didn't stray from the path he determined for me.

As usual in the church, the response to my letter was long in coming. In January I finally received the official notification that the cardinal was awarding me a "venia docendi," or habilitation, to teach at the Theological Faculty and was also establishing me as rector at the Church of St. Salvator with the task of renewing the university student chaplaincy there. I resigned from the clinic and headed to the Department for Church Affairs at city hall. It still included the former "secretaries for church affairs," although they were now obsequiously obliging. They drew up a letter of appointment and fixed my salary at 1,200 crowns a month, which was about a quarter of my previous salary at the hospital. I was satisfied, however, and started to learn how to make entries in a parish register, use liturgical garments and vessels, and learn other skills required of a chaplain in training.

▋ "INTEGRATION INTO PUBLIC STRUCTURES of the church," was more difficult, however, than I had anticipated. At the end of Advent in 1989, Bishop Škarvada arrived in Prague. He told me that he found the Czech church quite divided. Now that people were emerging from the shelter of their different groups, he was hearing various expressions of resentment toward members of other groups and even complaints from priests about people who had rendered enormous service, such as Mádr and Zvěřina. He said, however, that since my recent public speeches in Brno and Rome, he was hearing approving comments about me from everyone. But he immediately added that I should prepare myself for this to change before long, as soon as people became aware that I was a priest, since "invidia clericalis," clerical envy, was one of the worst diseases in the church. I would recall those words frequently in the years to come!

During the first days of December 1989, my friend Josef Hrd-lička, future auxiliary bishop in Olomouc, had invited me to a meeting of priests of the Olomouc Archdiocese to speak about the tasks now facing the church. I spoke there still as a member of the laity. On the way home in the car we heard a radio broadcast about proceedings in Parliament at which members had revoked the article in the constitution establishing the leading role of the Communist Party. It was clear that Communism had been defeated for good, and it would no longer be a matter of some internal reform of the existing system along the lines of "socialism with a human face."

On December 14, 1989, a historic meeting of priests of the Prague Archdiocese took place in St. Joseph's Church on Republic Square. Gathered together for the first time were officially approved parish priests, priests who were deprived of permission to follow public ministry, and priests who had been clandestinely ordained. I was presented by Father Mádr, who was the first to introduce me to all those present as their brother priest. I then gave an edited version of the speech I had given at Olomouc, and the text was later published in one of the first issues of the newly founded *Catholic Weekly*.

I tried to expound in ten points the concept of how the church operates in a free society. First I expressed my esteem for the parish priests who had operated publicly, and I thanked them for preserving what they could in difficult conditions. I told them sincerely that I would like most of all at that moment to go to each of them in turn and kiss their hands. I wanted to preempt the notion that the underground priests would now emerge as judges of those who were forced to make various compromises. What I wanted was forgiveness and unification. Concerning the regime-sponsored organization Pacem in terris, I said we must speak frankly about collaboration, identify it, and condemn it as a particular stance. But regarding the individual priests who had belonged to it, I said only God could judge; it was up to us to strive for forgiveness, healing, and reconciliation. I said we were not yet in the promised land but were only leaving Egypt for the desert, and we still had a long journey ahead of us. We should not fall prey to triumphalism when we see enthusiasm for the Catholic Church. Elements of Czech anticlericalism could still return, particularly if we failed to avoid certain dangerous mistakes.

> The aforementioned sympathy for the church . . . must not be overestimated, and we must realize that the church can easily lose it—particularly if it now succumbs to triumphalism, or thirst for power and property, or indeed anything that might be interpreted as such. Let us maintain humility, self-restraint, taste, and discretion.
>
> We cannot assume that the church will continue to attract all those who are dissatisfied with the previous regime. We cannot try to win the nation's support with a program that simply says: We are many, we are not afraid, we have suffered a great deal. Nor can we restrict ourselves to traditional forms of church activity. We have a duty to present the gospel message to the nation in a manner appropriate for the times, and strive for "inculturation" by entering as a competent partner into dialogue with the various religious and social movements in a pluralist society.

As the first point I proposed a truthful appraisal of the real state of the church, which would comprise sound sociological analyses. I warned against tendencies to restore the past—efforts to revive the "associational Catholicism" of the pre-1948 period and confine ourselves to a ghetto. I proposed the convening of a synod, which would mark a turning point in the life of the church. I requested systematic work on creating church structures in the spirit of the Second Vatican Council, starting with a bishops' conference with appropriate teams of advisers and including parish councils and, in particular, greater involvement of the laity in pastoral activity. I proposed the preparation and adoption of a long-term scheme of pastoral activity with clear priorities, which could base itself on the ideological ground plan of the Decade of Spiritual Renewal. I recommended a reform of church administration, whereby the previous model of territorial parishes established by Joseph II would be replaced by a more flexible structure, identifying productive zones and mission fields, which require different approaches. I proposed the establishment of a Christian Academy and the creation of an effective scheme of education in the church, including vital reforms of centers of theological education for future priests. I argued for the introduction of an institution of permanent deacons, who would need good spiritual direction, so that this service should find a spiritual identity in the church and not become some kind of centaur between clergy and laity.

I pleaded for appropriate care to integrating clandestinely ordained priests as soon as possible into the presbyterium as a whole, in order to avoid a leveling of the clergy and instead promote "unity in diversity." I said we ought not underestimate or forget the clandestine church's experience of linking priesthood with a secular profession.

> Let us cherish it as the apple of our eye and not eliminate it by the shortsighted transfer of all those priests to local parish administration! Let us respect the vocation and decisions of those priests who will want to continue working in secular professions, so that they may reach people to whom a parish priest will never have access, or by whom he will not be taken seriously. I know that the shortage of parish priests is an urgent issue, but I implore you on the basis of the experience of bishops and ordinaries over many years, which has been carefully considered from both theological and sociological standpoints: let us be far-sighted and generous; let us not think solely about today's momentary needs, but consider as of now, with responsibility and far-sightedness, the long-term future of the church in our country, and elsewhere.

I pointed to the danger of practicism, the fact that priests tend to consider education a kind of luxury and not a vital dimension of their vocation. I drew attention to the lack of theoretical detachment in theology and to its outdatedness. I prayed that our contact with the West should not lead us to succumb to one or other of two extremes: we should not uncritically embrace everything, nor should we fear the West and out of an unacknowledged inferiority complex delude ourselves with a false picture of the Western church as a seedbed of heresies and disintegration while telling ourselves that only here was there true faith and religious fervor.

I prayed that our church should start to learn internal dialogue, so that after being silenced for so long everyone had the opportunity to express themselves. Thus all suggestions and initiatives could be gathered, but above all teams of genuine experts should be set up, particularly from among laypeople.

I pointed out that we would have to find a balanced relationship with the political sphere, that the church must not have too close links with any political force but that it would have to learn to take a position on the problems of society as a whole in a very competent and opportune way. In conclusion, I once more drew attention to the importance of the Decade of Spiritual Renewal: "At a time when a few days of revolution have changed so much in society that many things suddenly no longer apply, and no one dares predict future developments, the Catholic Church stands at the heart of society as almost the only force offering a well-thought-out, long-term program for the reform of national life, one that does not compete with any political programs, because its aims go much deeper. It is aimed at that plane of the nation's life that is beginning to show itself to be fundamental, and without which any political and economic reforms would not achieve their ends, namely, the spiritual and moral plane. . . . It is now becoming apparent that the Decade project can achieve a profound link between the renewal of the church and the current renewal of the nation."

Finally I pleaded for us always to give priority to the movement of the Holy Spirit in all our proposals and plans, so that in prayer we would return constantly to the center of the church, which is the living Christ, and in the light of his Spirit we should examine the signs of the times and have the courage of Abraham, the father of all believers, who "went out, not knowing where he was to go."

Although my words were applauded by the priests, and many of them slapped me on the back, I couldn't help remembering the scene from Bernanos's *Diary of a Country Priest* when, after the priest has poured out the entire contents of his heart, the parishioners tell him, "You got nicely worked up!" I read mistrust in the eyes of many of my listeners: "Who is this person to presume to give us lessons? A few months ago nobody had heard of him and now his name is on everybody's lips." I realized I would have to a pay a toll for the period of underground activity, when I had worked anonymously in the shadow of Cardinal Tomášek. I discovered that a lot of priests were taken aback by being presented a vision of church life by someone who had not experienced the life of a parish priest like they had.

I still often wonder where I went wrong at that time. In hindsight, I would still have made the same speech three weeks after the November events. I think that subsequent developments fully confirmed that the entire concept was correct, as also was my warning. What more could I have done at that time to get those who were responsible for the church to reflect on these issues at least a little bit? I don't want to play the undervalued prophet whose words proved true. "History knows no 'what ifs.'" Nor do I want to judge anyone. If it is said that the church failed, then, as part of it, I can only say I failed also. Perhaps I ought to have repeated those ideas more patiently and more often and shared them in smaller doses. Maybe in subsequent years I ought to have devoted myself solely to thinking about the Decade and to promoting and organizing it and refused all the other tasks, particularly after my closest associates were overloaded with many other jobs: most of the members of the "upper consistory" became bishops, and Petr Pit'ha became minister of education, while people from the "lower consistory" departed for big politics or university posts.

But I am most inclined to think that I simply overestimated the situation of the church and its scope. After all, I had been moving in rather restricted circles, and I expect I subconsciously—and very naively—supposed that most priests were characters like Zvěřina and Mádr. I had to find out with regret that forty years of Communism had devastated the church to a greater extent than I imagined. That period of repression had an enormous impact, particularly on the clergy. And I have great respect for the priests. What I experienced was a mixture of human respect and enormous despondency. For so many years the absolute majority of Czech priests were deprived of contact with the world church, theological thinking, and the life around them. Some of them were splendid during the totalitarian years, but the onset of freedom caught them very much unawares. It was as if they were suddenly overcome with accumulated fatigue, and they aged by an entire generation. They no longer had the capacity to find their bearings in the new situation and lacked the strength for new tasks.

I realized that while I was perfectly in tune with many people from university circles, the media, politics, art, and other spheres, in clerical circles—with the exception of a few friends, mostly from the religious orders—I remained very isolated. The differences in our views became increasingly evident. Even now I must admit with regret that whenever I travel westward from our borders, I have the sense that the priests I encounter are truly my colleagues and brothers. We read the same books, we have the same concerns, and we ask the same questions. But as soon as I am back among the Czech clergy I feel like a foreigner—and sometimes even like someone who has been sent back fifty years or more in a time machine.

WHEN BISHOP ŠKARVADA ARRIVED IN Czechoslovakia before Christmas, I accompanied him around Prague. He had not been in his native city for over forty years. On December 23, I took him to the Špalíček building on Wenceslas Square, which was the headquarters of the Civic Forum in those revolutionary days, to see Václav Havel. It was just a few days before the presidential election, and by then people were fairly certain that Havel would win the vote. I took the opportunity of that visit to tell Havel that I was a priest. He told me that he had known it for a long time, and that I was a Jesuit. I told him that the secret police always thought I was a Jesuit, but that it was not the case. He laughed and said he had definitely not received the news from them.

During our conversation Václav Havel mentioned that if he became president he would very much like to invite the pope to Czechoslovakia, and he would like the visit to take place as soon as possible, even before the first free parliamentary elections. He wanted the visit to have a positive and calming effect on the atmosphere in the country, to "infuse it with spirituality." Bishop Škarvada didn't think it would be possible, as such visits involve at least two years' planning. But Havel responded, "Perhaps he could come for just one day."

I shall skip ahead a bit and relate the surprising subsequent turn of events. When Monsignor Škarvada returned to Rome, he dined with the pope and conveyed to him Havel's informal invitation. To his great surprise, the pope replied that it might be possible. That same evening he telephoned me in Prague and told me they would need an official invitation. So I went the following day—at the beginning of January—to the newly elected president, who was in the throes of moving into the castle, and gave him the news. The next day an official invitation was issued by the Office of the President, probably the first official contact between Hradčany and the Vatican in several decades. The Czech lands opened their gates for a visit by the head of the Catholic Church for the first time in their history.

Before Christmas, I led public spiritual exercises for students for the first time. At Midnight Mass on Christmas Eve I concelebrated Mass for the first time in public with Father Reinsberg. A few days later I watched the election of the president and the celebratory Te Deum on television. I then left for Wrocław with some friends for a European youth meeting organized by the Taizé Community. There we listened on a transistor to President Havel's New Year address, in which he also mentioned his intention to invite the pope to Czechoslovakia. It was already dark when we traveled back from Wrocław. It was frosty and there was snow in the air. That new-year evening reminded me of my journey from London to Bangor all those years before. Something new was beginning; something totally unknown.

■ ON THE EVENING OF JANUARY 25 my first Mass was celebrated belatedly at the Týn Church. The date was deliberately chosen as it was the Feast of the Conversion of St. Paul. I had always had an affinity with St. Paul the Apostle, and I also took into consideration that it was also an important day in the calendar of the reformed churches. I wanted my first Mass also to have an ecumenical character, because I regarded my concern for unity as an important dimension of my priesthood. During the service the composer Petr Eben performed his "Field Mass," and the concelebrants were Bishops Liška and Otčenášek and Fathers Zvěřina, Mádr, Reinsberg, Duka, Opatrný, and other friends. Two Protestant pastors, Alfréd Kocáb and Miroslav Heryán, stood near the altar.

On February 1, I took up my duties at the Theological Faculty and was appointed university chaplain at the Church of St. Salvator. After eleven years as an underground priest it was not easy for me to master liturgy in a church. One could count on the fingers of one hand the number of times I had worn a chasuble since my ordination, as I had been accustomed to celebrating Mass at home in my ordinary clothes, at a small, simply laid table, or at a weekend cottage, or outdoors in nature. Suddenly I had been put in charge of an enormous Baroque church in the center of Prague. People started to address me as they were accustomed to in church, which caused me a certain identity crisis. Those were days when the relations between church and state were changing. A legal framework for the free functioning of the church had yet to be established.

At the beginning of February, I took part in a tour of Austrian and German dioceses arranged for several of our priests, who were all associated with the Decade of Spiritual Renewal. We wanted to find out about the positive and negative experiences of churches in our neighboring countries and how the work of the church was organized in a free society. We discovered how different each diocese was. In some of the dioceses pastoral activity was very open, while others were fettered by bureaucracy. We finally arrived in Munich in a blizzard. While there, we heard on the news that one of our number, Miloslav Vlk, had been appointed bishop of České Budějovice. He had been told about it the previous week but was not allowed to speak about it. We celebrated it that evening, and the next morning Miloslav Vlk, František Radkovský, and I set off to an ecclesiastical outfitters to buy the necessary attire for the new bishop. The frivolous way in which we chose a solideo and miter aroused the suspicions of the sales clerk, who was used to serving distinguished monsignors and started to think we might be imposters. But he eventually believed us and joined in our fun.

On the last evening of that trip, when we were praying alone, an insistent vision came to my mind, which I shared with my friends the next morning: this would not be the last appointment of a bishop from our group, and we were not here by chance. Each of us—whether as a bishop or in some other role—would have a unique mission in the church, and we should cultivate our friendship, which we had experienced so spontaneously during those days on the eve of freedom, and we should support each other, even in our difference, so that we might bear this responsibility for the church in our country. And indeed in a short space of time, over half of the members of that trip found themselves at the head of dioceses in Bohemia and Moravia.

■ SHORTLY AFTER MY RETURN FROM AUSTRIA and Germany, Cardinal Tomášek invited me to the Archbishop's Palace. Waiting there for me was the papal legate, Archbishop Colasuonno, who handed me a flight ticket to Rome for the following day. He told me I was to spend about a month in the Vatican assisting with preparations for the pope's visit to Prague, and I must speak to no one about the actual purpose of my work. It was no easy task to prepare for my trip in just a few hours, because I had to change completely my busy program up to Easter and make all the necessary arrangements. I took the plane on the morrow and learned that I was to meet the pope the very next morning. I was told emphatically that I must appear in full clerical attire. This was another minor problem, as until that moment I had never owned anything of the kind.

I was awaited at the Rome airport by two Vatican representatives, who escorted me elegantly through all the customs checks, sat me in a car, and drove me to a house that was generally used for bishops' ad limina visits. The next morning I headed for a clerical outfitters to purchase the appropriate attire for an audience with the pope. It was very early in the morning, at least by Italian standards, and the store was still closed. As soon as it opened I dashed in as the first customer, still in my everyday clothes. I grabbed the nearest shirt with a clerical collar that I saw and a cassock. It turned out to be too small, but I squeezed into it somehow and ran, waving my new official pass, through the Bronze Gate into the Vatican, where the first preparatory meeting took place.

I attended the first papal audience with Bishop Škarvada and Cardinal Tomko. When I met Cardinal Tomko in the anteroom I told him that I was wearing a cassock and clerical collar for the first time. He then divulged that information to the pope, who laughed and blessed my cassock. That marked the start of a week of intense activity. I can't relate the details of the preparation, as I had to take an oath of secrecy, but I can share something of the overall atmosphere. Every day I got up very early and walked to St. Peter's Basilica in the light of dawn. There I would celebrate Mass at one of the altars in the crypt beneath the basilica. In the basilica's large sacristy one encounters many priests and bishops of all colors and from every continent. A group of servers was already there prepared, most of them pupils of church schools. I eventually became friendly with one young African server, who used to seek me out every morning and bring me a missal and chalice. Then I would select one of the altars in the Basilica, either the altar of St. Wenceslas or one of the altars of my favorite saints. Sometimes I said Mass down in the chapel containing the tomb of Cardinal Beran. Each time it was for me living communication with the tradition and history of the church, and I was very glad to be praying every morning at that heart of the church.

Then I would enter the Bronze Gate on my way to work. As I went along the corridors the Swiss guards would salute me with their halberds. I passed through the courtyards of the Vatican until I reached a classic elevator from the early twentieth century, in which I would encounter various prelates and cardinals. In the morning I shared an office with Bishop Škarvada. It was a beautiful room with a fine view of all of Rome. At first I doubted whether I would manage to tear my gaze away from the view and concentrate on my work.

In accordance with the rhythm of the Vatican, I worked until about 1:00 p.m., when I would go for lunch and, after the indispensable siesta, continue working until evening. At rare moments of free time in the evening or on Sundays, I would wander around the old parts of Rome, visiting churches and monuments. During my stay I had repeated opportunities to speak with the pope.

The pope made careful preparations for his trip. He wanted to find out as much as possible about Czech culture and history. I was surprised by the insistence with which he returned again and again to the question of Jan Hus and wanted to know why the Czechs had done nothing about it yet. I realized that this pope, who had rehabilitated Galileo, and for whom healing historical scars and coming to terms with the dark sides of the church's past was a major issue, viewed the case of Hus in the same light. Several times he reminded me with a smile that the only person to have defended Hus at the Council of Constance was a Polish theologian from Kraków. On one occasion the pope pointed to a row of books by Václav Havel on his desk and asked me which of them he should read in particular. Off the top of my head, I named about three titles that I considered the most important, and he said, "I've read those already." Seeing my surprise, he added, "The pope reads at night."

Pope Wojtyła had a great sense of humor. I had the impression that he did not really approve of priests with beards. Several times, at the beginning of our meetings, he would make some comment about my beard, and sometimes he would tug it jokingly. "He's got a full beard like an Orthodox, I think we'll send him to Russia!," he once remarked to his secretary. "But I can't shave my beard!," I objected, "Why?," the pope asked in surprise. "Well, because it has been touched by the pope—which means it is something like a relic!," I replied. The pope laughed and never spoke about my beard again.

A few years later my beard received a further honor. When a meditation with the Dalai Lama took place in our church many years later, the Dalai Lama said to me in the sacristy, "We're like brothers! Here"—he stroked my bald pate—"we're the same, but here"—he tugged me by the beard—"we are different." I am convinced that there exists no beard in the world that has been touched by His Holiness the pope of Rome and by His Holiness the Tibetan Dalai Lama.

■ BY SEEING THE VATICAN AT CLOSE QUARTERS in that way, it acquired certain human dimensions for me. I was able to see that it was also made up of ordinary people with ordinary problems. It ceased to have the aura of something mysterious and unearthly; on the other hand, it was clear that the journalistic view, which focused on scandals and the "dark mysteries of the Vatican," was equally naive and bore no relation to the facts. It struck me that the life of many top-level Vatican officials is fairly stereotypical, in fact. Saturday was also a workday, although the Vatican ordained days off for many of the church holy days. These people were evidently part of a great administration, and they often had no other dimension to their lives, neither family nor parish. They would just help out from time in one of the parishes of Rome, and on their free Thursday afternoons they would get together for celebrations or trips into the nearby countryside.

When I had the opportunity later, during my studies in Rome and on official trips, to get to know more fully the life of the Vatican dicasteries, it meant a great deal to me. I understood how wise it is when the church sends some of its priests to study in Rome, particularly those who are to shoulder responsibility in local churches. Only in Rome can one come to understand the entire scope of the Catholic Church. Priests who have grown up in their locality can scarcely have a full appreciation of it. I was almost within touching distance of a whole range of things that make up the church, from the catacombs and other places where the church started in Rome to the triumphal monuments recalling the times of the Renaissance popes to the present day. The dramatic history of the church is indelibly printed on the face of Rome. It is here also that we become aware of the universality of the church. At the college I encountered students of every color, and I spoke with them about the problems of the church in Asia, Africa, and South America. What I had known only theoretically up to that time, I now had direct contact with: the enormous universality of the church and its internal plurality. Only there does a priest realize what Catholicism means, what he belongs to, and what he is permitted to serve. He is then able to avoid two extremes: on the one hand, a pessimistic attitude fixated on just part of the church and its local problems; and on the other, illusions and ideological perspectives that fail to take account of weaknesses and the human aspect of the church.

I made friends with the head of the German section of Vatican Radio, a Jesuit, Fr. Eberhard von Gemmingen, who had accompanied the pope on all his trips. From my conversations with him I gained a well-informed picture of the problems in various local churches around the world. I also made the acquaintance of Opus Dei's top man in the Vatican, the spokesman of the Holy See, Dr. Joaquin Navarro Valls, a Spaniard, who was originally a psychiatrist. He was a man of superb intelligence who had an amazing grasp of world issues. He was very interested in developments in the post-Communist world. He invited me to call on him whenever I was in Rome, which I regularly did. With his recommendation I visited the center of the Opus Dei prelature. It is a remarkable place, located discreetly in a building in the middle of one of the richest quarters of Rome. There are several below-ground stories, one of which consists of a large sacred area, beneath which is the tomb of the founder of Opus Dei and of his sisters. When I spoke with people from the center, I noted that they were quick-witted men with broad general knowledge. But at the same time I realized that this was not a path for me.

I also came to know "Vatican Poland," namely, the pope's close associates, whom he had brought from Poland with him. In particular, I became friends with Professor Stanislav Grygiel, a philosopher from Kraków. At his home I also made the acquaintance of Professor Józef Tischner, a philosopher of phenomenological orientation and a perceptive analyst of the spiritual and moral problems of our times, who was one of the spiritual fathers of Solidarność. In later years Tischner and I would meet up again many times in various corners of Europe.

I made friends with a number of Italian philosophers, including Rocco Butiglione and some of his associates close to the Communione e Liberazione (CL) movement, and of course I was in contact with the group around the periodical *Il nuovo Areopago*, which used to print our texts during the totalitaritarian period. For a time, Butiglionne was known in Rome as John Paul II's "court philosopher." What gave rise to that nickname, tinged with a bit of envy and a bit of irony, was the undoubted fact that the two men were close, both personally and in terms of ideas. Butiglione was greatly inspired by the phenomenologist Ditrich von Hildebrant, who, apart from a rather unfortunate book about the evolution of the church after Vatican II— which he called "a Trojan horse in the City of God"—was the author of profound texts on the philosophy of religion, philosophical anthropology, and ethics. Hildebrant interested me because he grew up among those students of Husserl who tried to combine phenomenology with Catholic tradition, whether Thomism, classical metaphysics, or existentially oriented personalism and mysticism. The best known of them were Edith Stein and Max Scheler. Hildebrant's legacy was promoted chiefly by an international center in Luxemburg, and Butiglione was one of its main supporters before he went into national politics. Butiglione drew my attention to developments in American sociology of religion since P. L. Berger questioned the theory of secularization of the modern world and recommended that I read Richard Neuhaus. I think that it was chiefly due to Butiglione and Michael Novak that I was invited to the United States in 1994, where I met Berger and Neuhaus in person. But at the same time I realized that American neoconservatism would not become my spiritual home either.

Shortly before I flew back from Rome, I received a phone call from the secretary of the Pontifical Council for Justice and Peace, which dealt with implementing the church's social teaching in public life, particularly with respect to human rights and support for world peace. He told me that John Paul II had informed him of his intention to appoint me to this body in the future. However, the proceedings of the council were conducted chiefly in French, and my inadequate knowledge of that language would be an insurmountable obstacle. When I went to take leave from John Paul before my departure, he invited me once more to dinner, during which he expressed the wish that I should undertake postgraduate study in theology at one of the pontifical universities in Rome and then gain a doctorate in philosophy or theology in Poland. He thought that the linking of Prague, Rome, and Poland would provide a good basis for my future work. Monsignor Dziwisz promised me a grant from the Vatican's State Secretariat for Postgraduate Study, so at the very end of my stay in Rome I discussed with Professor Skalický the possibility that in the next academic year, if Cardinal Tomášek agreed, I would commence study for a licentiate degree under his direction at the Pontifical Lateran University.

That year, John Paul II bore me in mind on two further occasions. When he learned in August about the sudden death of Josef Zvěřina, whom he had appointed adviser for preparations for the European synod, he expressed the wish to appoint me in his place; however, as he had been unable to find me in Prague—I was at an international conference at Ampleforth Abbey in England—the post had to be taken by another candidate. And then I received a letter from John Paul II appointing me consultor to the Pontifical Council for Dialogue with Non-Believers, which, in the course of three years, opened the possibility for close cooperation with the Holy See.

The council was the brainchild of Cardinal König, who became its president. During my time with the council the president was the French curial cardinal, Paul Poupard. The council's mission was to study the evolution and forms of atheism in the world and find points of contact for cooperation with nonbelievers. This took the form of various programs, colloquia, and international conferences but also academic and publication activity, as well as taking part in certain talks with the authorization of the Holy See. The members and advisers were cardinals, bishops, priests, and laity from practically every continent. Each member was obliged to attend the main meetings once every two years in Rome; in the interim, various smaller meetings took place in various parts of the world. What also made it interesting was that the first day of such meetings was devoted to news from various continents about the situation of the church there. That provided me with a global overview not only of the church worldwide but also of the situation in the Czech lands, which could only be fully understood when seen in the global context.

At the end of the meeting there was usually a special audience with the pope, at which he would receive information about the proceedings and conclusions of the meeting. I made the acquaintance of many very interesting people there, and I made contacts that stood me in good stead during various international trips.

◼ I RETURNED TO PRAGUE ON THE LAST DAY of March 1990. Before the pope's visit I had several more meetings with Václav Havel, who also prepared himself very responsibly for the event. We had a meeting at the president's country residence at Lány on the afternoon of Easter Saturday and discussed various details, as well as a message I had brought to President Havel from John Paul II. Then he drove me back to Prague because he wanted to attend Mass at St. Gabriel's Church, where Václav Malý was then the parish priest. He persuaded his chauffeur to let him drive. During the journey he made one of his random "drop-ins": we stopped at one of the dive bars on the outskirts of Prague, where the president's unexpected visit aroused a great deal of excitement. I marveled at the bravura with which Havel was able to communicate with people, who genuinely behaved toward him without the appropriate diplomatic protocol, putting their demands to him and sharing various ideas. The first citizen of the state, who always seemed to me a timid person, managed to cope with these demanding situations in a unique way.

The first ever visit by a pope to the Czech lands, and of a Slav pope in the bargain, was regarded as a celebration of freedom. Václav Havel commented on it in the well-known words he used to welcome the pope at the airport: "I don't know whether I know what constitutes a miracle." The visit received enormous coverage from the media at home and abroad. Hundreds of journalists arrived, and I had to spend whole days talking to many of them about the history of the church in our country, as well as about its present situation and future prospects.

The visit itself was a splendid celebration. It was hard to believe that our country was capable of organizing everything in such an incredibly short time, virtually without any experience and without infrastructures in either church or society. The pope's speeches tackled key issues in the church and society, and it was also welcomed by people outside the bounds of the church.

Nevertheless, it was also obvious that certain political circles intended to exploit the event to their advantage before the forthcoming elections. This was unfortunately the case of the chairman of the Catholic-oriented People's Party, Josef Bartončík, who was soon exposed as a former State Security agent. Maybe those circumstances were the reason many people who previously had a friendly attitude to the church were now wary of it. I became aware of a certain degree of crisis in ecumenical relations. I started to hear from some representatives of non-Catholic churches that we were behaving as if we were the only church in Czechoslovakia and that we had somehow forgotten they existed. Anticlerical murmurs started to surface, which increased in intensity in the coming years. I also noticed that some of the Catholics who had converted to the church when it was persecuted and clandestine—particularly young converts—continued to have a psychological aversion to everything official, and the ecclesiastical officialdom associated with the pope's visit took them unawares. The church took advantage of its new scope of activity, but some of us got so carried away by this that we became less sensitive to the rest of society. In a certain sense, the pope's visit in April 1990 marked the end of postrevolutionary euphoria and the beginning of everyday life.

■ AT THE BEGINNING OF THE 1990S, I became a student again. I commenced a postgraduate course in theology and religious studies at the Pontifical Lateran University in Rome. Because of my other commitments it could only be distance learning. I was released from my duties in Prague for just a few months in fall 1990 and spring 1991, and then briefly to defend my thesis for my Licentiate of Sacred Theology. I had to prepare and sit for exams in twenty different subjects and write a thesis. When in Rome I stayed at the Nepomucenum, the pontifical Czech college, which trained many priests who had greatly influenced the life of the church in the Czech lands in previous generations. It was gratifying to experience, at least briefly, something similar to what they had known. Although as a priest and postgraduate student I was not bound by the rules of the seminary, I wanted to experience them at least for a little while, and I added some extra stipulations to make them stricter. I used to get up at 5:00 a.m. and take an ice-cold shower (imagining that nothing worse could possibly befall me during the coming day). Then I meditated in a cold chapel, said Mass, and spent the rest of the morning working.

After lunch and a brief siesta, I went on working until the evening meal. Afterward I took a walk in the park of the Nepomucenum, before resuming my work until one o'clock in the morning. I kept up that rhythm without break for several months, except for Sundays, when I would visit various sites in Rome.

This system of dividing up the day suited me. I used to joke afterward that a siesta is part of my Roman Catholic identity and an expression of my solidarity with the Holy See. A daily rhythm like this gives one the opportunity to enjoy the blessing of two very productive times of day—early morning and late evening. In general people are divided into those who rise very early and those who work late into the night. Thanks to the siesta I discovered that it is possible to combine both to great advantage.

The physical conditions of my study were very unfavorable, because there was almost no heating in the college. The bedrooms were austere cells with ceilings almost four meters high and uncarpeted marble floors, and the windows were single-glazed. That winter was unrelentingly fierce. At first I studied wrapped up in blankets, with a cap on my head and wearing two sweaters. Then a seemingly fairy tale solution presented itself: a certain Czech noblewoman married to an Austrian diplomat to the Vatican telephoned me to say she that the idea came to her during Mass to make me a present of her gas-fired heater. The trouble was that the heater leaked, so I often had to choose between dying of cold and asphyxiation. When the fumes in the room made it too hard to breathe, I would open the window and let the freezing air in, and when I started to turn into an icicle, I would turn the heating back on.

At their St. Nicholas's Day party, the students came up with a splendid lampoon of these freezing conditions: they acted out a scene in which the college of cardinals discussed whether they should canonize the vice-rector of the seminary, who had frozen to death in the Nepomucenum; the cardinals came to the conclusion that it was a martyr's death and that the new saint would be appointed patron saint of Greenland, and the Vatican's first ice-breaker would be named after him.

I spent Easter in Rome, and took part in all the ceremonies in St. Peter's Basilica. On the morning of Holy Thursday, all priests present in Rome renew their vows. On Good Friday, together with the pilgrims, I ascended the Holy Staircase close to the Lateran basilica on my knees, and at night I followed the stations of the cross in the Colosseum, led by the pope. During the pope's Easter vigil Mass, I distributed the sacrament and thereby took a direct part in this sublime liturgy. During that Easter Week we also received news that my friend of many years, Miloslav Vlk, had been appointed archbishop of Prague.

My postgraduate study in Rome was very useful "revision," but I also acquired much additional valuable knowledge; I was able to draw extensively on my years of intensive study with Professor Patočka, as well as on my independent underground theological studies, lectures at seminars in private apartments, and my own texts, which I had written during the previous twenty years without hope of publication. I eventually completed my course summa cum laude. I subsequently reworked my thesis and published it in book form. I was intending to continue further doctoral studies in Rome but received an offer from the dean of the Pontifical Theological Faculty in Wrocław. In view of the special circumstances and the fact that I had a doctorate in philosophy, he said that I could acquire associate professor status in practical theology, specializing in the church's social teaching, on condition that I first took several entrance tests and submitted a requisite set of at least eleven specialized studies for approval. I imagine that the offer was prompted by John Paul II, who wanted me to complete my postgraduate studies both in Rome and in Poland. Although I would have preferred to spend more years in Rome, I was already forty-five, and pressing duties awaited me in Prague, at the university, in my parish, in the Conference of Bishops, and in the Christian Academy, a situation I could scarcely contemplate nowadays. I therefore fulfilled all the requirements demanded by the Polish Pontifical Theological Faculty, and after defending the submitted set of studies, I presented a lecture on the concept of culture in light of the Second Vatican Council before the Academic Council, which comprised professors from theological faculties from all over Poland and was chaired by Archbishop Nossol, chairman of the council of bishops for theological education. The graduation ceremony took place the same day and was presided over by Cardinal Gulbinowicz, archbishop of Wrocław and great chancellor of the faculty. I received the appropriately decorated diploma later by post.

At that time in Prague I could legally apply for the title of assistant professor on grounds of exoneration, because during the Communist period I could prove that I was not allowed to teach at the university for political reasons and that I had lectured for years in underground seminars. However, I decided not to take this easy route and underwent the regular habilitation for assistant professorship in sociology at the Faculty of Social Sciences. My habilitation lecture was on the sociological aspects of John Paul II's social encyclicals. The dean of faculty and my tutor at the time was Professor Petrusek, who had already known me as a student and had closely monitored my development in subsequent years, during which neither of us was permitted to teach at our faculty. Thus the previous quarter of a century of silent independent study finally bore fruit in rapid succession.

■ AFTER THE POPE'S VISIT, THE CZECH conference of bishops was established. The newly appointed bishops included many of my friends and collaborators from the committee of the Decade of Spiritual Renewal. Paradoxically, this would prove fateful for the work of the Decade, because those who had promoted it were now absorbed in many new tasks. It was sad to see that a number of them allowed themselves to become too preoccupied with short-term needs and seemed to forget about longer-term policy, so that programs like the Decade of Spiritual Renewal were no longer a priority for them. Only two bishops, Liška and Otčenášek, continued systematically to promote the idea of the Decade. The other bishops were good, pious, and conscientious, but because of their particular theological training and attitudes about the church, they were more anchored in the past and less open to the future.

I was now faced by the question of where my place was. Was I to devote myself to pastoral activity at the Church of St. Salvator and at the faculty, or was I continue to work closely with Cardinal Tomášek? Admittedly the cardinal had led the church over the threshold of freedom, but he was now truly an old and sick man. Just prior to the revolution, a number of bishops had been appointed in Czechoslovakia on the basis of a compromise between the Communist regime and the Vatican. Although they had not been members of the regime-sponsored Pacem in terris, the well-informed State Security bodies had agreed to them because the church would not particularly flourish under their leadership. The important post of vicar general for Prague was given to the aforementioned Jan Lebeda, about whom Zvěřina stated aptly, "I've known him for over half a century. He was already an old man in high school!" Nevertheless, he was a bishop, and people from Cardinal Tomášek's circle of advisers took a backseat somewhat of their own accord. And lo, nobody asked about them. Not even Mádr or Zvěřina was engaged by the Theological Faculty after the revolution. Zvěřina was eventually given the formal post of honorary dean, but he was blatantly ignored by Wolf, the newly appointed dean.

In this situation, I learned that some of the younger bishops were considering proposing me as candidate for the post of general secretary of the conference of bishops. It would mean I would be able to ensure continuity between the circle that had stood by Cardinal Tomášek in the years before the collapse of Communism and the present church leadership in the new circumstances. General secretary of the conference of bishops—particularly at the time when foundations were being laid—was a very responsible position; would I be able to combine it with my other tasks as a priest and university teacher, to which my heart was more spontaneously inclined?

I decided to maintain my inner freedom in the matter and leave it up to the bishops to decide and to accept that decision as God's will. I was quite relieved when it was decided at the first meeting of the joint Czech and Slovak bishops' conference that the general secretary should be one of the bishops, not a simple priest, and the choice fell on Bishop Radkovský. But shortly afterward, the bishops decided to elect secretaries for the separate Czech and Slovak parts, and this time I was elected and appointed secretary to the Czech bishops' conference. Although Cardinal Tomášek had indicated to me that he would release me from my other commitments in the church, he then sort of forgot about it, on the grounds that it would be hard to find a replacement for me in the faculty and at the university church. And so I became not a "pluralist," as the post was honorary and unpaid, but a "multifunctionary," which was probably not very wise. For several years I lived with the feeling of having fallen into a raging torrent of multitudinous tasks that far exceeded the powers of a single individual. The beginnings of the bishops' conference were inauspicious. At its first meetings I became aware that many of the newly appointed bishops were ill prepared for their new posts. Most of them had no previous experience of leadership and managerial work and had no idea how to organize time, how to choose, direct, and motivate their colleagues, how to delegate tasks or run meetings. I had spent ten years at the Institute of the Ministry of Industry teaching the sociology and psychology of management, so I tried to lend a hand but ended up convinced of the truth of the dictum that no man is a prophet in his own land.

But help arrived from abroad: a rich Swiss businessman and Professor Zulehner of Vienna. The bishops' conference was offered a management training program geared to the management of church activities. It consisted of three weeklong courses spread over eighteen months. The first was held in Austria, the second in Passau, and the third in Jerusalem in fall 1992. It was very practical training led by a team of psychologists and sociologists, which was very similar to what I myself had once taught. It employed active social learning methods, particularly role play. The program was interspersed with theological lectures and meditations by Professor Zulehner, and the spiritual director of the entire course was a very likable bishop from Brixen in Italy. One of the workshops was attended by Cardinal König, emeritus archbishop of Vienna, who was one of the architects of the Second Vatican Council and probably the main inspiration for the election of the Polish pope at the final enclave. I first made the acquaintance of Cardinal König during a brief official trip to Vienna in 1988 to attend a psychological congress, and afterward we would meet almost every year on various occasions. I recall with gratitude every conversation we had together, because I regarded him as a true aristocrat of the spirit, as well as the model of a modern pastor of the church, one of the greatest figures of twentieth-century Catholicism. I saw him for the last time when I received the Cardinal König Prize from his hands. On that occasion, the oration was penned by President Václav Havel and read on his behalf by the future Czech foreign minister Karel Schwarzenberg.

OF COURSE, SOME OF MY PUBLIC appearances, program articles, and activities of those days gave rise not only to positive responses but also to much controversy and tension. Some of it was certainly due to that "clerical envy" mentioned earlier, but I too was at fault for having promoted my visions with a degree of stubbornness, pig-headedness and impatience. Moreover my relations with certain bishops underwent certain trials and crises during those first years.

"How is your relationship with the hierarchy?," foreign friends would ask me in those days. "My relationship is like a good coffee," I used to reply. "Strong and stimulating but not too sweet."

New Foundations

The summer of 1990 was marked by the tragic death of Josef Zvěřina. I received the news of the unexpected death of one of my teachers just before leaving for an international conference in England.

Zvěřina died suddenly while bathing in the sea near Rome. One of the eyewitnesses to his final moments told me a curious story. Before celebrating Mass with a group of young people on the day of his death, Father Zvěřina apparently said to them while preparing the altar, "I had an odd dream last night. I dreamed I was entering a space where there were all of my friends who are now dead. But whereas all the other priests were properly dressed in albs and stoles, I was only wearing swimming trunks!" A few hours later he appeared before the Lord and the communion of the saints in his swimming trunks straight from the depths of the sea, which he so often compared to the love of God. The last words he spoke were in response to a question about how he was feeling: "Fine. Like an old sailor returning to his sea."

At the Theological Faculty, where he exercised a kind of moral patronage over the studies of lay students since he was not permitted to teach theologians, his loss was also felt deeply. We had hoped that his influence might have helped raise the rest of the faculty to a standard compatible with developments in Europe.

I soon inherited another of Zvěřina's posts: I was elected president of the Christian Academy. We had contemplated the founding of the academy during the time of underground seminars. In December 1989 I had proposed it in my introductory words to the priests at the meeting at St. Joseph's Church. I was convinced that an institution should be created in our country that would be a platform for dialogue between the church and Czech culture and a place for meeting "sympathizers," those who later would become known as Zaccheuses in this country, after one of my books. The work of setting up the academy was undertaken by a group of young people, and they logically asked Josef Zvěřina to head the institution, as a living symbol of the moral and intellectual regeneration of Czech Catholicism.

At that time Zvěřina promoted the idea that the Academy should not be a church institution but instead a civic association with a certain formal independence from the church and that it should be consistently ecumenical in character. This was extremely prescient. I succeeded Zvěřina in December 1990 and was then reelected again and again. I have now headed the Christian Academy for over a quarter of a century.

The Academy now has over seven thousand members, making it one of the biggest not-for-profit organizations in the country. It has local centers in sixty-seven communities in almost every large town. We place emphasis on the functioning of local groups of the Academy outside Prague, as the capital city has been saturated for years now with many national and international conferences and lectures of every kind. But in some of the smaller towns, a few dozen kilometers outside Prague, the Christian Academy is often the only institution organizing regular lectures and cultural activities. The Academy also has corporate members, such as the Association of Catholic Doctors, the Church Law Society, and the Catholic University Students Movement, as well as a number of specialized sections: philosophy and theology, history and art history, and education, not to mention natural science and technology, ecology, economics, political science, and psychotherapy. The foreign guests who have lectured for the Czech Christian Academy over the years have included Cardinals Ratzinger, König, Cassidy, Schönborn, and Kasper; Bishops Wanke, Laun, and Kapellari; the political scientist Michael Novak; and other outstanding figures from the West and the East.

When I became a member of the informal community of intellectuals who regularly came together at President Václav Havel's summer residence at Lány to discuss the situation of Czech society and provided the president with critical feedback, it struck me that something similar was lacking in the church. And so I initiated a tradition of regular discussion evenings with invited guests under the auspices of the Czech Christian Academy. We are always seeking new guests, according to the topic chosen, to take part in monthly events at which we freely discuss crucial social issues. These discussions have also been attended as equals by several bishops, including Cardinal Vlk, as well as by Jesuit and Dominican provincials and leading representatives of non-Catholic churches. I particularly remember one evening when we were discussing the role of the army in a democratic society, the function of military chaplains, and the theory of just war. We had invited senior representatives of the Czech army, the Ministry of Defense, and the General Staff, together with commanders of the air force and antiterrorism units. They all accepted our invitation, and there was an exceptionally lively debate, after which we received almost emotional thanks from the generals, who declared that they would never have thought they would have discussions with a cardinal and professors of moral theology and that the meeting had been very valuable to them. There are many other groups, some of whom have never had any close contact with the church, who have valued this "laboratory of dialogue."

The Czech Christian Academy also organizes international colloquia on specialized topics, as well as engaging in publishing activity and research and in ecumenical and interfaith dialogue. In spite of some reservations and even a certain mistrust in the early period, our bishops have come to appreciate the Academy, particularly those who regularly cooperate with us. We have made it clear that the Academy is not primarily an internal educational institution of the church, even though it sometimes fulfills that function, but that its main mission is to be a bridge with secular society. To that end it is essential that it maintains its independence and broadly ecumenical character.

ANOTHER DREAM THAT WE TRIED to realize during the Prague Spring of 1968 finally came true in 1990, when a student chaplaincy was renewed at the Church of St. Salvator near Charles Bridge. The chaplaincy came to an end in 1948 when Monsignor Alexander Heidler went into exile, and all the priests who had worked with the students—Oto Mádr, František Mikulášek, SJ, and Antonín Mandl—were arrested one by one. St. Salvator was the Jesuits' first church in the Czech lands, and it has an illustrious and checkered history. The English missionary and martyr Edmund Campion was ordained in the church, and those who have served there include the Blessed Charles Spinola, a Jesuit missionary martyred in Japan, Bohuslav Balbín, a Jesuit historian and Czech patriot of the Baroque period, Bernard Bolzano, philosopher and mathematician, and, in more recent years, Professor František Kordač, the first archbishop of Prague after the creation of the Czechoslovak Republic, and Michael Schmauss, professor of theology at the German University in Prague and one of the teachers of Josef Ratzinger. Two German priests who served there during World War II paid with their lives for their anti-Nazi stance.

I took over the chaplaincy on February 1, 1990, from the auxiliary bishop of Prague, Antonín Liška. During his time there, only one Mass was said each week, at 2:00 p.m. on Sunday afternoon, and it was attended by only a few elderly ladies.

I recall a number of oddities from those first months that were characteristic of the times. There was a man, for instance, who would wave his rosary beads around during the Mass and keep on kneeling. He very much wanted to meet me. He turned out to be a former member of the Communist Party who was still a top official at one of the ministries, where the minister was an active Catholic (and a future friend of mine). That man also brought his adolescent daughter to see me to arrange her baptism, although she herself was not in favor of it and was clearly embarrassed. He thought that Catholicism would be the new ruling ideology in our country, and it would ensure his exculpation from his previous political connections and allow him to continue in comfort in his present post. I encountered more such cases. I tried to explain to those people that even if all the ministers of state were Catholics, the church did not demand loyalty of that kind. I told them that faith neither was nor could be an ideology of the state or a ticket to a career. People would not be forced to attend church in the way they were once obliged to attend Communist May Day parades. Faith was of value only as a free act. I subsequently noted that people like that, who were frustrated in their hopes after several months as "Catholics," would often turn away and display great animosity toward the church. However, I do not regret the loss of such supporters of the church.

At first I celebrated just the Sunday afternoon Mass that I had "inherited," being true to the principle that after a priest arrives in a new parish he should spend a year studying it before making any major changes. Then we gradually broadened the spiritual program of the student church. Regular preparation for adult baptism started to be organized, as well as Tuesday masses followed by discussion. Particularly in those first years after the fall of the regime, we focused our efforts on those who had converted during the final years of Communism, often chiefly for reasons of political sympathy with the church as political and moral opposition. Only now were they given the opportunity to acquire systematic knowledge of the Bible and the church's teachings. In the Tuesday discussions I was able to make use of my experience in active social teaching and group psychotherapy. I realized how important it is, particularly when dealing with young people, for a priest to avoid presenting himself as someone with a ready answer for every question. It is necessary to encourage young people's independent thinking and searching. Specifically, this means not being a monologic pedagogue but rather a moderator and facilitator, asking questions, ensuring the widest possible participation in the debate, and gently questioning overconfident and superficial answers. I have always had an aversion to the kind of religious agitation I knew from certain evangelical groups. Everything needs to be considered from different angles. It was already clear to old Socrates, with his *technē maieutikē*, that what people come to understand through their own thinking, provoked by well-chosen questions, is imprinted much more deeply on their consciousness.

I wanted St. Salvator to be an open place, somewhere non-believers or seekers might come without some evangelizer—crazy for God—forcing himself on them with missionary zeal and asking, "Brother, are you saved? Come on Tuesday!" I was guided by a principle I adopted from Fr. Enomiya-Lassalle, one that I also impress on my colleagues: All are invited; nobody is forced. All new arrivals have the right to choose freely how closely they wish to be involved in the activity of the parish. If they so wish, they can remain simply silent observers and guests. All "seekers" are entitled to their questions, doubts, and objections; one must take into account that these young people may come from an environment in which they have only heard negative things about the church, as well as prejudice and the usual media clichés. Everyone must be respected, and not even the most naive comment must be subject to mockery.

Gradually the number of young people started to grow at the church near Charles Bridge. With each new academic year there appeared another large group of those who had come to study in Prague or had only just found out about the student church. For over a quarter of a century the number of newcomers, including recent converts and those interested in baptism, has continued to grow. In the course of those years I have baptized or confirmed almost two thousand adults, mostly university students and sometimes university teachers—and always after thorough preparation lasting almost two years. There is an even greater number of those who—like me—

were christened as infants but grew up without religious education of any kind and only came to faith during their studies; they have also undergone similarly lengthy preparation for confirmation and first communion.

Religious services, courses in the fundamentals of the faith, and open discussions were not the only things offered by the pastoral program of the student church. From the outset there were evenings of silent meditation before the exposed Eucharist, at which time we were available for the sacrament of reconciliation or private conversations. Ever since my student days, Eucharistic adoration was an important component of my personal spirituality. For almost a quarter of a century, every Thursday evening, providing that I am in Prague, I listen until late into the night to those who have come for confession or to seek advice regarding spiritual or other problems.

After the fall of the Communist regime in 1989 many activities of the Catholic church in our country proved to be an expression of short-lived euphoria, which gradually evaporated. The impressive number of candidates for priestly or monastic vocations gradually decreased until it reached a level similar to the crisis of vocations in many Western European countries, and the number of people in census returns who declared themselves members of the Catholic church fell drastically from year to year. In opinion polls the profession of priest was regarded as one of the least prestigious, and trust in the church was shown to be in constant decline. Long-running disputes over the restitution of church property confiscated by the state after 1948 were exploited in a populist manner by a number of politicians and political parties and contributed once more to a rise in an antichurch atmosphere. People started to say that the church had failed to lived up to expectations in our country. The Czech Republic, alongside Estonia and the former GDR, was, and still is, labeled one of the most atheistic countries in Europe if not of the entire planet.

However, the vitality of the constantly changing community of young people at the Church of St. Salvator, which subsequently became an independent personal parish called the Academic Parish of

Prague, has not waned since its creation. A number of young people have chosen priestly or monastic vocations, and my current close colleagues came from among them. One is the Jesuit Petr Vacík, chaplain of our parish, who is an expert on modern film and less common forms of spiritual exercise, particularly "spiritual exercise with films"; another is the Carmelite nun Denisa, the first female Doctor of Theology at the Prague Catholic Theological Faculty since its founding in 1348. When I was lecturing in Brussels a few years ago, I encountered in the space of three days about eight young people who introduced themselves to me as "children of Salvator." They were now employed in Brussels in various jobs with the European Parliament or the European Commission or at the Czech embassies to the European Union and the Kingdom of Belgium. I similarly came across "Salvator children" at Czech diplomatic missions in various countries and also in my own country in many departments of state, the academic world, and the mass media.

Sound recordings made during Mass and services of the word are available on the parish's website, so they are listened to by "Salvator children" and many Czechs living in various parts of the world. Salvator has ceased to be just one of many parishes, but has become a spiritual movement of a kind and a school—one of the distinctive faces of contemporary Czech Christianity.

Over the years, the Prague Academic Parish has been transformed into a lively place of ecumenical and interfaith dialogue. We have welcomed into our midst the Dalai Lama, a number of rabbis from different countries, Buddhist monks from Tibet and Japan, an imam from Iraq, the chief priest of the imperial Shintoist shrine in Japan, and many others. After the Dalai Lama took part in meditation and discussion with us, some priests reproached me for spreading "religious indifferentism" among the young. This was not true. I have repeatedly come across students who were taught in catechism the usual simplistic clichés about Buddhism and other religions, and later—as happens nowadays—on their travels—unlike those who taught them the catechism—they actually made the acquaintance of

Buddhists and adherents of other faiths. They discovered that what they had been told in Catholic circles about other religions was merely a lot of prejudice and ignorance and a reluctance to understand others. As a result, some of them lost faith not only in the priest who put forward such views but also in the credibility of the Catholic Church and its teachings. That is why I have always tried to present to my students other religions as they really are and, where possible, "at first hand," emphasizing that in order to be faithful children of the church, we do not need to belittle and malign other religions.

The Prague Academic Parish has also gradually become a very lively workshop for art and culture in general. Regular exhibitions of modern art take place there, as well as concerts of classical music. Young writers come and read their poetry or short stories during musical evenings, and artists exhibit their drawings, sculpture, and photographs. The large Baroque hall of the sacristy is occasionally the setting for theatrical performances, just as it was at the time of the first Jesuit missionaries. Some young composers have had the world premieres of their works—including liturgical works during Mass—in this, their parish. Every year "Artists' Lent" is organized in the church, a traditional confrontation of the worlds of faith and contemporary art, during which art exhibitions are held, plays are premiered, and concerts are given.

A specific feature of pastoral care in the Academic Parish, and one that has predominated in recent years, is various spiritual exercises and joint meditation, which take place every week, as well as weekend or weeklong courses of meditation or experimental forms of spiritual exercise. In a country that has been proclaimed all too hastily—on the basis of statistics about attendance at church Mass—an atheist nation, sincere interest in developing spiritual life is growing.

For years pastoral activity at St. Salvator was described as a one-man show, and something similar used to be said about Father Reinsberg's activity at the Týn Church. However, that ceased to be the case long ago, thank God. Capable coworkers have grown up around me, and I am beginning to be guided by the words of the Gospel: They must increase, I must decrease.

■ AT THE BEGINNING OF THE 1990s I had the feeling that fate was compensating me for everything that I had long been denied. It was like living in a dream. I was able to work at the university and receive academic titles; I could work at establishing and expanding a lively center for pastoral activity with students, as well as academic platforms for dialogue between church and society; I held an important post in the secretariat of the bishops' conference and in a Vatican dicastery; I could start to travel the world, and I had access to the mass media. There were now people in leading positions in politics, the church, and academe with whom I had been close friends since the time we worked together in dissident circles. I was on a first-name basis with the then president of the republic, the chairman of the bishops' conference, and the rector of the university. I had known them well for years and still had unlimited access to them.

Sometimes I was afraid of waking up again to the gray dawn of "real socialism." Even more often it struck me that although I had been granted more than I had ever asked for, it had come at a terrible price: my life was running away at a frightening rate, and it was constant exertion; I didn't have a moment to appreciate it. At no moment could I say those fateful Faustian words: "Stay a while, you are so beautiful!" I was not dissatisfied. It was simply that the swollen torrent of life rushed onward at such a tempo that I sometimes lost all awareness of time, and in my memories, which are so clear at other times, whole months totally coalesce.

But at such a moments, something happens that is described in beautiful mythopoetic language at the beginning of the Book of Job: "One day, when the sons of God came to present themselves before the LORD, the satan also came among them." The time had come for me to be tested and refined, so that I should be rid of much and give up many things, so that the path to greater depth might be opened.

TEN

The Experience of Darkness

I have a vivid memory of my first journey to my new place of work—the Cyril and Methodius Theological Faculty—at the beginning of February 1990. I traveled with Josef Zvěřina the forty miles to Litoměřice, where the faculty was then located. Zvěřina had been appointed honorary dean of the faculty, but he was unable to have any involvement with the running of the institution, probably on account of people who disliked him. Neither Mádr nor Bouše were ever asked to assume any teaching duties. At that first meeting I also made the acquaintance of the revamped faculty. Although I was looking forward to my work, my first impression, for reasons that are hard to explain, was one of extreme unease.

I had been assigned to the Theological Faculty by Cardinal Tomášek in November 1989, in response to a request from theologians. At that time "social sciences," which used to be taught by representatives of the Communist regime, had been removed from the curriculum, and I was to replace it with the discipline "practical psychology and sociology." Within the sociological component, emphasis was to be placed on the church's social teaching, in other words, a subject that had been totally excluded from the faculty during the Communist regime; even before that it had been taught only as a marginal part of moral theology.

I realized that the entire faculty bore the heavy burden of the previous forty years. In the 1950s it was forcibly separated from the university, moved out of Prague, and excluded from the sphere of higher education. It was placed under the total control of the regime, which was concerned that its standard should be as low as possible. Initially the bishops actually forbade, or at least strongly discouraged, priests loyal to the church to teach at that bogus Communist-sponsored institution or candidates for the priesthood to study there. The bishops later tolerated it for want of any other possibilities, but it was obvious to any reasonable person that this "high school for altar boys," as its students called it for years, had no real standards, and its atmosphere as a whole had nothing in common with a genuine university theological faculty. A provisional attempt at improving its level at the time of the Prague Spring was soon stifled, so once more almost all of the competent teachers were dismissed, apart from a few exceptions in nontheological disciplines. After November 1989 the overall situation in the faculty was not remedied, even after the dismissal of the most compromised members of the teaching staff, the restoration of links with the rest of the university, and the return of the faculty to its original building in Prague.

One of the faculty's great paradoxes was the fact that it tried to link two things that are almost impossible to combine in my opinion: a basic theological school of the diocesan seminary variety and a university faculty. At the beginning of the 1990s, only a few of my students were up to the standards commensurate with undertaking university study. Most of the students and the teaching staff were at best at the level of a diocesan seminary. Only a handful of the teachers had personal experience of university work. They tried to introduce a university style but were met with incomprehension on the part of the other teachers and most of the students.

I still had vivid memories of my experience during the favorable period at the Arts Faculty during the 1960s and at a British university. I later came to know the pontifical faculty in Rome as well and started to be invited to lecture at various universities in Europe and elsewhere. I therefore tried to implement some of my good experiences from abroad at least partially. I was convinced of the need for seminars, in addition to the traditional lectures, at which there would be more discussion and students would be encouraged to think independently and undertake independent scholarly activity. I also believed that they should write papers each year, as well as master's theses. Such things were all quite unusual at the Theological Faculty in those days, and whenever I tried to encourage some discussion, at least within the lecture framework, the students were totally disconcerted. One student actually reported me immediately to the archbishop, saying that I kept asking my students questions, which proved that I was unfamiliar with the syllabus and was trying to learn it from them. Other students asked me not to deliver my lectures too fast; in effect they wanted me to dictate the lessons, which they were accustomed to in high school. There existed almost no contemporary specialized theological literature in Czech, and most of the students' standard of linguistic expression was abysmal. This could all have been excused on grounds of the objective difficulties of the unpromising beginnings, but the administrators of the faculty in those days did nothing to alter the situation. Whenever I visited some theological faculty abroad, its members would complain to me bitterly that the dean of the Prague faculty refused their offers of cooperation and sincerely intended assistance—whether in the form of visiting lecturers, specialized literature, or study visits by students and teachers of the faculty—and reacted to it as some hostile attempt at ideological diversion from the West.

Many Christians who had lived for years under siege were now incapable of living without an enemy. When the Communist enemy fell they had to find something to replace it. "The decadent West" was handy. I realized that some Catholics referred to the West in precisely the same terms as the Communist potentates once had. That was one of the reasons I started vigorously to oppose the stereotypical opinion that they were decadent and we were the good guys.

A number of conservative Catholics visited us from the West in those days and tried to win support here. They approached our church as if they were a fairy tale prince and our church was Sleeping Beauty, who, under Communism, had blissfully slept through the periods of turbulence and Vatican II, and they would now awaken it with a magic kiss into the delightful immaculate state of the premodern church. This seemed to be such a disgraceful slight to everything that had happened here, because we had neither slept nor lived in Czechoslovakia in a kind of vacuum. They congratulated us that there were no "theological excesses" here as in the West. I told them in reply that those who vaunt the fact they do not have tooth decay should ask themselves first of all if it wasn't perhaps because they had dentures instead of real teeth.

The management of the Theological Faculty isolated itself not only from the world but also from the other university faculties, and in particular it avoided ecumenical contacts. It gave no support at all to scholarly publishing or research and automatically returned any offers of grants. There was a faculty meeting only at the beginning and end of the academic year, and it was purely formal. The different departments did not cooperate with each other, not even within the framework of the faculty, and nothing was done to prepare a new generation of scholars. If the administration of the faculty had at least hinted that it considered this state of affairs temporary and inadequate, I would have understood; but instead it sanctified its inactivity by presenting itself as, above all, the guardian of orthodoxy, and whoever criticized them was opposing the orthodoxy. In fact, those of us who opposed this state of affairs were not taking a stand against orthodoxy; we were simply trying to rouse the faculty from its inaction and lethargy.

Something similar was deeply familiar to me from the totalitarian period. Those in power identify their position and their views with the ideology itself, and no one can criticize them. But at that moment the entire system stops evolving. That is the secret of the apparent stability of all totalitarian systems but also of their inner decay. Such statements as, "When you criticize us, you are actually opposed to the Party; are you aware of this, comrade?," were extremely familiar to me, and they differed only slightly from, "When you criticize us you are actually opposing the Holy Father; are you aware of this, professor?" When the cards were dealt like that, any real dialogue was already out of the question.

For nearly twenty years I had looked forward to returning to the university, but what was happening under the roof of the Theological Faculty truly had little in common with a university. I asked myself anxiously what and how these future priests would preach, since they had had no contact with what had been happening in the field of scholarly exegesis over the previous decades. What would be the pastoral activity of those who had been taught a pastoral theology that ignored the findings of the humanities? How would those who had no experience at all of how to lead a genuine discussion be able to discuss with seekers and nonbelievers? All this filled me with feelings of deep depression. The faculty was not open to the laity, who could only enroll for correspondence courses of a scandalously low standard. One of the students told me at the faculty that "the main thing for a priest is to keep the laity at arm's length." When I experienced how the leadership of the faculty treated the two nuns who were awarded the privilege of studying there—they were not allowed to eat with the other students, or even with the members of faculty, and were made to sit at a table in the corner of the refectory—this offended me so much as a man, a Christian, and a priest that I demonstratively joined them at their table; maybe that was the psychological beginning of my dispute with the faculty's administrators.

But in all honesty I must add that I was dissatisfied not only with the overall environment of the faculty but also with my own work. Admittedly I gave my students a bit more than was customary at that time, but I did not give them as much as I could or should have. Although I had always tried to teach even during the totalitarian period, at least in underground seminars, at university I had to learn to teach. I lacked the patience needed to guide my students away from the style of learning they had been used to and accustom them to the sort of participatory manner of study I had come to know at the British university. I failed to tune in sufficiently to my students, and I expect I spoke over the heads of many of them. When I became aware that the dean had informers among the students, who would ask me provocative questions with the aim of "catching" me proclaiming some heresy, I was unable to rise above it, which totally demotivated me. Nowadays, even when I am tired, I always look forward to teaching; at that time I did not enjoy my work, and that is always apparent.

My students were accustomed to simplistic explanations of the catechistic type, and the apologetic character of the teaching was evident, whereby the opinions of opponents and "heresies" were always quickly and easily swept aside. Chesterton had taught me that "heresies are truths gone mad," that heresy—as it was also understood by medieval scholastics, which grew out of free university disputations— has some grain of truth, which much be deciphered and freed from one-sidedness and integrated into a broader context. Josef Zvěřina taught us that Catholicism's basic principle is "not only but also"— that it is necessary to see the other side of everything. Only when one learns the art of the hermeneutical approach to the mystery of faith does theology become an exciting adventure of learning. But the students of those days were totally deprived of that.

I knew that there were several members of the teaching staff who were linked with the murky past of the faculty and the church. I was not surprised to find that some of the names appeared in the unofficially published lists of secret police informers. Indeed I was beginning to sense enormous personal animosity toward me from those individuals. I had a very complicated relationship with the dean of the faculty. I respected him and did not doubt his political integrity; I found him likable, and our initial contact seemed to be developing fairly well. The dean himself was a successful teacher, beloved by generations of his students, particularly those who liked things to be neatly pigeonholed. Although he was not an independently minded or creative theological thinker—throughout those many years he had not written a single book or published a scholarly article of any significance—he could nevertheless be considered a competent expert on the neo-Scholastic theology of the turn of the twentieth century. The problem was rather the fact that he clearly did not recognize any other type of theology. He was a gifted linguist, well traveled, and a sportsman; at first sight he was nonconflictual and pleasant, with a ready smile. Nor did his lectures lack humor, although the more attentive listener would register an undertone of irony and an almost aggressive denigration of other opinions. I was very glad that there was someone like that in the faculty capable of giving the students a clear and simple introduction. But there was a need for others who would teach them to look at things from other angle, and understand that behind apparent certainties there are layers of additional questions inviting them to go deeper and creating that dramatic and thrilling landscape of perception. When I look back at my philosophical education with hindsight, I am extremely grateful that alongside Professor Svoboda, who introduced us to the ABCs of philosophical traditions and systematics, we had Professor Patočka, who was able to introduce us to the dramatic U-turn made by philosophy when, with Heidegger, it took a radical look at the forgotten assumptions of the entire Western metaphysical tradition and began to ask about new starting points.

I later got to know that dean better. It struck me that in the depth of his personality there was an unusually intense fear. Apparently he himself had once been a very open-minded theologian, who had had the opportunity to study and obtain a doctorate in a West German university. However, his contact with the environment of a German university in that period seems to have been not only a culture shock for him, but to have caused him some kind of psychological trauma, as a result of which he henceforth resolved to fight against the influences of modern theology and, above all, against everything that came from the German-speaking countries. He reminded me of a type of priest that I had encountered quite frequently: people who had grown up in a predominantly feminine environment and had a strong fixation on their mothers, which was sometimes transferred to the institutional aspect of the church; nothing irritated them or made them feel threatened more than those who had greater inner freedom and were able to have a somewhat more adult relationship with "mother church."

In time it was clear that I was starting to become the embodiment of everything that that person feared. I had been ordained in Germany, and I made no secret of the fact that my thinking was inspired chiefly by the works of outstanding theologians from the German-speaking world, including Balthasar, Rahner, Ratzinger, and Kasper. Maybe that is why I became an ideal screen on which to project his image of the enemy image, and our relationship started to take a dramatic turn. People who are afraid have an immense need to have others fear them; that man was afraid of me, and he was unable to cope with the fact that I did not fear him. But I neglected to pay timely attention to the fact that I had failed to placate his fear of me and instead had unwittingly increased it still further by many of my reactions.

Tension increased when I returned from postgraduate study in Rome. It was the ones who were linked with the faculty's inauspicious past who saw me as some kind of dangerous competitor, and they used all sorts of hearsay and slander to try to turn the dean and the administration as a whole against me. Things worsened even more when the faculty received an invitation to a congress of the European Society for Catholic Theology. At that time the administrators put pressure on the members of the teaching staff not to attend the meeting. I thought it was vital that Czech theologians should not drop out of that working association. I had spoken about the association personally in Rome with the pope and Cardinal Ratzinger, and although I sensed that the Vatican initially had reservations about the initiative, I certainly did not get the impression that they wanted us to boycott it. Zvěřina had come to a similar conclusion when he talked to the pope previously about the proposal to create the Society. I was sincerely convinced that it was important that the founding congress, which had been planned for so long, should be attended by theologians from Central and Eastern Europe, precisely because their experience was different from that of their Western colleagues. I therefore decided to attend.

On my return, the dean called me in. It was clear from that interview that I was no longer persona grata at the faculty and that the dean and the people around him were looking for a pretext to get rid of me. He no longer regarded me simply as a possible competitor and rival; I was now an adversary, with whom one did not discuss. It was from that standpoint that the dean viewed a strange private misunderstanding, which I still do not fully understand, because it involved indiscretion from other parties and false interpretation of some things said in private conversation. Before Easter I sent the dean a letter in which I asked his forgiveness if I had unwittingly offended him in some way. I suggested a brotherly conversation as a way of mutually clarifying matters and achieving reconciliation. He never replied to my letter and repeatedly refused to meet with me privately. Instead the faculty secretary interrupted me in the middle of a lecture to bring an official notification that "disciplinary proceedings" had been instituted against me, and I was subsequently summoned to those proceedings: "If you fail to present yourself the proceedings will take place in your absence." I requested in writing to know what the proceedings related to, so that I could prepare a defense. As usual, I received no reply.

Those "proceedings" took place at the beginning of June 1992, and looking back, it was one of the most traumatic experiences of my life, though at that moment it seemed to me more like a farce or something between an absurd play by Václav Havel and some screening process from the Communist period. The administration set up a kind of tribunal that was absurd not only with respect to the points of the "indictment," but also its legal form. The constitution of the university did not permit "disciplinary proceedings" against a teacher. In response to my opening question regarding the legal nature of our meeting (a question I was trained to ask at secret police interrogations), the dean stated on the official record that it was taking place at the behest of the archbishop. That statement later turned out to be a lie. Doctrinal questions did not figure at all. Neither then nor at any other time previously had a single sentence of mine been criticized by any church or theological body for diverging from the church's teaching or for preaching heresies. The accusations concerned my influence on the students, to whom I had allegedly voiced criticism of the faculty's philosophy. That was true; I had criticized the faculty for contravening church policy by preventing the admission of the laity to regular full-time study. The other objections leveled against me were clearly just a pretext. I felt I had made a sufficient defense and that the entire matter was resolved. In conclusion, I asked what the outcome of the proceedings was, to which the dean replied that he would not be making any conclusions, as it was a matter for the archbishop to decide. Scarcely had I closed the door behind me than the dean dictated a postscript into the official record: "Conclusion: after hearing the entire case, and in the light of all the circumstances, the faculty members of the Catholic Theological Faculty of Charles University present have come to the conclusion that the continued engagement of Dr. Tomáš Halík at this faculty is no longer desirable."

I am convinced that those people did not even listen to me, and their "verdict" was already prepared in advance, like it used to be in Communist courts and screening committees. Quite simply, I was an obstacle to them, and they wanted to get rid of me. Nothing else interested them. I realized that some people, whom I was supposed to regard as my brothers in faith, did not care about the truth. That disconcerted me like nothing before in my life.

I wrote an appeal to the archbishop, describing to him the real reason for the conflict, namely, the lamentable state of the faculty, and I begged him to start finding a solution to the situation at last.

The archbishop annulled the dismissal but recommended that I leave the faculty in order to calm the situation. After lengthy reflection I accepted this solution. I requested a year's unpaid leave and the termination of my contract at the end of that period.

Several years later, when I was already teaching at the Arts Faculty, the same dean made another attempt to damage my reputation, and it was timed just before my professorship was being considered. I asked the rector of the university to investigate the accusation made against me by the dean of the Theological Faculty. A thorough investigation was carried out by an independent commission consisting of several deans and lawyers, and in the end I was morally vindicated in full. As a result the dean's final action against my person had a more beneficial than negative effect on my standing with the representatives of the university. "A doctor would never do anything like that to another doctor, nor would a lawyer to another lawyer. Why would a priest do that to another priest?," I was asked by one of the members of the university's academic council.

Shortly afterward the dean of the Theological Faculty allowed himself to be unlawfully reelected to his post, thus placing himself in conflict with the archbishop and the university management. He lost his position in a truly inglorious manner.

■ IT WAS A TRAUMATIC EXPERIENCE, but I owe a great deal to it. Until that time I could not imagine that the church had repugnant aspects. When I heard media commentators talking about the church as a totalitarian organization, I was affronted and believed them to be influenced by Communist propaganda. I and my friends who converted during the Communist era knew the church from a completely different angle. Suddenly I had experienced at firsthand that even nowadays someone in the church, in the name of protecting its structures, can cold-bloodedly place power above truth. In my mind I apologized to all those who had ever thought or written bad things about the church and who I had considered liars. I don't share their negative view of the church, but I admit that they did not lie: they had their own negative experience of the church.

But I also realized that the abominated secular pluralist society, with its Enlightenment ideals of tolerance, human rights, and civil liberties, protected the church from any temptation to relapse into bad behavior. It is good that we live in a democratic society; I do not yearn for a "Catholic state." Were there an attempt to make a state ideology out of faith, I would probably be the first dissident—in the name of faith and of liberty.

I have no wish at all to dramatize what happened to me. Compared to the difficulties faced only a few decades ago in the church by people much more significant and estimable then I am, including such theologians as Yves Congar, Jean Danielou, Hans Urs von Balthasar, and Henri de Lubac—to mention only those whose fidelity to the church subsequently received papal acknowledgment—my troubles were a mere flea bite. I did not doubt for one moment that the church authorities would soon verify the true state of affairs at the Theological Faculty and vindicate me in this dispute. It did not cause me any existential harm. At that time I was beginning to acquire a certain professional reputation and knew that I would have no difficulty finding employment in any arts faculty in my own country or at a university abroad. Very soon I started to lecture again, first at the Faculty of Social Sciences and sometime later at the Faculty of Arts, where I continue to work today.

Yes, I repeated to myself, looked at entirely rationally and objectively, nothing particularly bad happened to me. I convinced myself that I had to behave as a courageous man, and as a priest I must always be capable of sacrifice. I swallowed my feelings of bitterness and started to work even harder. However, this is a solution I would not recommend to anyone. One is not just coolly rational. One has emotions, and has the right to them. I don't think one should allow oneself to be ruled by them. One should process them, but in order to do so honestly—which takes a long time—one must have the humility to let them enter one's consciousness and admit them.

I didn't want to admit to myself that I felt frustrated with the church that I loved, and for which I had risked my skin, and which now turned to me a face that I knew only from Goya's caricatures of the Inquisition. I didn't want to admit that I felt disappointed by the behavior of the bishops, not one of whom stood up for me then and lifted a finger to help me. I thought a priest had no right to such feelings, so I gritted my teeth and soldiered on.

Everything I knew from psychotherapy, and would be capable of advising others to do, I failed to do when it came to my own situation. That was a mistake. Suppression of one's feelings is not as moral or effective as is sometimes thought. It is not possible to escape one's heart.

During a conference in Spain a few months later, I suddenly came down with stomach problems and violent fevers. When I went for a medical examination on my return, it turned out that the results of the liver function tests were extremely high; one of the doctors said he suspected a malignant tumor. I recalled a line of verse that my father had quoted to me at our last New Year's celebration together: "Death is looking over our shoulder."

The psychosomatic nature of various illnesses, including tumors, is well known. I knew that many patients who are diagnosed with malignant cancer have, during the previous two years or so, generally suffered a serious traumatic event in their lives with which they have not been able to come to terms.

I don't think it can all be attributed to the conflicts at the Theological Faculty and my enormous disillusion at the attitudes of the church authorities. I was totally exhausted and weary unto death. The years prior to the change of regime and the first years afterward had been so hectic and full of work and events that my body had to rise in revolt. Happily the next medical examination ruled out cancer; my symptoms were the result of severe stress and long-term overload, and I returned to health within six months. But anyone who has lived for just a few weeks with that suspicion is aware of how useful that experience is and how different it is from the moments when, in the silence of spiritual exercises, we allow ourselves to meditate on preparation for death.

And I was unable to pray. God was silent. It was night. Shortly before I reached my forty-fifth year of life I had reached rock bottom, as that old priest once predicted I would.

◼ MOST BELIEVERS, INCLUDING PRIESTS, probably undergo a major spiritual crisis at least once in their lives. It can be provoked by interpersonal conflict or disillusionment with human behavior in the church. It can take the form of an overall crisis of confidence in church institutions or in a particular community. In the case of Catholic clergy, it can be a crisis of one's celibacy and the shaking of one's priestly or monastic identity. Crisis can be the result of exhaustion and overload: the burnout syndrome is quite common even among priests. Sometimes it is a question of the "noonday demon of acedia," a state of sudden languor and torpor that occurs in midlife. It can also be a "closing doors syndrome," when someone feels they are getting old and the horizon of their life expectations and motivations starts to shift. It can be a crisis of faith, when, as the result of some stressful events and unheard prayers, their previous notion of God clouds over, and they start to doubt his kindness and closeness and sometimes even his existence. Sometimes people feel a total aversion to everything religious and spiritual, including prayer, even when it previously meant a great deal to them. Who is able to distinguish these often complexly interwoven levels of spiritual, mental, physical, or interpersonal suffering?

There are countless inauspicious ways of solving such crises. In the case or priests and other clergy I have come across various typical reactions. Some of them de facto lost their faith, without being capable of admitting the fact to themselves, and they became religious tradesmen. Others have tried to drown out this unacknowledged loss of faith and compensate for it; such cases account for the majority of the fanatical defenders of orthodoxy, who project their own doubts onto others, whom they zealously persecute, thus unconsciously punishing themselves. Another form of compensation tends to be contrived piety, hectic activity in various movements in the church, and increased missionary and pastoral activity. But there also exist familiar reactions in the form of alcohol, career fixation, property (sublimated sometimes in various types of "collecting"), giving up the ministry, or a covert sexual relationship. And let us not forget the zealots from the opposing camp: many campaigners for church renewal, implacable critics of "the hierarchy and Rome," passionate campaigners for the abolition of celibacy and in favor of a female priesthood, as well as "antifundamentalists," are sometimes recruited from those who indulge in such activities to smother within themselves their loss of faith—a faith that they actually secretly envy the so-called fundamentalists.

A spiritual administrator of a monastic community once told me a long time ago that X-rays of the nuns' stomachs would say more about the convent than the alterations to the chapel or the singing in the choir. Stomach ulcers and other problems can often tell more about the real state of relations within a community, about the stresses that sometimes remain masked, unacknowledged, inwardly suppressed, and transmitted through the internal organs, than fixed smiles. In my youthful idealism, what he said seemed almost blasphemous to me, and I was even more astonished by his opinion that maintaining a pious atmosphere and ensuring that souls were not soiled by anger, as was so strongly recommended, was actually no more than a cowardly shifting of a spiritual task from the soul to the body.

I now know that what I was told by that experienced priest is the psychological and theological truth, in contrast to the heaps of would-be pious, ascetic vademecums with their heretical pelagian emphasis on "ascetic exercises," clichés, and reprehensible psychological naïveté, which have inflicted inner suffering on so many devout people and twisted their personalities. I still have a lot of people coming to confession who are severely damaged by having been taught by such pamphlets. Thank God there exist books by Anselm Grün and others that draw on a deeper and more authentic tradition, from the spirituality of the desert fathers, or the first Benedictines and Franciscans, and are able to link it creatively with the perspectives of depth psychology.

Many traditional lives of the saints, as well as sermons and treatises on asceticism and morality, presented an idealistic image of the believer, and particularly the priest, which was totally alienated from real life, and in the spirit of them many priests used to create a mask behind which they concealed their true self from others, from themselves, and from God. The pressure for perfection sometimes led to tragic hypocrisy, so that those people simply displaced from their consciousness everything that was problematic or "inappropriate." As a result, those problems were magnified, and those people then truly led a double life, often without being able to admit it. On several occasions, I was invited as a priest with psychotherapeutic qualifications to talk to priests who in the past had signed an agreement to collaborate with the secret police. I think that something similar was at play in those cases, as in the cases of certain priests who sexually abused young people. These people had totally "forgotten" it—had utterly displaced it from their consciousness! The pressure of external expectation, cultivated by the romantic ideal of the holy priest, together with the psychological pressure created by the internalization of that ideal in the course of seminary training, never allowed those clergy to admit that they were not capable of meeting that ideal. I realized how important and profound was Jesus's criticism of similar "religious professionals" among the Pharisees of his day.

"He who wants to play the angel plays the beast," Pascal said. People should vigorously fight the temptation to play the angel in order to forestall serious splitting of the personality and real demonic breakdown. Even believers who have spent years trying to live in accordance with moral demands should meekly, and without fear, admit that they are not perfect, that they still have unsolved problems within themselves and from time to time feel tremors of anger, disappointment, sensuality, narcissistic self-centeredness, aggression, and rebellion. To deny and displace this part of our nature, which we share with our forefather Adam since the Fall, is not a virtue but self-deception. Such self-deception is more dangerous than many of our negative inclinations, weaknesses, and failings. One wise confessor once told me something I will never forget: there is a commandment that precedes the Ten Commandments, namely, "You shall not delude yourself or the Lord your God! You shall not pretend you are better or other than you really are, either to yourself or to Him!"

Whenever we immediately "moralize" these inclinations that appear in our feelings and "moods," whenever we blame ourselves for them, we make it worse. The first thing to do is to say that such things are quite natural, that such shadows exist inside us; they will only become a moral defect if we allow them to control our lasting inner attitudes, our way of thinking, or our behavior. Indeed, if we reject them too hastily by force and displace them into our unconscious they are capable of governing our behavior and our disposition more powerfully than if we confront them calmly in our conscious mind. If we displace them, we can find it harder to process them and regain control of ourselves.

In his spiritual exercises, Anselm Grün interprets a story about a man who taught himself to understand the language of animals, and this led him to find a treasure. One should understand this language of instincts and emotions, particularly those one is loath to admit to, and enter into dialogue with what can be heard deep within one. People are all too willing—foolishly, superficially, and hypocritically—to identify only with what shines in the light, what accords with their ideals, and what they can be proud of. They are scared of what is in the shadows and deeper; they immediately regard everything that is complex and ambiguous as sinful and are unwilling even to touch it.

At the beginning of the Mass, we confess that there are many things we ought to have done but did not do, and we have sinned by neglecting what is good. We should pay greater heed to that! We have existential debts. I would think we all have things in our unconscious that we have displaced there, or that we have never lifted out of the mighty potential of our being. A debt is not the same thing as sin. But debt can become sin if it is neglected and unpaid. We often focus on "sins" that are failings with respect to certain laws or ideals or that are simply an expression of the fact that we are weak and imperfect people. But our gravest faults can be our unpaid debts—the things "we ought to have done and have not done," when we have skipped certain of our lives' tasks, when we have been shallow and untrue, when we have swerved off the path to maturity. When will we at last take the gospel seriously and care more about sincerity and integrity in our lives than listing our good deeds and our "purity."

C. G. Jung rightly suggested that we should strive for wholeness and integrity rather than perfection. We should not live only on the surface and identify solely with just one aspect of our being, but we should assume responsibility for our lives as a whole. His words shed new light for me on Jesus's preference for those who are aware of their sinfulness, and yearn for redemption, over those who make a show of their righteousness. For many Christians it is still incomprehensible and unacceptable that Jesus habitually preferred tax gatherers and prostitutes to the truly moral, just, and pious Pharisees— who were, however, rigidly and inwardly closed. A humble awareness of sinfulness can be a good starting point for following Christ; the pride of those who are settled in their righteousness is a slippery slope to hell.

During the Confiteor, it once struck me how important it was that we say, "It is *my* fault." This is not primarily depressing self-recrimination with respect to some static ideal of virtue and certainly not superficially casting our debts as far away from us as we can. On the contrary, it is a matter of accepting them, and assuming them, in the sense of recognizing that "this is also me." As soon as I am capable of this humbling integration, of drawing back all the darker aspects into myself, into the sphere of my own responsibility—whereas formerly I projected them onto others or blamed external factors—then they lose a great deal of their dark power over me. Unlike people, "public opinion," or my own tendency to make myself out to be better than I am, God accepts me just as I am. And when I stand before him humbly—in other words, sincerely and truthfully—with all that is within me—good and bad, light and dark—he starts to lead me along the path to maturity. If I can experience that God accepts me in this way, I can gain the courage also to accept myself fully—and then I can learn to accept other people just as they are and not as I would like them to be. Conversion, repentance, forgiveness, and reconciliation: this is not some exercise in pious feelings but a process of maturing toward responsibility, adulthood, and integrity, of which self-acceptance and self-knowledge are an integral part.

My weaknesses, my dark aspects, and conflicts are tasks and opportunities. Often in the confessional, I tell people who are depressed about always having to confront the same weaknesses, "Wouldn't it be boring if we didn't have something to deal with in ourselves and were like angels?" Proximity to the angels is something we can look forward to beyond the gates of death but something we should not foolishly try to play at on the earthly battlefield. Let us bear our ambiguous and problematic earthliness as an ongoing task. Let us not stagnate in the naive conviction that we have already reached our goal. You can't get to heaven by skipping your earthly nature. This is also a case where "gratia supponit naturam," grace presupposes natural behavior.

■ ANY ATTEMPT BY US TO STAY SILENT about the weaknesses and conflicts in the church would be in clear opposition to the words of John Paul II that the church must be "a house of glass," that we must be transparent and not seek to cover anything up. In a media society, whether we like it or not, nothing can be covered up, and any attempt to do so only worsens the situation and leads to loss of credibility.

I am not saying that people should run to the media with every little injury and place all the information about the darker aspects of the church's environment at the mercy of a gutter press that feeds on scandals in the church in the slow news season. We must make a distinction! When someone talks about the bad things he encountered in the church but hasn't come to terms with it and simply wants to publicize it in order to slam the door behind him and justify his stance to himself and others, it is usually embarrassing. But if people have suffered something of the kind and are able to offer others a sincere testimony about where the path can take them, and how not to allow oneself to be envenomed or broken by such shadows, then they can be helpful to a lot of people in a similar situation. Then the truth, however bitter, subjective, and partial—human truth is always partial—can be greater help than any prettification or obfuscation. It is necessary to talk about problems openly but also to emphasize that others have the right to see things differently. Even in the eyes of the public, the church is more credible if it can show that in its ranks there are people capable of viewing it critically. This is the best way for us to counter truly destructive and hostile criticism. Only the truth will free us.

THERE ARE CERTAIN SPIRITUAL CRISES during which people have the feeling that they have lost their faith. Faith is a serious thing, so we should speak about its loss in a responsible manner. Losing one's faith is not like losing one's wallet. And if people have the feeling they have lost their faith in that manner, then they have nothing to regret, as probably all they have lost are religious illusions. Of course it is possible to neglect faith and not take care of it, just as one can neglect a marriage and not take care of it and then be surprised when it collapses. But sometimes the "thorns of earthly cares" can so overgrow the human soul, that faith can't get a word in, so that it ceases to influence a person's thinking and actions; and there are many other possible situations when faith becomes stunted, to which the gospel parable about the seed refers so plainly and eloquently. But I am not speaking about that here.

I am speaking about the moments when the image that someone has created of God becomes dim or disintegrates, and they find themselves in a kind of vacuum. When people undergo a serious crisis, which can sometimes be sparked by something they have suffered in the church, they often hear from priests or from friends who are believers pious encouragement along the lines of, "Pull yourself together. It's not so bad! The Lord Jesus also suffered; you have to make sacrifices and carry your cross! Where's your faith?" The Book of Job is full of similar good pious advice from Job's wise friends. But fortunately it also includes the scene in which God finally decides to speak, and the first thing he does is to severely criticize Job's friends for their pious advice and moral encouragement, and he takes the part of Job who had argued strongly with him in a manner that the pious considered blasphemous. "You have not spoken rightly concerning me, as has my servant Job," God says to these and all other similar well-meaning individuals. "Let my servant Job pray for you that I do not punish you."

When you ask people like that what they mean by bearing one's cross and sharing in the Lord's suffering, they are often disconcerted, because often it is simply a meaningless pious phrase that they trot out, or they offer you some heretical pelagian ideal of the moral athlete. Saying things like, "Your situation is not so bad objectively speaking, and all in all it is no big deal," may often be the "objective truth," but it is not the truth about your situation and your life. As the Czech proverb has it, "The one who is sated does not believe the one who is hungry."

My recommended response to the question, "Where is your faith?," is, "I'm not sure. Sometimes I think I've lost it." Then they'll run off as if you have leprosy, mumbling that they will pray for you. Jesus asked the apostles this question, when they were standing together on a boat buffeted by the storm and the waves. But those people not only do not have the power to calm the storm buffeting you, but above all they are not in your boat and are far from the whirlpools that shake you.

Carrying one's cross and sharing in Jesus's suffering definitely does not mean gritting one's teeth and letting oneself be persuaded that all the dark things one is experiencing are actually rosy. On the contrary, it means entering into the moments of Jesus's darkness and his agonizing question, "My God, my God, why have you abandoned me?"

It is extremely important to realize that such moments, when people's entire spiritual life is shaken, when God seems to have died for them, when their faith is dimmed and they are truly at rock bottom, are important and of value. It is necessary to accept precisely this moment as a pivotal religious experience. Sometimes this can mark the abandonment of "religious notions" and the beginning of real faith.

There are people who turned away from faith at a time of God's silence, because they came to the conclusion that God did not exist. It would have been more honest to say that their previous notion of God no longer worked. A God who operates in accordance with human notions truly does not exist; it is an idol, from which one is right to free oneself. Those people are right in a way, but they remain in a "halfway house." The point of breaking away from idols is to make a space to encounter the living God. Indeed, that moment of eclipse on the spiritual journey can become a decisive encounter with the living God. Often in hindsight we realize that it was God himself—and no internal or external obstacle—who was blocking our previous spiritual journey. He hid in silence, and darkness, and reduced himself to nothing—but it is precisely there that one must meet him.

I WAS ASSISTED IN THAT CRISIS BY the writings of mystics connected with so-called negative theology, such as Meister Eckhart, St. John of the Cross, and Teresa of Avila. Since then they have been my constant spiritual guides and teachers of the faith.

Meister Eckhart says, God is truly *no-thing*. We won't find him in a world of existing things, of many "some-things." God is not part of it, not "something." Nor is he a "supreme being." And now comes the most important point: in order to encounter God, who is nothing, you yourself must first become "nothing," nobody—knowing nothing, wanting nothing, being nothing. That means not being fixated on any thing; not identifying oneself with anything such as property, a social role, or even ideological property, knowledge; being inwardly free and totally open; not clinging to any ideology, "images," or idols (even our notions of God, as well as concepts and definitions, can be objectivizing and misleading idols). God is no-thing, and you must become nobody, free of all attachments, freed from your very self. Only then can you encounter God—"in mutual nakedness."

And you will not encounter him only during the performance of some particular sacred activity or in some sacred place; this free God is also "all in everything," and you can be just as close to him, says Eckhart, when you are milking a cow or when taking part in adoration in a church. When you will be a free "nothing," God will fill that nothingness and totally permeate your life, because he will not encounter any obstacles there from your ties to things. In the language of mystics, nothingness and fullness are two words for the same thing.

And John of the Cross? He presents a map of the journey to Mount Carmel. As with Eckhart, that path leads through "*nada*"— wanting nothing, knowing nothing, being nothing. And on the mountaintop? Again nothing. John of the Cross speaks to people for whom "God has died," whose faith has faded, and they are walking through the night. He reinterprets this situation as an experienced spiritual therapist. Do nor terrorize yourselves with moralizing reproaches! This darkness is not God's punishment for your sins; it need not mean that you have neglected your faith. And it certainly doesn't mean that your journey to this point has been pointless. This dark moment, this contact with the loneliness of our Lord on the cross, is a moment of transformation and purification, of your death and resurrection.

First the world fell silent, when, like one in love, you flew freely to a loving encounter with God, as one runs with love in one's heart through a summer night. Isn't this darkness in fact being blinded by

excess of light? Doesn't this "dark" moment signify that you are looking into the sun?

It came to me: yes, that was that answer. This was the spirituality that corresponded to the life situation I found myself in. John
speaks to someone who is shaken, to someone in crisis, exposed to
the desert of God's silence. He tries to show him that his crisis is an
opportunity and a visitation. He neither moralizes nor offers quick
and easy solutions. We are to accept this situation, because this is
one of the ways that God communicates with people. It is in fact one
of the profoundest ways of contact with the human heart. He comes
to the wounded and the parched. Smashing our existing piety is an
opportunity for a childish and naive form of faith to die within one,
a chance to experience the fall of idols. We always have a tendency to
turn God into an idol, to mold him into the shape of concepts and
images. It is only at the moment of the fall of those images, when
they called into doubt and silence, that we can realize that God is
far beyond and above them, that he is greater than anything we can
imagine about him.

When, many years later, I reread the essay "Ego dormio," which
I wrote, at Václav Havel's request, for a collection to commemorate
his fiftieth birthday, I was surprised to find that I had addressed a lot
of these ideas many years before and then seemed to have forgotten
about them, as if they were some kind of musical theme that has returned in different variations throughout the composition of my life.
I had only reached for the essay out of intellectual interest. Now it
was illuminated by my experience, like when the sun shines through
a cloud. The time seemed dark, but now golden rays were beginning
to pierce the darkness. I realized this was my spiritual path. I had
touched bottom: and lo, that's where God was.

■ THEN SOMETHING ELSE STRUCK ME: what John of the Cross
says about individual souls could be applied to entire cultural epochs.
Isn't our epoch, which many describe and truly experience as the era

of the "death of God," also a kind of "dark night of the soul"? Isn't the atheism of our time—and I mean existential atheism as attested by Nietzsche, Heidegger, or Sartre, not the shallow atheism of those who never ask themselves any spiritual questions—also a kind of religious experience?

The spiritual experience of my encounter with mysticism, which helped me clarify and inwardly process my inner crisis in 1992, was reflected in my lectures at the faculty and also in my pastoral service to people who were seekers and doubters. Mysticism and negative theology went on to make a considerable impression on my theological thinking, which was reflected in my books, and eventually helped me initiate a creative dialogue with contemporary postmodern philosophy of religion and philosophical theology.

When I returned to the Arts Faculty, I started to work intensively on the history of modern philosophical atheism, particularly on the theme of the death of God as dealt with by Hegel, Nietzsche, and others. With the insight I received from my encounter with Christian mysticism, it struck me that everything those authors wrote about, whether we call it the loss, eclipse, or death of God, need not be something "outside" the history of faith and the experience of faith. Wasn't the "dark night" also part of the journey to God? It was then that it first struck me that atheism—or at least one type of atheism—was simply "part of truth" rather than "untruth"?

The dialogue between faith and atheism can take a deeper form than beating each other up with arguments. It can be an enriching sharing of experience. If I could show an atheist that I can share his experience of the eclipse of God, would this not provide me with an opportunity to offer him my experience of the closeness of God?

An elderly nun once said something to me that I did not understand at the time: "As I get older God seems to me both closer and more remote at the same time." Sometimes it takes many years of spiritual life, and at least three serious crises of faith, for one to realize that faith is not an unchanging, static "certainty" but a journey during which light and darkness alternate. If it is possible to catch a glimpse of God—like Moses "glimpsed" him on the mountain—then it is precisely at the moment when day and night interpenetrate.

■ THEN TWO OTHER THINGS HELPED ME: my trip to the Holy Land and the proximity of students.

Jung, who would seem to have gone through a similar crisis in the years prior to World War I, stated that two things had helped him: he understood his crisis as a kind of anticipation and "mystic sharing" in the crisis that suddenly engulfed the world during the war and the fact that he kept his struggle within his heart and did not interrupt his work with his patients, or his duties toward his own family, for a single day.

It is not my intention to tempt people who have serious problems not to seek psychotherapeutic assistance. That would be irresponsible of me. On the contrary, in many cases undergoing psychotherapy can be a sensible, humble, and courageous emergency step. It is also good to have intimate friends and speak to them and sometimes to get it down in writing, have a good cry, or scream your rage and heartache into a pillow. There are plenty of therapeutic and spiritual tools and aids that are inadvisable to disdain. Even someone with psychotherapeutic training should not disdain psychotherapy if it concerns their own problems, and spiritual leaders should seek spiritual advice concerning their situation. Indeed doctors often neglect their own illnesses. And for those in the caring professions such advice can seem like that given to Jean-Gaspard Deburau, king of pierrots, who is said to have visited a doctor incognito when he was in a state of deep depression, and the doctor advised him to go to a pierrot show by Deburau to cheer him up.

At that time I did not seek the help of a psychotherapist, as my crisis was more spiritual than psychological in nature. Of course I spoke about it with my confessor and several close friends. I thought that on this occasion I would receive "help from on high," and I did receive it, particularly in the Holy Land. On the natural level, it was a great help that I could perform my service to students every day, both in church and in the university lecture hall. Fortunately I had not been denied for long the university environment that I need like a fish needs water.

■ MY FIRST TRIP TO ISRAEL in November 1992 was actually the third part of the "managerial training for bishops" that I referred to earlier. It consisted mostly of exercises in which a pleasant young bishop from Brixen, a friar with great spiritual depth who was also an excellent exegete of biblical texts, accompanied our bishops to places where Jesus pursued his ministry and trained his apostles. In meditations at the holiest places in the Holy Land, he tried to demonstrate "Jesus's style of human leadership." The horizontal component of the course, in which the bishops studied the rational organization of work, was now augmented by a vertical and spiritual dimension: it was an outstanding feat.

I already had by then a deep affinity with Israel and Judaism. For centuries Prague was an important center of Judaism. From my early years I read Prague's Jewish authors with great enthusiasm, particularly Franz Kafka, Franz Werfel, Max Brod, and Gustav Meyrink. Later I studied the Jewish philosophers Martin Buber, Franz Rosenzweig, Emmanuel Lévinas, and Hans Jonas, and later still— with a sense of great like-mindedness—I read the books of the rabbis Abraham Heschl and Jonathan Sacks. One of my favorite books is *Nine Gates to the Hassidic Mysteries* by Jiří Langer.

But there was one remarkable and totally unexpected meeting that opened up to me a truly personal attachment to the Jews and Judaism. It was sometime in the early 1990s. I had taken part with Czechoslovak bishops in talks with Polish bishops at the Bishops' Conference center in the Warsaw. Afterward we had to wait five hours at the airport for our return flight to Prague because of bad weather. Near us stood a group of American Jews who were traveling around Europe visiting Jewish sites and were now returning to Prague from

Poland. Suddenly an elderly bearded man—he looked a bit like Martin Buber or one of the Old Testament prophets—separated himself from the group and came over to talk to me. I don't know why he came to me of all people; my clerical collar must have told him what I was, and I was surrounded by bishops. He told me I was the first person he had spoken to in several days. A few days earlier he had visited Auschwitz, where most of his family perished, and it had been such a dreadful experience that since then he had been unable to speak or eat. He said he couldn't understand how his wife could just go shopping here. And with reproach in his voice he asked me, "What did you Christians do to stop something like that happening? When a piece of meat is burning, you can smell it all over the house. But six million Jews died here, and you didn't know anything?" He claimed that the roots of anti-Semitism and all those horrors were actually to be found in Christianity: "You didn't want us. You didn't want us as Jews. You thought that Judaism had no legitimate place after the establishment of Christianity." He spoke about it with pain and anger.

Not only did I know plenty of counterarguments, such as the church's help to persecuted Jews at the very least, and I also knew there was a fundamental difference between Christianity's anti-Judaism and the neopagan anti-Semitism of the Nazis. But at that moment I realized I must remain silent. But I was aware that he was speaking to me in a language full of pain, similar to that used by Job in the Bible. And suddenly I caught a glimpse of our shared history seen through his eyes. And I listened to him in that way. Then we sat next to each other throughout the flight and I went on listening to him. When we parted at the Prague airport, we hugged each other. He felt that I understood him and that I had taken his testimony to heart. It was such a powerful emotional experience for me that ever since I have felt duty-bound to speak out in Catholic circles against all forms of anti-Semitism and to support a positive attitude toward the values of Judaism. After all, in the words of Pope Benedict, Jews are truly "our fathers in faith."

In Poland, I once visited the former extermination camps at Auschwitz-Birkenau, a place sanctified by the pain and suffering of millions of Jews, and also many Christians, including several Czech Catholic priests. So-called post-Auschwitz theology, both Jewish and Christian, has been a significant inspiration for my own spirituality and theological thinking. I too have honestly sought an answer to the question, "Where was God at Auschwitz?" I have adopted the answers of two Jewish thinkers, Lévinas and Rabbi Kushner. First, God was there with his commandment "Thou shalt not kill!" And second, the right question is, Where was *humanity* at Auschwitz? When we shift our human responsibility onto God, we turn him into a screen onto which we project our wishes, our pain, our anger, and our moral indignation. "God on the captain's bridge," somewhere above the waves of our pain, hovering like a deus ex machina wherever we humans have created hell out of the world he entrusted to us, such a God has indeed died—and he certainly died for many as a result of tragedies, such as the world wars, Auschwitz, and the gulags. Such a god was a human projection.

I subsequently spoke on many occasions with the Prague rabbi and representatives of the Prague Jewish community. In the University Parish we have organized many meetings with Jews, and I am extremely pleased to note that not only is the younger generation of Christians not anti-Semitic, but they are actually philo-Semitic. Many young Catholics have a lively interest in the Hebrew roots of Christianity, and some of them have gained a liking for traditional Jewish music and Jewish dance as an expression of prayer. At Easter some Christians in their homes share in something like the Pesach Seder, at which the Eucharistic rite was instituted.

Over the years I have made the acquaintance of numerous rabbis, including the former rabbi of the Westminster Synagogue, Albert Friedlander; Rabbi Melchior, who held an important post in the Israeli government; and later, Rabbi David Rosen, who is an outstanding representative of Jewish dialogue with Christianity. For years I have been in contact with the Centre for Jewish-Christian Relations in Cambridge, which studies relations between Jews, Christians, and Muslims, where I was a visiting fellow in 2003. Together with the present archbishop of Prague, Dominik Duka, I took part in the founding of a branch of the International Council of Christians and Jews in our country, and we are both members of its board of honor. When I was awarded the honorary title "Man of Reconciliation 2010" at a Warsaw synagogue by the Polish Council of Christians and Jews in recognition of my services to Christian-Jewish dialogue, I was particularly moved by the fact that I was allowed to speak in a synagogue for the first time, and it was a synagogue in the middle of the former Warsaw Ghetto where horrifying events took place during the war.

But let us return to my visit to the Holy Land. Those ten days with Czech and Moravian bishops in the holy places was also a much needed vacation for me, as I set out for it completely exhausted. It was shortly after the stress I experienced at the Theological Faculty. In addition, I had only recently been through the habilitation process at two universities, in Prague and shortly afterward at the Pontifical Theological Faculty in Wrocław. I was successful in both cases, but it was an additional burden of course, and so I flew from Prague in such a wretched state that Archbishop Vlk told me later that he was worried whether I would actually cope with the trip physically. A really nice, friendly, and relaxed atmosphere reigned during those few days with the bishops, without the slightest personal tension. The bishops were also naturally happy to be relieved of their duties for a short time, and they were amazingly rejuvenated. I wish anyone who imagines the conference of bishops to be some power center of gloomy hierarchs could have shared those jolly moments and seen venerable bishops leaping around with balls on the beach. I realized that in spite of all my reservations, I liked them all very much, and they too have all come to know me well over the years, and they have learned to accept me the way I am.

But the visit was not just an ordinary vacation; it was a pilgrimage, and if it is taken seriously, a pilgrimage is always an opportunity for re-creation, a small step on a person's journey of renewal in the many levels of his or her being. The sacred places of the Holy Land truly have a healing power for believers of the three monotheistic religions, as well as for every spiritually aware person, of course. There was still all that aridity and darkness inside me, but contact with places like the Holy Sepulcher, Bethlehem, Nazareth, Mount Tabor, and many others brought light.

Recovery—even in the spiritual area—generally starts with the symptoms of the illness making themselves felt at maximum intensity, as if giving us the opportunity to enter into dialogue with the mystery of our pain. There were dark moments for me there too. I will never forget wandering alone one evening on the shore of the Sea of Galilee, in the place where Jesus summoned his apostles, and suddenly feeling very old. How terribly I had aged in the course of those years after the fall of Communism and the conflicts of the previous year. I was struck by an idea that Nietzsche expressed at some point: Jesus died too young. What conclusions would he have reached if he had grown old? What does he have to offer an old man? Suddenly Christianity seemed to me like something for young enthusiasts. Shouldn't I leave to others my net, my vocation of being a "fisher of people" for Christ? Wouldn't the coming phase of my life have more in common with the autumnal wisdom of the old Buddha?

I imagined that if Jesus arrived and appealed to me, like the apostles, to leave everything and follow him, it would arouse in me a great deal of confusion, even resistance. I was tempted to respond to this appeal of Jesus: "Lord, find someone younger. Let me stay sitting here. I'm not going anywhere. I'm tired and disillusioned. I've had enough."

On the shore of the Sea of Galilee I dragged all my pain and weariness out from the depth of my heart and entrusted it to the one who once walked through these parts. I begged him to draw my steps back to the footprints he once made in the sand of this shore once upon a time. On our return from Caesarea Philippi the next day, I mentioned this to Bishop Škarvada when we were alone together for a moment. He just laughed and said, "Perhaps the Lord will rejuvenate your heart again."

I didn't experience any dramatic "second conversion" there, but I did return "different" from when I left. After all, that's the point of a pilgrimage, isn't it?

ELEVEN

The Path of Politics, Challenge or Temptation?

The year that saw me cut my ties with the leadership of the Theological Faculty, 1992, also saw the death of Cardinal Tomášek, a man who had meant a great deal to me. My last meeting with Cardinal Tomášek forms a kind of triptych.

When I visited him at the end of July, he was in his bed and on the verge of death. "Father Halík is here," the nurse told him. He opened his eyes, smiled, and said in a surprisingly clear voice, "He brings good tidings!" Those were the last words I heard him speak. I said Mass at his bedside and passed a spoon to him with the Blood of Christ. Before leaving I placed his hand on my head and thus received his final blessing.

Bishop Škarvada telephoned me on the afternoon of August 4. "The cardinal has just passed away. The papal nuncio was with him. There is no one else now in the palace but myself and nuns. Can you come?" I helped him place the cardinal in the coffin, draft a press release, and send a telegram to Archbishop Vlk, who was then in

Switzerland. Then I said the first Mass for the departed in the chapel of the Archbishop's Palace, encircled by nuns. It was the first time I had pronounced his name in a different part of the canon.

A few days later I was the commentator for live TV coverage of the cardinal's funeral, direct from of the royal crypt of the cathedral. My memories of our various meetings in the course of the previous quarter of a century passed through my mind in succession like a film. The person being buried was more to me than just a church superior. I became aware of a strange coincidence: my father was born on June 30 and died on the night of August 4; the cardinal was also born on June 30 (two years earlier) and died on August 4.

When the coffin was being lowered into the tomb of the Prague archbishops, I had to switch the microphone off for a moment. I was ashamed of being unable to completely control myself. "What's happening? I can't hear you," came the voice of the operator from the studio. "It's OK, I'll continue," I replied after a moment, in a voice that was quite calm, and I added by way of explanation, "I loved him."

The evening after the cardinal's funeral, I realized that a lengthy phase of my life had now come to an end. I decided I would not stand for another term as secretary to the bishops' conference and that I would withdraw from those hierarchical circles, in the same way I had withdrawn from the Theological Faculty. In any case I had only undertaken that work as a bridge between the period when I was assisting Cardinal Tomášek and a time when a new hierarchy would be fully functional. Once more I had to ask myself where God was calling me to go and where my main place would be.

■ BETWEEN MY FORTIETH AND FIFTIETH birthdays enormous changes occurred in my life. On my fortieth birthday I happened to meet Father Reinsberg, who told me, "That's the best age for a man— no longer a young fool and not yet senile." Then he shared with me a very wise principle he had heard from a Jesuit: "Until you're forty, choose the company of the old, after that choose the company of the young." I had overshot by five years.

After leaving the Theological Faculty and the bishops' conference, I decided to continue working chiefly with students, as a university teacher and also as university chaplain. Wasn't it the students who had largely been instrumental in the events of November 1989? Didn't they deserve something in return? I devised a schedule over several months as a way of organizing the transition, and I nicknamed it jokingly "Operation Guardini." Romano Guardini is the person I model my life on: he was a philosopher of religion who lectured at a secular faculty while also being a university preacher and spiritual administrator. Through his lectures, preaching, spiritual exercises, books, personal interviews, and student vacation camps, he prepared a whole generation of high-minded and well-educated people, and he did much to bring about a lively dialogue between Christians and the cultural world of those days.

Operation Guardini was a success. Once more it turned out that those who had tried to do me harm had achieved the opposite, and the erstwhile dean of the Theological Faculty deserves sincere thanks. Even before the leadership of the Theological Faculty managed to formally expel me, the dean of the Faculty of Social Sciences offered me the opportunity to lecture externally as well as complete my habilitation there. I then accepted an offer of the post of associate professor at the newly created Department of Religious Studies at the Arts Faculty. My feelings on taking up my duties at the Arts Faculty were quite the opposite of what I had felt on joining the Theological Faculty. I was coming home to the environment in which I had studied and had spent the most inspirational years of my youth. The teachers at the faculty included many of my former fellow students, and the students were a colorful, responsive, and demanding public, in whose midst I am still very pleased to be. Most of my colleagues and students are people who have little in common with the church, but I have never had the feeling of being rejected a priori on account of being a Catholic priest. I have always been careful never to favor believers over other students, and if there happen to be some of my "parishioners" among my examinees, they know that I will tend to be more demanding of them than of the rest. I think the students appreciate the fact that I have accepted the rules of a secular faculty, and although I never conceal my views, a shallow apologetic approach is entirely alien to me. When expounding any opinion or religious system I try to be faithful to the way it understands itself. My return to the Arts Faculty, where I wanted to teach one day when I was still a student, was one of the natural stimuli that gave me a new lease of life.

On the threshold of my fiftieth birthday, however, a new theme appeared in my life story. For a long time I was not sure whether it was a challenge or a temptation.

■ I EMBARKED ON MY FIFTIETH BIRTHDAY WITH an early-morning silent Mass in a side chapel of Prague Cathedral. Then I went to the Church of the Infant of Prague to pray briefly. From there, in the company of my nearest and dearest, I headed to one of the cafés in Malá Strana for breakfast. I brought a handful of morning newspapers to the table with my coffee, and each of them, sometimes on page 1, carried the news that President Havel had proposed Tomáš Halík as his successor! The question they all asked was, "Will a Catholic priest be the next Czech president?" I wondered whether this could be a reaction to my conversation with Václav Havel on the popular radio show "Conversations from Lány." "A great start to my second half century, if it's true," I lamented sarcastically.

Scarlett and I had been invited to dinner that evening at the presidential chateau at Lány. Seated around the table were several of the president's close friends and colleagues. A few of them, as well as Havel himself, shared their memories of my father. On the way home, we got out of the car, and from the fragrant meadow behind the cemetery at Lány where T. G. Masaryk is buried, we watched the sun go down. Exactly half a century ago, on the eve of June 1, I had my first contact with the world outside my mother's womb. Is it true, what Freud writes, that the baby cries and screams in terror because birth is a trauma caused by losing the safety of the mother's womb? Is this anxiety at the unknown similar to the feelings with which people often leave this earth and are born into eternity?

We spoke about the custom in India for a man on his fiftieth birthday to leave his family and occupation and become a pilgrim. In Christian tradition this was done by Nicholas of Flüe, to whose hermitage in the heart of Switzerland I once made a pilgrimage.

Is the topic of the presidential candidature a sign that the world has encroached far enough? Does it mean I have reached this point and should now let go of everything and set off on a spiritual journey—even though it need not involve a secluded mountain chalet in the mountains? Scarlett tends to favor that option. Or does it, on the contrary, mean that I should bring the spark of the Spirit, which I was endowed with for my journey so far, to the life of the community, the polis? This need not mean, of course, that I should be a candidate for president. At the end of the well-known Buddhist story, the pilgrim returns from isolation to the marketplace of the world; in Christianity a similar idea can be found in the legends about St. Gregory.

Although on June 1, 1998, I did not think it feasible that I should stand as candidate for presidential office, I had a sense that the strange coincidence of the emergence of this topic on the very day of my birthday heralded something that I could not dismiss out of hand. What did it symbolize or presage for the years to come? That was a riddle I would be puzzling over for several years from that moment, at various different levels.

◼ WHEN I WAS INVITED TO TAKE PART in a dialogue with President Havel on the radio show "Conversations from Lány," I subconsciously suspected that the presenter would ask about this matter.

My name had figured among possible candidates for the future president of the republic several times in various opinion polls and surveys—in fifth, fourth, and once even in second place. The idea was voiced for the first time by Havel some two years earlier in reaction to a speech I gave introducing a book of his presidential speeches. On that occasion, everyone tended to regard it as a pleasantry. But it was reported in the newspapers and on the radio, and people started to stop me in the street: "Listen here, Mr. Halík, I'm not a believer, but I consider you to be a fair-minded and sensible fellow, and I'd very much like to have you as my president!"

When I started to get more and more reactions like that, I found it rather irritating and reacted to it with various witticisms prepared in advance. The last time I had wanted to be president was probably at the age of seven, shortly after I stopped wanting to be a polar bear. (Had some fairy godmother in recent years offered to grant one of those two childhood wishes, I would probably have found transformation into an animal more attractive.) After that I wanted to be a polar explorer, then an astronomer, before I eventually decided to become a writer and historian; that lasted almost until high school graduation, when it gave way to a desire to become a professor of sociology (like Masaryk) and, finally, a priest. The last two wishes had been granted, and in both those professions I was happy and content, so why should I now return to my childish notions and yearnings?

It must be pointed out that the role of the president in the Czech Republic has a very specific character, quite different from that in countries that have "presidential systems," such as the United States or France, or in countries where the president plays more of a ceremonial role. It was Professor Masaryk, above all, who lent the presidential role an exceptional aura, and Václav Havel drew on that tradition. As has been demonstrated in many surveys and opinion polls, Czech society wants a president who is not primarily a political functionary but a spiritual leader, above all, and a spiritual and moral authority.

■ WHEN I WAS PREPARING MYSELF for the radio interview with the president, I walked up and down the garden, agonizing over every aspect of the question I feared most: Would you be ready to stand as a candidate in the presidential election? At that moment, it was not a matter of whether someone would be willing to officially propose me and certainly not whether, or in what circumstances, such a candidacy would have a chance of success. Of course I could simply brush off the entire proposition as being totally improbable, particularly since in those days the president was elected by the deputies in Parliament, whose composition was unfavorable at that time. Although I realize that "miracles" occasionally happen in politics—precisely because I am a realist—I was fully aware that I had no financial or political backing and was confronted by a dark cloud of prejudice against the church. I also knew that although the constitution allowed a priest to stand for election just like any other citizen, from the church's point of view, and according to canon law within the church, I would have to request a papal dispensation (an exception for reasons of serving the public good, like Petr Pit'ha had received), or request temporary release from priestly duties or the priesthood, or, in extreme cases, request laicization (as the future government minister Daniel Herman did). Even in those cases the relevant church authority can cancel the suspension and enable the priest to work again in a parish after leaving politics; even in the case of laicization, ordination is "an irrevocable sign." Of course it was obvious to me that I would miss the altar enormously, and such a step would be a great sacrifice on my part, so I hoped that the Lord would not require it of me.

On the other hand, there were a number of reasons not to say an absolute no in advance. An absolute no only applies to situations that are in themselves morally wrong. I said that kind of no when the secret police tried to force me to collaborate with them. Agreeing to stand for president was risky, of course, and unusual but not immoral. If President Havel, who was best acquainted with the demands of presidential office and also knew me, expressed the opinion—which

I had already heard from a number of level-headed people—that I could hold that office with dignity and honesty, then, I said to myself, it would be irresponsible to say no out the outset, whatever the chances of success. Even if in the end I did not present myself as a candidate—which I still thought would be the likeliest outcome—the fact that the name of someone like me would figure in the campaign for a space of time would help enrich the discussion about the future president. It would not be confined to a narrow circle of predictable names of party officials. If it would help ensure that another interesting name might emerge from the world of culture or academia, so much the better.

In a democratic state the result depends on other mechanisms than the wishes of an individual. All I needed to do now was to decide whether it was a typical temptation by some "noonday demon" to divert me from my proper mission or whether it was a challenge from God. I decided to combine the technique of honest inner dialogue, which I had mastered as part of psychotherapeutic training, with the method of "distinguishing spirits," as used in Ignatian exercises, and which I considered to be the most valuable way of discerning God's will.

I started from what seems the most superficial element, the emotions, which nevertheless strongly affect our decision making. What feelings did the idea arouse in the deepest, most deeply buried, prerational levels of my soul? Those feelings were contradictory. Every guy wants to be president in some secret corner of his soul. But maybe it is more than just a question of arousing masculine vanity and ambition. In the Czech lands, mostly thanks to Masaryk, the presidential ideal corresponds to something extremely ancient in the gallery of Europe ideas, dreams, and myths—the Platonic philosopher king. On many occasions abroad I discovered that people esteemed President Havel above all because he was not a run-of-the-mill politician but managed to enrich the spectrum of statesmen with something distinctive—an ability to see and enumerate cultural, philosophical, and moral aspects of politics. Those who were aware that Masaryk already did something similar expected that this asset would remain the Czech presidential tradition's permanent contribution to European political culture. In view of my general disposition, it was scarcely conceivable that I would not find such an archetype attractive and appealing.

My second emotional reaction was unequivocally negative. I had recently come to the conclusion that as far as the external circumstances of my life were concerned, I had achieved everything I wanted. My scholarly and teaching activity at the university and my pastoral work with students as a priest all gave me a sense of satisfaction, usefulness, and being fully occupied as the right man in the right place. As an independent intellectual I could express my opinions in many ways, and in that role I was freer and more credible than any holder of political office. In recent years I had lectured and published a great deal abroad, so I was gradually becoming one of those "public intellectuals" who, on every possible occasion, are asked to express their opinion in forums at home and abroad, as well as in surveys, colloquia, TV debates, and radio broadcasts, or asked to sign various petitions or lend their support to some initiative or other. Moreover, I enjoyed taking an active part in exchanges of opinion across national and cultural boundaries—definitely more than a lot of things associated with discharging a political office. What did I lack? What could motivate me to abandon it all, everything that, since my student years, I had only been able to dream of and use up my energy, and quite a bit of my lifetime, arguing with Mr. Klaus, the prime minister, or others of his ilk? Why should I make myself a permanent target of tabloid snoopers? Why make myself for many people simply a screen on which to project either their need to idolize or (more frequently) their malicious need to vent their life frustrations and find a symbolic culprit or enemy? Do I need that? What could politics provide me? Money, fame, power: such things truly meant little to me. What I really needed, I already had.

I shifted from emotional to rational considerations: here further questions confronted me. What was society's real need, and how could I respond to it, or not? What could I actually offer? I tried for a moment to think about myself from a third person's viewpoint. Yes, I had "clean hands." Not that I had never made a mistake or was some kind of saint, but in my life it would be hard for someone to discover some political, financial, or sexual scandal that could open me up to blackmail. And perhaps it was fair to say that my "clean hands" held something of use: I had experienced quite a lot of things in my life, after all, and stood the test. My sympathizers could probably argue that Czechoslovakia's first two presidents, Masaryk and Beneš, were in the same profession as I was: they were both professors of sociology at Charles University. I wasn't "in politics," but I had already looked quite attentively over the shoulders of a couple of politicians and learned a thing or two thereby. But I also had a lot of characteristics that were not favorable: I found it hard to make up my mind about things, always seeing a lot of pros and cons at the same time. I am not thick-skinned, which a politician probably should be for the sake of peace of mind; I find it hard and painful to confront human malice and stupidity. When I receive rude and vulgar anonymous letters, what irks me is that I am sorry for the authors and I feel ashamed on their behalf; I am totally unable to communicate with ill-bred people. Someone in an exposed position, and the target of constant attacks, ought to be a lot more resilient than I was.

Then I came to the final area, spiritual considerations. There was one thing I had learned from years of Ignatian spiritual exercises: if some matter is such that of itself it is neither bad nor good and there are many reasons for and against, it is necessary to liberate oneself of all partiality and achieve what Ignatius calls "indiferentia," which is translated better as "inner freedom" rather than "indifference." To let go of it, as it were, and place it in God's hands. This is no smug passivity: acting according to what sober assessment tells us but having the capacity to observe things impartially and wait. Not craving for one or other alternative but also not fearing either of them. If we have inner calm and freedom, the right decision or solution will arrive in due course. Incidentally, not only the founder of the Jesuits but also the Zen masters say something similar.

After a few hours of such reflections, I was ready for the interview. I traveled to Lány and the anticipated question was indeed asked. I answered into the microphone, "At this moment I would say 97 percent yes, 3 percent no. I don't count on it, but I also don't rule it out. I could even imagine myself taking part in the election campaign simply in order to draw attention to certain values and make things a bit more difficult for the other candidates, and if someone else was elected it would not bother me too much." As my first election speech it was probably very weak, and most likely counterproductive, but I wasn't making an election speech, simply stating what I thought.

Václav Havel was asked the same question. I think he was probably unprepared for it and answered spontaneously. He said that in his view I would make "a fine president" but added that in view of the present disposition of political forces it would be highly unlikely that a candidate without strong links with a political party could succeed. He said the present parliament would tend to opt for some party big wheel or a harmless "octogenarian professor of Egyptology."

Sometime afterward—again in a TV interview and with the same "postscript"—Havel mentioned my name among those he might theoretically imagine as his successors. I expect the president had no idea how much his answer would complicate my life. For years after that I was always having to answer questions of this kind from someone. Representatives of two political parties approached me suggesting that I consider standing for president.

When, in 2001, I received an offer to be a visiting professor and fellow at Oxford University I welcomed it for many reasons, including the opportunity to escape the world of Czech politics for a few months. At Oxford, my love of university surroundings and academic work grew intense once more. A university career combined with pastoral care of students and independent public activity were what allowed me to feel I was in the right place. Thoughts of a political career ceased to worry me.

■ VÁCLAV HAVEL WAS SUCCEEDED AS president by Václav Klaus—Havel's antithesis. It would be hard to find two people with such contrasting political styles, political philosophy, value orientation, or character traits.

Of all my personal encounters with Klaus—including conflicts of opinion in front of TV cameras—the first of them is most strongly embedded in my memory. We first met at a TV studio in Brno on an evening discussion show, when Klaus was still prime minister. "Watch out," Václav Havel warned me—he had appeared with him sometime before on the selfsame widely watched show—"Klaus always arrives as a matter of principle at the last moment and immediately insults and denigrates the other participants in the debate. It's his style, he does it regardless of the circumstances." I was grateful to Havel for that warning. Five minutes before the show was due to start, when the entire TV crew was already very nervous, the prime minister entered the studio, having just flown in by helicopter from Prague.

"Halík—that's you, is it?" he said turning to me, having seen me for the first time in his life. "You're the devil incarnate! I've read all your articles, every single one! And I know that my greatest enemy in this country is not Miloš Zeman or the Communists but Halík and those moralists! But I intend to give you a hard time now." I laughed. "Fine, Mr. Prime Minister! I prepared two scenarios for this evening's show, a 'soft one' and a 'hard one.' If you've chosen the 'hard one' . . . " Klaus immediately changed his tone. "Oh, come on, it's a tennis ploy. . . . You have to put your opponent of their guard before the match, don't you?"

We then faced the cameras, and there followed quite an interesting ninety-minute debate about the state of society. At the end Klaus took a moment to insult the moderator of the evening's debate, but he invited me to dinner at a nearby pub. At one point the topic of the conversation shifted to Karel Čapek and Hermann Hesse: "You see, everyone says I am only interested in economics, but you and I can chat about literature! It's a long time since I've had such a pleasant conversation. Here's the direct telephone number to my secretary. We could meet again some time if you like."

It was a long time before I took him up on his offer. The president of Germany, Roman Herzog, had just invited representatives of the Czech Christian Academy and the Ackermann-Gemeinde, a Catholic organization for German-Czech reconciliation, to Berlin, to thank us for our contribution to Czech-German dialogue. I telephoned Václav Klaus, and when I told him I would have an opportunity to speak with the German president, he immediately invited me to the office of the prime minister. To a certain extent it was a replay of the previous scenario. "What was that I read in the bishops' letter about reconciliation between the Czech and the Germans? What reconciliation? Aren't you reconciled, then? I don't understand it!," he said to me by way of greeting. "Yes, I also had to explain to a lot of people why you criticized that document. I told them that you weren't opposed to the document but simply didn't understand it," I replied. "How dare you!," Klaus exploded. "I understand it only too well. It's you who don't understand!" But shortly afterward he calmed down and changed his tone as always when he could see his browbeating wasn't having the desired effect. The conversation then became quite calm and workmanlike and even had a humorous denouement. When his secretary entered to inform him that his next visitor was waiting, I said to her, "But the prime minister is in confession, you mustn't disturb us!" This time Klaus reacted obligingly, and he said to her, "Yes, it's very good, you should try it sometime."

When, in 1997, Klaus was forced to resign after a corruption scandal came to light involving fake sponsors of his party and almost the entire political scene, including his closest colleagues, turned against him, I was one of the very few who publicly came to his defense in the press. I expressed the view that he would prove capable of accepting the political responsibility and withdraw from politics to reevaluate and change his political style and that perhaps he would one day return to the scene as a real statesman. I was naive. Klaus didn't change. There is a story by Karel Čapek in which he differentiates between cleverness and wisdom. Cleverness is an attribute, while wisdom is a virtue.

That was the main difference between our first two post-Communist presidents. Klaus was clever, but Havel was wise.

"ADVENT. THE SUNDAY LAST OF ALL. Angels, wakening, start to call." Every year I used to recite this line by the poet Bohuslav Reynek during Mass on the fourth Sunday of Advent. However, on the fourth Sunday of Advent in 2011 my voice was shaking. On that day the angel of death awoke. Václav Havel had died.

What Masaryk had been for the generation of my parents, Havel was for mine: not simply a head of state, but a symbol of the values that we acknowledged, and for which we had worked, and of the hope we kept alive. And for me, in addition, he was a dear friend of many years' standing.

There was no time to mourn. I was invited to one TV or radio studio after another to reminisce about the president and assess his political and moral contribution to Czech society. The following Tuesday I said a requiem Mass for the president in the presence of his relatives, the rector of Charles University, the foreign minister, Karel Schwarzenberg, and many of my friends, Havel's former colleagues. But the church was above all packed with students.

My friend, the philosopher Václav Bělohradský, whose views often conflict with my own, wrote a column about notable funerals in Czech history. At the funeral of T. G. Masaryk in 1937, the Czechoslovak Republic was virtually interred with him: the Nazi occupation was approaching. When President Beneš was buried in 1948, freedom and the hopes of a postwar renewal of democracy were buried with him, after which came Stalinist terror. When we buried Jan Palach, we buried the hopes of the Prague Spring, and there followed twenty years of "normalization," the moral suffocation that was so damaging to the Czech character. Were we now burying with Václav Havel the hopes for renewal of democracy that people had in 1989? Would his funeral now be followed by a time of venality and corruption and arrogant political leaders devoid of moral scruples? Would Wojtyła's and Havel's great dream of a united and free Europe now collapse in the near future due to national selfishness? Were there people of authority on the European political scene capable of confronting these dangers?

The fears that could not be concealed I had expressed in my sermon at the requiem for Václav Havel. But immediately afterward I had recalled the moment in Beethoven's Ninth Symphony when suddenly there is heard, "O Freunde, nicht diese Töne!" But what would give us the strength to sing the Ode to Joy, the song that united Europe had chosen as its anthem?

Young people, who were not yet born when Havel first entered politics, streamed until late at night into the Church of St. Anne, where his coffin was displayed. The never-ending funeral procession proceeded through Prague to St. Vitus Cathedral, where his former fellow prisoner, Archbishop Duka, took leave of Havel, along with politicians from many countries of the world. Possibly only twice after the year 2000 was the death of one particular man covered by all the world's newspapers: when John Paul II died and when Václav Havel died. It was the day before Christmas Eve. The city's department stores, which every year are teeming with people at this time, stood empty. The country fell silent.

■ THE STATEMENT THAT VÁCLAV HAVEL repeated to the excited Czech public in the November days of 1989, at a time when he was known by only a small fraction of the population, was very simple: truth and love must triumph over lies and hatred.

What became Havel's election slogan, and then rapidly appeared on all the posters of the November revolution, has long become a favorite whipping boy of all political cynics and pragmatists as being the essence of what they regard as naïveté. Those of us who still claim allegiance to Havel's moral and political legacy, and try to further it, tend to be mocked as the "brotherhood of truth and love." The reality of the post-Communist world certainly does not resemble a battlefield in which the banner of truth and love waves victoriously over the ruins of the citadel of lies and hatred.

So did Havel's slogan simply express the naïveté of an idealistic dreamer who wandered briefly from the world of his plays onto the political stage? Or an even worse objection and suspicion creeps in: didn't his moralistic rhetoric actually conceal his real intentions, a lust for political power? Did Havel that time perhaps abandon the world of underground philosophical seminars and assent to the black-and-white populist division of reality into the evil empire and the promised land of freedom and present himself to people thirsting after a better future as a knight of truth and love? Did he promise them something he knew was unattainable?

From history we know how dangerous religious rhetoric can be in politics—dangerous for politics, for religion, and for the history of humanity. So is something else at play here perhaps? For thousands of years the terms *truth* and *love* were used as names for God.

The concept of truth has special meaning in the context of Czech religious culture. The presidential banner that was unfurled over Prague Castle in the final days of the dramatic year of 1989 in honor of the newly elected president Havel, bears the words "Pravda vítězí" (Truth Prevails). These words are a secular version of the famous Hussite slogan: Pravda Páně vítězí! (The Truth of the Lord Prevails!). For centuries Czech patriotism regarded Hus as a witness to the truth and a martyr to the truth. In Czech culture the word *truth* has similar authority to the word *ordo* (order, orderliness) in Latin culture, the word *shalom* (peace) in Hebrew culture, the word *raison* (reason) in French culture, the word *Wesen* (essence) in German culture, the word *sense* in English culture, and so on. These words are difficult to translate because each of them has its own "Sitz im

Leben"—a wider horizon of meaning, associations with a particular social or cultural context, which cannot be conveyed by a simple translation. *Pravda*, the Czech word for "truth," means far more than equation or conformity (*adequatio*) of thing and intellect, as the well-known scholastic definition has it. *Pravda* is something that one must answer for with one's life. That is why the Czechs chiefly regard martyrs as witnesses to the truth—from the saints of early Christianity to Hus and Jan Palach, as well as the victims of the two totalitarian regimes of the twentieth century.

So how are we to understand the statement about the victory of truth? Those witnesses to the truth are above all witnesses to the fact that truth is on the losing side in this world. Witnesses to the truth are among the defeated, the victims, those who lose—and in the end lost that which is of greatest value, their own lives. Or does the victory of truth become apparent solely in the fact that there are people for whom fidelity to the truth prevails over the fear of death, people who have shown that truth can be worth more to them than their own lives?

Those for whom the key to the understanding of life and the world is the story of Jesus of Nazareth were aware that only those who were willing to be losers in this world, to bear a cross, could "bear witness to the truth." And part of that cross is Pilate's cynical question: "What is truth?"

Truth is a dangerous word, and contemporary postmodern culture assents to the skepticism of Pontius Pilate. Havel's statement has been criticized on those grounds. Those who want to eradicate the question of truth (so that none should doubt the self-legitimizing sacrality of power) use clever arguments nowadays. They lay at our door that if we speak about truth, we are haughtily and arrogantly setting ourselves up as prescient *owners of the truth* and are in reality dangerous agents of totalitarianism, whereas they are defending freedom and democracy from us.

But these people are lying: we do not regard ourselves as "owners of the truth." We ask for the truth. And precisely asking for the truth has the capacity to undermine the monopoly of power, which the mandarins of politics rightly suspect and rightly fear.

I too am convinced—and have said and written many times— that to identify with Truth and profess to be an owner of the truth is the same sin as ceasing to care about the truth and joining the camp of cynics. Anyone who starts to regard truth as *his or her own property* has lost in advance the battle with cynical political power, not only physically and politically, but, above all, morally. At that moment "power confronts power" (and in the end it is impossible to tell them apart, like the people and the animals at the end of Orwell's *Animal Farm*), and the definite loser in that struggle is truth itself. Truth is a book that none of us has yet read to the end.

Lessing once wrote a beautiful sentence: "If God were to hold all Truth concealed in his right hand, and in his left only the steady and diligent drive for Truth, albeit with the proviso that I would always and forever err in the process, and to offer me the choice, I would with all humility take the left hand." TRUTH should probably stay in the hand of God; it is too big and also too fragile for our clumsy human hands.

So can truth and love prevail over lies and hatred? Probably not in this world, and yet this ideal must remain the object of our eschatological hope. "Things impossible for people are possible for God; nothing is impossible for God," is something we read in various parts of scripture. And this hope must revive again and again our search for truth and confront the temptation to despair.

I expect we will never definitively win the struggle with lies and hatred, stupidity and malice, corruption and violence. But we must never give up, right to our last breath.

Windows on the World

After almost twenty years of "vacation abstinence," my paths led me to all the continents
on planet Earth. Usually it was not tourism but
official travel, visiting professorships, or study
fellowships, although I would also find time to
visit local museums, galleries, and historical or natural sights, as well
as for meetings and long conversations with interesting people. My
memories of journeys beyond the boundaries of Europe, including
three trips to Australia, one to Canada, and sojourns in Morocco,
Burma, Istanbul, Vietnam, Hong Kong, and Taiwan, would fill an entire book. After the fall of Communism and the Iron Curtain, I suddenly had the possibility to visit the entire world, and I welcomed it
with enthusiasm, since I have always regarded travel as part and par-
cel of education.

As soon as the borders were open I took a vacation trip to Greece
with the Vasiluks and their children—my godchildren. It was a marvelous encounter with the cradle of European learning and also with
places that were dear to me from my reading of the New Testament.
In particular, I remember the moment we stood in the Areopagus in

Athens, and I had a mental picture of my favorite scene from the Acts of the Apostles, which took place there: Paul preaching at the altar to the "unknown God."

As part of that Greek pilgrimage we also visited the "monastic republic" on the island of Athos, that ancient center of Orthodox spirituality imbued with mystery and legends. It was not easy to reach by any means. Although I had a letter of recommendation from Cardinal König, I was obliged, as a Catholic priest, to have special permission from the ecumenical department of the Constantinople patriarchate, whose headquarters were in Athens. Only the male members of our group reached there, because, since time immemorial, women are banned from Athos. We visited several monasteries, even the less accessible, which hang like eagles' nests on cliffs above the sea, and we were accommodated in one of them. In the middle of the night monks and pilgrims are roused by a bell, and this is followed until dawn by an unending morning liturgy, which is very moving but also very alien to the Western mind-set. At a Russian monastery we talked to a monk who had been a Soviet soldier in Prague in August 1968; his experience probably contributed to his conversion. He left the Soviet Union soon afterward in fairly dramatic circumstances, and now he spends his time in a place that is so beautiful that we felt pangs of regret when we had to leave it a few hours later.

■ I THEN MADE THREE TRIPS IN QUICK succession to my beloved England, after twenty years' absence. First I took part in an international congress in August 1990 in the delightful surroundings of the English Benedictine monastery at Ampleforth. That congress was perhaps the first attempt after the fall of the Iron Curtain to enable Christians from Central and Eastern Europe to discuss freely with their Western counterparts and speak about their experiences in a Western environment, in order to come to a collective awareness that this part of Europe was no longer "the second world." While there I made the acquaintance of several interesting people from the East and the West. I particularly remember with pleasure my conversations with the English primate Cardinal Basil Hume, who was once the head of this monastery. One could see the enormous affection he felt for these surroundings. He was a true Benedictine and a wise and kindly man. He could have served as an illustration for Cardinal Newman's well-known definition of a gentleman. He was a man with a truly ecumenically open heart, who was recognized by non-Catholics as the most striking representative of British religious life.

On a recommendation from Cardinal Hume, I was then invited to an ecumenical colloquium at Windsor Castle, a residence of the British royal family. The entire surroundings and the spirit of the meeting were imbued with the purest essence of English culture, which was a balm to my soul. I was unpleasantly surprised, however, at the Windsor colloquium by the naïveté with which, for decades, certain leading representatives of the British Council of Churches took seriously various representatives of "Christian peace committees" from Central and Eastern Europe, who were actually agents of the Communist regimes, voicing Soviet propaganda. Even after the collapse of Communism, most of them were incapable of shedding their illusions, let alone admitting their failure to distinguish lies from the truth, although they had plenty of opportunities to ascertain the real state of affairs. It reminded me of the visit to Prague and Moscow by the well-known evangelist Billy Graham. He stayed at luxury hotels and let himself be led by the nose by collaborators and representatives of the regime, and in the end he issued a statement declaring that there was no persecution of Christians in Eastern Europe.

I went to England the third time to lecture at a conference at Cambridge University in the summer of 1991 marking the hundredth anniversary of the encyclical *Rerum novarum*. I had just returned from the Vatican, where I had become accustomed to a very formal and traditional Mass, but here I encountered for the first time, the distinctive style of American liturgy, as I concelebrated Mass in the Cambridge college chapel with Bishop Sullivan from America. It gave me a shock when, in place of the customary "osculum pacis," he gave me a "sign of peace" by thumping me good-naturedly on the back and exclaiming loudly, "All the best, Thomas! For you and for Czechoslovakia!"

I returned repeatedly to England in the subsequent years, and I had the honor of lecturing at the two most illustrious British universities, Oxford and Cambridge. I spent an entire term at Oxford in fall 2001. I have a very special attachment to Oxford. I will never forget the moment when I first came to the city as a twenty-year-old student during my 1968 vacation. I must point out that I do not believe in reincarnation, but at Oxford I had an intensive and thrilling sense of déjà vu—as if I were returning to profoundly familiar surroundings. I walked enraptured around the historical buildings of the university and could not overcome the powerful impression that I really did remember that that was the gate to the quadrangle, that was the way to the chapel and the dining hall . . .

Afterward I dreamed about Oxford countless times, and I still have dreams about it. However, at that time—August 19, 1968— I also experienced a very sad moment in the garden of Magdalen College. I came upon a bench with the inscription "Reserved for Senior Fellows" and realized bitterly that I was a foreigner from a Communist country, whose exit permit was about to expire. I had just one remaining five-pound bill in my wallet, and I was here for the first and maybe the last time. I must admit that I bitterly reproached the Lord at that moment: Why did you send me into the world at such a moment and in such a place? If I had been born here, in different circumstances, I might be a student at this university, and perhaps one day I would have the right to sit on this bench! And I was still unaware that at that moment tanks were already stationed on the borders of my country and in the course of the next forty-eight hours they would consign it to even greater isolation and subjection for the next twenty years.

When I returned to Oxford thirty-three years and three weeks from that moment as a visiting senior fellow I went to find that bench on the evening of my arrival, and I sat down on it with a feeling of enormous satisfaction, gratitude, and happiness. I also apologized to the Lord for my youthful reproaches and impatience. "There is a time for every purpose under heaven," we read in Ecclesiastes.

Fourteen years later I was invited to the ceremonial inauguration of a lecture hall named after me in an Oxford college, and the year after that, Oxford University awarded me an honorary doctorate, something I truly had never dreamed of before.

■ IN 1990 I MADE THE ACQUAINTANCE in Prague of the Chilean journalist Christiana Raczynski de Valdes, who conducted a lengthy interview with me for the daily *El Mercurio*. On her recommendation, I later received an invitation to lecture at the universities at Santiago de Chile and Valparaíso. I was there in August 1991.

The flight to Chile was extremely long, so I had two stopovers, in Madrid and New York. In the Spanish capital I was taken care of by my good friend from Rome, Monsignor Fernandez Martinez, who was then auxiliary bishop of Madrid. On the way there he gave me a tour of Madrid, and on the return journey we took a trip to Toledo for a few hours. I will never forget the moment when, on the way there, he suddenly stopped the car, and when we got out on an absolutely empty plain, where there was nothing to be seen for miles around but scorched grass beneath a cloudless sky in blinding sunlight, he told me, "Look. This is the landscape where the works of St. Teresa and John of the Cross came to fruition—this is the *nada*—nothing, nothing but the soul and God, parched soil and dazzling sun."

I flew from Madrid in the company of a Polish aristocrat and intellectual, Adam Potocki, with whom I subsequently lectured in the same university seminar. During our stopover in New York we saw on TV the attempted putsch in Russia, which led to the fall of Gorbachov, and after the putchists' failure, the rise to power of Boris Yeltsin. "This is finally the defeat of Communism in Russia and the beginning of the inevitable collapse of the empire," Potocki commented farsightedly.

It was confirmed for me on many occasions that the Poles are best informed about Russia and have the most realistic perspective on it.

Chile is not a very typical South American country. Chile and Argentina are sometimes called the "Britain of Latin America." I did not come across the sort of poverty that occurs in surrounding countries. I managed to do a bit of traveling during my stay in Chile and meet a number of interesting people. In addition to my lectures at the university, I gave a lecture on the problems of the post-Communist world for several members of the diplomatic corps and was able to talk to several economists, who, during the dictatorship of General Pinochet, had achieved a rapid revival of the Chilean economy, which had been damaged by the socialist experiments of the Allende government. My impressions of Chile were certainly one-sided to a great extent, as I moved in a milieu of extremely wealthy people with right-wing views. *El Mercurio* newspaper invited me to its family headquarters at a chateau deep in the Chilean countryside, which was surrounded by extensive orange and lemon groves. There was a private family cemetery there, as well as a private polo ground, and in the middle an exotic garden. And above it all loomed the snow-covered peaks of the Andes. In every room a fire burned in a hearth. During our conversation, the servants, who lived there in a kind of patriarchal coexistence with the owners' family, brought us one dish after another. The entire atmosphere was reminiscent of a historical film or a fairy tale. I recalled St. Paul's words, "I know what it is to have little, and I know what it is to have plenty," and I had to ask myself what effect it would have on me to live in such an environment. The gospel warns us that the eye of the needle is narrow, and wealth is a risky environment for the human soul. Would I be capable of being true to myself in such conditions and preserve my independent view of the world?

▌In 1995 I had the opportunity to visit two other non-European civilizations, which are commonly perceived as the extreme poles of poverty and wealth: India and the United States. It was my first major experience of the United States. At that time, I had no inkling that I would be returning frequently to the country during the next twenty years, mostly for visiting fellowships at American universities, the longest of which so far was a trimester at the University of Pittsburgh in summer 1999 and two semesters at the University of Notre Dame in Indiana in the fall terms of 2015 and 2017.

Shortly after the collapse of Communism, a travel grant was established with the help of several leading American foundations to assist people of the younger and middle generations with potential for intellectual or moral influence, particularly in the post-Communist parts of Europe. The object of such trips was to obtain "intensive experience of the United States," build a network of useful contacts in that country, meet with important people from one's field and from public life, and get to know something about American institutions and the American way of life. Grantees would also be given a certain amount of publicity in order to share something of their experience and achieve some sort of renown in America.

Almost every day involved taking a plane somewhere. I traveled from San Francisco to Charleston. As part of my sojourn I lectured about the experience of the church under Communism at seven American universities and colleges, including the Jesuit Fordham University in New York, Calvin College in Michigan, and Marquette University in Wisconsin. The program was physically strenuous and mentally demanding. I realized that those "future leaders" probably tended to be younger than I was. The schedule was precisely arranged from early morning to late in the evening. It started with a working breakfast, and afterward I generally had a lecture at a university or at some club, after which I would meet with interesting people from academe, politics, or the church.

In Washington I got to know a number of people from among present and former White House staff. My most interesting conversation was with Jeane Kirkpatrick, who had been U.S. ambassador to the UN and was one of the architects of President Reagan's foreign policy. At that time I had a certain sympathy for American neoconservatism, and I became personally acquainted with a number of its proponents, in particular, the "holy trinity" of Michael Novak, George Weigel, and Richard John Neuhaus.

The political scientist and theologian Michael Novak, a leading American theorist of democratic capitalism and recipient of the Templeton Prize, would later exercise considerable influence on certain circles of Czech society. He was a right-wing exponent of Catholic political and social thinking, who tried to bridge the tension between the American tradition of liberal conservative thinking and traditional Catholic social doctrine. Novak sincerely welcomed John Paul II's social encyclical *Centesimus annus*, and it was rumored that he and the Italian Christian-Democrat politician Rocco Butiglioni, among others, had done much to inspire it.

Michael Novak had a profound knowledge of political life in the United States. As an active member of Reagan's team with a particular focus on the promotion of human rights and a member of the board of Radio Free Europe, he had many close links with Eastern European dissidents and had a good understanding of our situation. He was not one of those Western thinkers who came to our country simply to preach to us and pity us; he was able to listen attentively to our experience. Novak was a most pleasant person. We subsequently met on many occasions in America and in my own country, where he lectured under the auspices of the Czech Christian Academy and at Prague conferences of Forum 2000. Although my perception of developments in the world and in the church, and my political opinions—particularly after Bush's unfortunate intervention in Iraq—later diverged considerably from those of the neoconservatives, our personal friendship did not diminish in the least.

I still regard my meeting in New York with the third member of the "holy trinity" of American neoconservative thinkers, Richard Neuhaus, to have been very useful. Unlike Novak and Weigel, he was previously unknown to me. Neuhaus was a Catholic priest, theologian, and leading adviser to the American episcopate and a number of politicians on matters to do with social teaching, political ethics, and international relations. He had undergone an interesting personal development, in the course of which his views had considerably evolved. He started off as a Lutheran pastor and close collaborator of Martin Luther King Jr., taking part in anti–Vietnam War demonstrations and other left-wing events. Then he underwent a religious and political conversion. He became a Catholic priest and prominent representative of right-wing thinking and a theorist of democratic capitalism. His ordination as a Catholic priest at the age of fifty-two was attended by several American cardinals and bishops. He was founder and director of the Institute on Religion and Public Life and editor in chief of the influential journal *First Things*, which subsequently published a number of my articles.

He was a very genuine person and an avid champion of New York. His apartment in the center of Manhattan resembled an artist's abode. He had a "writer's bunker" in the basement, with an enormous library. A short staircase led from it to a small courtyard with shrubs, sculpture, and a fountain, surrounded on all sides by the Manhattan skyscrapers. We spent almost a whole night there under the stars talking about many, many things. We interrupted our hours of debate at three o'clock in the morning, when he took me on a tour of the whole of Manhattan in a taxi. We ended up at the Republican Party's club near Central Station on Fifth Avenue.

I returned to the United States on many occasions. I particularly like to recall a visit in spring 2010 when I lectured at Harvard University and when Martin Palouš, who was then Czech ambassador to the United Nations, organized a presentation of my book *Patience with God*, at the UN headquarters in New York, with contributions by speakers from three continents: Archbishop Migliore, the Holy See's permanent representative at the UN; the Sudanese and Indian ambassadors to the UN; and the Japanese deputy to the UN secretary-general. In his toast at a gala dinner at the Brook Club—which betrayed the nostalgia for British culture of Americans in the past century—Palouš recalled how we had both been detained by the Czech secret police thirty-three years earlier in a boiler house, where he was employed as a boiler operator. On that occasion, we were both interrogated overnight, and while we were waiting together at dawn for the first tram on that chilly November morning, I said to him, "You'll see. One day we'll happily reminisce on this as we sit in comfortable armchairs by a warm fire with a glass of whiskey in our hand!"

◼ IN 1995, SEVERAL MONTHS BEFORE my first visit to the United States, I made a trip to India. I had long been interested in Eastern spirituality, so I happily accepted an invitation from Thomas George, an Indian Catholic priest and professor of religious studies at the University of Madras, whom I had met the previous year during a study fellowship at the University of Eichstätt. To my great surprise, he had shown me at Eichstätt an article I had written, along with my photograph, that had been published in an Indian journal. I had no idea that any text of mine had appeared in India; it was a translation from an American journal. My Indian colleague had been impressed by the article and brought it to Europe. He recognized me from my photo during lunch in the university dining room, and the outcome of our many conversations together was an invitation to a study fellowship in Madras and at a priestly seminary in Mumbai.

I flew to India at the end of January 1995. My stay in India got off to a rather dramatic start, because my plane arrived in Mumbai many hours late, and at the airport I discovered that all my baggage had been lost en route, and the person who was supposed to take care of contacts with all the other places in India was not waiting there to meet me. I was totally lost. Some strangers very willingly offered to help, but they soon turned out to be a gang of swindlers who preyed on tourists who were unfamiliar with the local language, currency, and customs. They took me—dog-tired after the extremely lengthy flight and interminable haggling at the airport—to a hotel, where they started to systematically fleece me. "A terrific start," I said to myself. "It can hardly get worse, so I can look forward with hope to the days and weeks to come."

At the close of day I managed to get from the hotel to the priestly seminary, where I received a cordial welcome. I got to know a number of interesting Indian Jesuits there, who helped me put together a detailed plan for my journey and telephone Madras. The next morning was Ekta Day, also known as Unity Day or Martyr's Day, the anniversary of the murder of Mahatma Gandhi. At the hour when the assassination took place, sirens sound and work is interrupted; people on the street stand still and hold each other's hands, thereby creating a huge symbolic chain across the subcontinent. I was standing at an intersection in the middle of Mumbai when it happened, and I found it extremely moving. That evening I lectured to a group of priests and seminarists on the roof of the seminary in the middle of a garden of ancient palm trees. The city beneath us was submerged in a purple haze, and above us vultures flew toward the nearby Tower of Silence, a gloomy structure, where Parsees leave their dead on a spiral staircase.

At the seminary I would concelebrate Mass with the superiors of the seminary. It included some elements of the Indian liturgy; for example, kissing of the altar was replaced by the typical Indian *namaskar*, bowing with hands brought together in front of the face. Many gestures and liturgical garments have been adapted to Indian customs and culture. I later celebrated Mass in Christian ashrams and Jesuit missions, where the adaptation of the liturgy is even more marked: one sits in the lotus position on the ground at an altar amidst an abundance of flowers, and joss sticks replace incense. On one occasion the main celebrant in a huge church invited me to dance a "Czechoslovak dance" during the Eucharist, as dance is a beautiful element of celebratory Indian liturgy. I excused myself, saying that the only dances I could recall from my dance lessons of long ago were the czardas and the tango, which I enjoyed dancing, but it was not the most suitable liturgical dance, nor was I sure that my archbishop would approve; they realized that in our country, alas, we do not express our joy in the Eucharist Christ by dancing.

I stayed in India for about another month. Almost every day I took a plane and crisscrossed the country, meeting many people. Indians were often shocked by the number of places I had visited and also by my lifestyle. When I told them my program, they would react somewhat disapprovingly: "You can't mean you're flying off tomorrow at 16.40. You're here now, so stay here a day, a week, or a year, maybe, and when you grow tired of it here, then you can move one. You can't be doing something all the time. You never stop working! A human being can't work the whole day like an animal. It is good to work for a while in the morning, but in the afternoon it is better to sleep and enjoy the peace."

I stayed at Christian monasteries, mission stations, and ashrams and at several Buddhist monasteries, and I also visited a center of interfaith dialogue. All in all, I came away with a very good impression of my meetings with the local Catholic church. In parts of India they truly live in a manner that recalls the early Christians, particularly with respect to solidarity. I remember how in one town I telephoned the local bishop and went to pay a courtesy visit. He was an exuberant, very dark-skinned man, who immediately asked where I was staying. When he heard I was at a hotel, he was very cross: "A priest staying at a hotel? Don't you realize the bishop is your father? As long as you are staying in this town you will live in my house and eat at my table. Or don't you recognize me as your bishop? Take a rickshaw and fetch your things here straightaway!" He then sent me to the next bishop, and so it continued. Most of the bishops considered it the natural thing to invite a priest to stay with them, and the same applied to priests. I once arrived in the middle of a mealtime and was about to excuse myself and leave, but it turned out that the bishop regularly took lunch with all the priests of the town and its surroundings, and there was always a place left empty next to the bishop for a chance visitor.

One evening, the bishop in the state capital of Goa, where there are lots of historical sites from the time of Portuguese colonization, took me to his library to identify the European saint whose Baroque statue had stood for centuries in the bishop's study. I had to smile: standing there, with a halo of five small stars around his inclined head in friendly greeting, was our very own John of Nepomuk.

At Jaipur, the "pink city," the local priest asked me to deputize for him at an Ash Wednesday Mass at a girls' school on the outskirts of town. I made the trip on the crossbar of a cycle rickshaw. At first we passed cars, but soon there were only bicycles, rickshaws, people on horseback, then only elephants, and then every kind of domestic animal ran past us, and on top of that, a dust storm started to blow. I arrived at the school soaked to the skin and covered with dust. I changed my clothes and started to celebrate a Mass in English for little girls with chocolate-colored skin in school uniforms. I had to make changes to the sermon I had prepared on the way there; when I started to talk about fasting, I realized to my shame that many of them had never had a proper meal in their lives. Since then, every time I distribute ashes on Ash Wednesday I remember making the sign of the cross with white ash on chocolate-brown foreheads, as I looked into their beautifully shining eyes and said slowly, "Remember, man, that you are dust . . . "

The Catholic church in India has systematically focused on education for a long time now. It has created a network of schools attached to parishes and missionary centers, which are open to all children, regardless of religion or social class. The church also takes care of the training of priests. Candidates generally enter seminaries after attaining a bachelor's degree in another subject, such as English literature. At Goa I stayed at an institute that young priests attend for a year of further education after completing a year of parish practice. On the weekend they serve as chaplains in their parishes, and from Monday to Friday they take part in courses that often comprise practical pastoral training, and the theoretical component concentrates on deficiencies that the novice priests identify when starting their practice. On my travels across India I also visited several Christian centers, where Catholics have joint meetings with believers of other faiths. Occasionally they even celebrate together the festivals of a particular religion and thereby get to know each other better. Indian Muslims, Hindus, and Buddhists particularly enjoy celebrating Christmas, the birth of Christ, with Christians, because they all have great respect for Jesus. As they are relatively few in number—although 2 percent of the Indian population is still an enormous number of people—Christians are perceived as a group that does not present a threat to anyone. They are therefore able to create a platform where Muslims and Hindus are able to meet, although otherwise they treat each other with hostility in India. These were modest beginnings, however, and much courageous and responsible theological work needs to be done in order to overcome mental barriers dating back millennia. My positive impressions were later somewhat tempered by news of violence committed against Christians in various parts of India by believers of other faiths.

I visited Hinduism's holiest site, Varanasi, on the banks of the Ganges. I stayed with the local Catholic priest, who accompanied me and two Dutch priests before daybreak to the Ganges, where he gave us a lengthy meditative talk about the place where death is transformed and people undergo purification. "This is a holy place," the priest said. "There are two holy places: Varanasi and perhaps Rome. This is a holy river, which has been visited by millions of people in the past millennia, who come here with an awareness of sinfulness and a need for purification. This is a place of death, to which millions of people have come to die in the belief that through here they will pass to redemption. This is a place of tolerance, which Hindus and others come to—rich and poor, healthy and sick. This is a place of silence: the basis of all reality is silent. Words are simply imitation."

We saw Indians who came with small lamps while it was still dark to take a ritual bath, and also those who were bringing their dead and burning their bodies. At first we were alone, but then people started to arrive one by one and then in the scores and hundreds, until by dawn the entire shore—tens of kilometers—was full of little flickering lights, like swarms of fireflies. The other—accursed—shore was empty, without a single light or living being.

When the first rays of the rising sun could be seen, we embarked on a punt and sailed along the holy river, shrouded in a mist from which emerged scenes taking place on the shore, now occupied by tens of thousands of pilgrims. The Indian priest pointed out to us with emotion three windows behind which there lived for a long time Raimundo Panikkar, a Catholic priest of Indian and Spanish origin, who was a remarkable and controversial philosopher of religion. "Panikkar is a genius like Teilhard de Chardin. It will take a hundred years for mankind to understand him," the Indian priest said with great reverence. I heard many people in India talk reverentially about Panikkar, even his former bishop, although the priest had long since de facto parted company with the church. I made Pannikar's personal acquaintance in Prague, when he attended the Forum 2000 at my invitation.

We alighted from the punt and went to take breakfast with the Little Sisters of Jesus, who, according to the tradition initiated by Charles de Foucauld, live as the poorest among the poorest. In that miniature rooftop courtyard between the entrance to a small shared chamber with three mats and an even smaller chapel with a view of the Ganges, I felt an emotion like I had felt many years before at Assisi on the spot where St. Francis composed his Canticle of the Sun. Rarely in this world have I been aware of so much inner light, peace, and joy.

My journey to Bodh Gaya, where the Buddha attained enlightenment, was very complicated. I traveled there from the Jesuit college at Patna on the frontier with China and did not heed the advice of the fathers there to buy a first-class ticket. The cheaper second-class accommodation meant that I first hung for almost two hours in a cluster of people gripping the outside of the train door with one hand. Dozens of people traveled on the roof of the car. I then managed to penetrate the press of perspiring bodies inside the car, where vendors were constantly passing among us and cute little Indian children danced on our heads. Then I found accommodation at a poor little parish at Gaya and traveled to the holiest site of Buddhism by bus and rickshaw.

It was getting dark when I sat down in meditation beneath the tree where "Lord Buddha"—as he was called by the Little Sisters of Jesus with whom I had supper—received enlightenment. When I opened my eyes it was already dark. All around shone hundreds of little lamps, and I bowed with reverence before the light that illuminated the Buddha's teaching in the hearts of so many people.

The British historian Arnold Toynbee wrote that when historians come to evaluate the twentieth century, they will remember it not for the technical achievements, the wars, or the conflict between capitalism and socialism but as the moment when Christianity and Buddhism finally made contact. I visited Buddhist monasteries at several places in India and Nepal and spoke at length with monks there. One encounter started in a very comical manner. I had been walking around the ancient rock temples and monasteries at Ajanta, one of the most interesting archaeological sites in India, in the company of a group of shaven-headed Buddhist monks in saffron robes. After a while the monks approached me and asked if they could take a photograph of me with them. The purpose of their request seemed obvious to me at that moment: We'll have some fun back at the monastery when we show our brother monks the oddball we came across: this bearded fellow, in a T-shirt and jeans! We started talking, and I learned they were young monks from Thailand who were studying economics, political science, and psychology at the university in nearby Aurangabad, so as to use this knowledge to the benefit of their country. When I told them who I was, their first question was, "Why did you separate from the Slovaks? What is Václav Havel doing?" I felt ashamed at how little we know about Thailand.

They invited me to dinner—I was also staying in Aurangabad with the local Catholic bishop, a charismatic healer—and in the course of it a very interesting debate unfolded. First we talked about Asia's political future. Like the Indian Catholic bishops, and many intellectuals with whom I later spoke in New Delhi, they anticipated dramatic force-field change in the world when China gets rid of its Communist regime and starts down the road of economic prosperity and superpower status in the world. Then we dealt with spiritual matters and interreligious cooperation. "You Catholic priests are celibate like us, aren't you? That is very good for spiritual life!," they told me.

Again and again I have ascertained that Buddhist monks often have a rather ironical attitude to the popular form of Western Buddhism and the Europeans who go around with shaven heads and play at being Buddhists. Generally they have much greater respect for those who are categorically rooted in their own religious tradition. I have even heard of masters of Zen meditation who sent Europeans home to read Meister Eckhart and St. Augustine first; Thomas Merton speaks about it in his memoirs. People who don't have a spiritual home anywhere and float in a mist of sweet-sounding clichés, or flit from one tradition to another, cherry picking, do not build any spiritual bridges. Am I in the position of God to pass judgment on different religions, including the winsome assertion that all religions are equal? All I can say is this is my home, here are my roots, this is the path I have followed, and I want to be faithful to it. At the same time, however, I look at your path with respect and interest, and I don't rule out the possibility that we have something to learn from each other for mutual enrichment, without denying our own identities.

Originally I planned to travel as far as Shrinagar in Kashmir. Instead I stayed in New Delhi, where I was due to meet with the philosopher Ramchandra Gandhi, the grandson of Mahatma Gandhi, but we just missed each other, as had previously happened in Prague. Our planned meeting finally took place on the third attempt, several years later at Caux in Switzerland. In Delhi I stayed at the secretariat of the Indian Catholic Bishops' Conference, where they strongly warned me against traveling to turbulent Kashmir. So on their advice I changed my travel plans and flew to the neighboring country of Nepal for a few days.

I stayed at a Jesuit residence in the capital, Kathmandu. Sir Edmund Hillary had lived in the house before he climbed Mount Everest, and his friend, the Jesuit superior, who was linked to him by radio, broadcast from that house the news that the first man had set foot on the "roof of the world." The local community consists chiefly of American and Indian Jesuits, with whom I had splendid rapport, and I would spend most of the night in their wonderful library. In the dining room they had a large photograph of John Paul II embracing the Dalai Lama, and they highly commended Václav Havel for having invited those two great religious figures to our country.

The Jesuits arranged for me to fly over the Himalayas in a small fourteen-seater plane. We came very close to the peak of Mount Everest, through which the Indo-Chinese frontier passes. Nepal is a unique synthesis of Nepalese, Chinese, and Tibetan culture. I felt greatly at ease in the Tibetans' monasteries. I have admired their culture for years, and I always express support for this remarkable people's struggle for freedom from Chinese domination.

While with the Nepalese Jesuits, I met a remarkable young Catholic priest from Romania. He was originally a mathematician, and among other things he was an excellent pianist and extremely gifted at foreign languages. After ordination he was appointed university chaplain. When his students kept asking about Buddhism and Eastern spirituality, he sensed that he could not go on giving them "secondhand" replies. He sold his piano and computer, asked his bishop for a two-year vacation, and set off for India on a study trip. He had worked in the houses of Mother Teresa in Kolkata but was soon confronted by the bureaucracy and open hostility of certain Indian institutions. A local official, a representative of allegedly unbelievably tolerant Hinduism, openly admitted that he was deliberately frustrating the activity of Christians in India. He said the poor people whom Mother Teresa served deserved their poverty because of sins in previous lives, and they were supposed to redeem themselves by suffering. Attempts to help them simply "spoiled karma." Well, I suppose every religion has its "fundamentalists."

When they refused to extend his residence permit in India, the Romanian priest moved to Nepal and was studying Buddhism under the guidance of the Jesuit fathers. "Everything they told us at the seminary and theological faculty about Buddhism was a lie. They said that they are actually atheists, but just look at the way Buddhists pray. Have you ever seen such fervor and such a level of contemplation among us Christians?" And he was always taking me from one sacred site to another. I could see he was up to his ears in love with Buddhism. Should I, as his brother in faith, disprove it and prove to him the superiority of our faith? I pondered on this at night for a long time, and I prayed. But one cannot dissuade from loving. It was important for him to pass through this phase of his journey in order to reach awareness, not just by cold reason but also with an eager heart. I was confident that this path he had taken, led by his eagerness for the truth, could not end in any other way but in the embrace of Christ, and perhaps he will see the beauty of his Lord in new colors and new dimensions, enriched by this spiritual experience. He was neither apostate nor defector, and he had not gone astray. There was a pure flame in his eyes. After all, he was someone who had "tried out the ways" instead of asking the way. I believe that the one who is the Way will not allow people like that to lose their way.

■ MY SUBSEQUENT JOURNEYS TO ASIA took me to Thailand, the Republic of China on Taiwan, to Myanmar, and twice to Japan. Later still I visited Vietnam and Hong Kong, where the first translation into Chinese of one of my books was published in 2015.

I first flew to Japan at the beginning of August 1998, two months after my fiftieth birthday. I traveled from Osaka Airport straight to the sacred Mount Hiei above Kyoto, which is covered in monasteries that preserve the oldest and most exalted form of Japanese Buddhism. I was accommodated in the small hermitage of one of those monasteries. On my arrival, the superior of the monastery welcomed me with typical Japanese courtesy: "I hear that your president is seriously ill at this time. Would you mind if we prayed together for him his evening?" I naturally assented, as I knew that Václav Havel had great esteem for the teaching of the Japanese monks of Mount Hiei. That evening I took part in a ceremony in the main temple, during which—as my invaluable guide explained—the celebrant symbolically cast the Czech president's illness and suffering into a blazing fire and burned them. That same night I watched the latest CNN news on the internet. They mentioned that Havel had been in a life-threatening medical condition but was now in an Austrian hospital, and he was alive.

A few months later I visited Václav Havel in Prague, and because there was mention of his wife's impending visit to Japan, he told me—although I had not previously related to him any of my experiences in Japan—that when he was in that critical condition in the Austrian hospital he had had a weird dream in which he was in some Asian prayer room surrounded by Buddhist monks and that for some time after he emerged from narcosis, "Asian motifs" worked their way into his normal perception. It was not hard to calculate that his critical condition more or less coincided with the ceremony I mentioned above. Sometimes the strangest things do happen in monasteries, both near and far.

I ARRIVED IN HIROSHIMA ON THE EVE of the anniversary of the atomic bombing. That evening, at the local cathedral, I concelebrated a Requiem Mass for the victims of the explosion, together with Japanese bishops and many priests from all over the world. That Mass, and the tour of the Hiroshima monument, had a profounder effect on me than I expected. I had an interesting conversation with the bishop of Hiroshima, followed by a discussion with my friends among the Buddhist monks of Mount Hiei, which lasted until the early hours of the morning. I could not help smiling when I viewed the scene with detachment: a bearded Catholic priest in summer attire surrounded by four Buddhist monks in traditional robes, seated at a café table in the Stardust bar on the fifty-second floor of a modern luxury hotel. In front of us we had glasses of Pilsner beer, and around us couples danced. Through the roof window could be seen a dark sky with myriad stars, while through another window we could see far below us the lights of modern Hiroshima. We spoke about the theme of suffering in the Christian theology of the cross and in Buddha's teaching about redemption, as well as about the attitude to nature in both spiritual paths. We did not part company until the stars started to grow pale. If there is some ear that listens over the millennia to the occasional conversations between the disciples of the rabbi of Nazareth and the Master of Bodh Gaya, then let it judge whether I am right in thinking that we made not inconsiderable progress along the path of understanding that night.

Joint religious services of representatives of all religions operating in Japan were to start the next day at 5:00 a.m. These would be followed by a very long secular assembly, after which, according to the program, I was to give to a short speech before lunch for the religious representatives.

I had a brief and troubled sleep. When I awoke I felt as if I had fallen into an abyss of light. I went out onto the hotel room balcony, and the sun was rising right in front of me. Beneath me lay Hiroshima. It was August 6, the Feast of the Transfiguration.

As I gazed at the rising sun—the eloquent symbol of Japan—several images and associations crossed my mind. "Brighter than a thousand suns"—that sentence from the Bhagavad Gita came to Oppenheimer's mind when he first witnessed an atomic bomb explode. "His face shone like the sun and his clothes became white as light," says the reading for the liturgy of August 6, the Feast of the Transfiguration of our Lord on Mount Tabor. Japanese Christians were possibly meditating on that very sentence on their return from early-morning Mass fifty-three years before, just before they were engulfed by "fire from heaven." The previous day in the cathedral I had thought so much about them and their lives that were cut short in an instant. It was as if they were visiting me now with the rays of the rising sun.

I prayed the Dawn Prayer from the breviary and briefly read the gospel reading for that feast. And then another image came to my mind: "And behold, two men were conversing with him, Moses and Elijah." An odd thought struck me: were only those two there with Jesus?

Two days before, in a small store near the station in Kyoto, I had bought a colored picture depicting a fictitious conversation between the Buddha, Confucius, and Lao Tzu. That scene had come to mind a couple of times during my lively disputation with the monks the previous night, and I think it also flickered in my dream. It was no wonder, then, that it now became entwined with the image that emerged from today's gospel, like another layer. Yes, Jesus converses before the gaze of the apostles with the long-dead Moses and Elijah, and it dawns upon the trio of fishermen what they were probably incapable of describing in words what only an image enables them to see. Peter, John, and James, as the first of the Twelve, are to discover that Jesus is more than just a "good master." In his face shines the luminous cloud of the fullness of God's presence, which once shrouded Mount Zion, which accompanied the Ark of the Covenant on the journey through the desert, and which filled the temple when it was to be consecrated. God's radiance similarly shone from the face of Moses after his encounter with God, and the sparks of that fire ignited the hearts of the prophets. Jesus is the key to the Law and the Prophets; he is the way to a new and fuller understanding of Moses and Elijah. He is no lesser authority than the two greatest authorities of the Jewish world: that is the message of Mount Tabor. He did not come to disown them, however; he converses with them. Fulfillment of the Law and the Prophets happens in dialogue with Jesus—and we can only fully understand Jesus's mission, if we too enter into conversation with Moses and Elijah, if we perceive him together with them, in their company. They converse, they understand each other—and they *mutually interpret each other*. The deeper meaning of the Law and the Prophets lies in their openness to the Word, which Jesus is. And that Word cannot be properly understood when it is taken out of the context of Judaism.

The gospel of the Feast of the Transfiguration does not need to diminish Moses and Elijah in relation to Jesus. They conversed with him and spoke about his death. The text indicates that it is they who are communicating something important to him. In light of this scene from the Gospels, later Christian depictions of the synagogue as a blinded woman with bandaged eyes, which we know from the portals of Gothic cathedrals, seem absurd and insulting. Moses and Elijah, the exalted pillars of Jewish tradition, are Jesus's partners in dialogue on Mount Tabor; the dialogue of mutual respect between the disciples of Jesus and the disciples of Moses should never cease. I am glad that many theologians and several living spiritual movements in our day have accepted as a "sign of the times" and a call from God the need to renew a deep and perceptive conversation between Christianity and Judaism.

But doesn't the scene from Mount Tabor lead us still further, beyond the horizon of Judaism? It would seem that the Greek fathers of the church already dared to take a further step into the depths of this mystery of dialogue across the frontiers of the ages, when they understood and accepted Plato and other philosophers of antiquity as partners in a "conversation with Jesus." What Moses was to the Jews, Plato was to the Greeks, the holy fathers maintained. In their view, the ancient philosopher paved the way for the Christ, and the Christ was their fulfillment. Anyone familiar with the history of Christian thought knows the importance of the role played by the dialogue between the Christian faith and the "pagan masters"—the ancient philosophers and Hellenic culture as a whole. Admittedly the first generations of Christians preferred to die in the jaws of wild beasts rather than sprinkle incense on the altar of the state cult of Rome, but the beginnings of Christian art in the Roman catacombs testify to the fact that at the same time Christians—probably the same ones—used a whole range of "pagan" symbols to articulate their faith, and they did so with great inner freedom and as something quite natural. The whole of patristic literature is interwoven with references to the culture, mythology, poetry, and philosophy of antiquity. If the Christians in those first centuries had been afraid to open themselves to the culture and spirituality of their day, Christianity would probably have remained an insignificant sect on the fringes of Judaism and would never have become the spiritual and moral current that transformed the cultural face of Europe and of a large part of this planet, to a greater degree and more permanently than any other teaching.

On their famous missions to Asia, the Jesuits did not hesitate to accept Confucius and other sages of the East as witnesses to the truth, and they were even more accommodating to local spiritual traditions than Paul was at the "altar to the unknown god" on the Athenian Areopagus. Christ in the dialogue of cultures and spiritualties is by no means a wild novelty of the postmodern era and globalism but the legacy of the entire Catholic tradition of Christianity—catholic in the most powerful and profound meaning of the word. My daybreak vision at Hiroshima—Christ in dialogue not only with Moses and Elijah but also with many who symbolize spiritual paths remote from Europe—was not something that a Christian should find astonishing or offensive. What was astonishing was the intensity and exceptional urgency with which that image penetrated my inner world. As if I had heard: enter more deeply into the cloud of that transformative mystery; take part in that conversation between spiritual traditions; help to create and promote space for that dialogue.

The sun now stood high above the horizon. I managed to hastily note a number of ideas that coursed through my head and heart before washing and dressing and joining the brightly colored crowd of Buddhists, Christians, Shintoists, Hindus, Jews, and Muslims that was moving toward the place where the death-dealing bomb dropped fifty-three years before, in order to pray together for the healing of the world.

■ I HAVE VISITED THE AFRICAN CONTINENT four times. I was twice in North Africa and once in the Republic of South Africa—areas that were relatively closest to our own culture—and once in Angola, albeit only briefly at a university. I have the feeling I have yet to penetrate the true heart of "black Africa."

My first African journey took me to Egypt. I spent the entire first week in Cairo. During the day I visited Muslim and Coptic historic sites and walked around that immense city, in which one cannot fail to notice, in addition to the monuments of the past, the dreadful sea of dirt, chaos, and poverty. My meetings and conversations with Muslim and Coptic theologians and intellectuals mostly took place in the early evening. During an opulent dinner in the luxury apartment of a Muslim representative to Europe, who spent most of the year in Paris, the discussion with the clergy present, who included the vice president of Al-Azhar University, chiefly concerned possible cooperation between Muslims and Christians in the field of social ethics. It was only at the end of the evening that I managed to steer the conversation toward theological and philosophical matters and the comparison of Muslim and Christian mysticism.

At an audience with the Egyptian minister for religious matters, I could not help feeling the minister was mostly seeking to use the meeting for political and propaganda ends. So I wasn't too surprised when, at our embassy the following morning, I was shown an article from the leading Egyptian daily, which stated that in conversation with the minister I had expressed great satisfaction with his policy vis-à-vis the Coptic Christians.

At the headquarters of the Coptic "pope" Shenuda, I had a lengthy conversation with his representative for theological and interreligious questions, Archbishop Bishoy. That imposing and self-assured man told me categorically that the accommodating attitude of Vatican II toward non-Christians was a betrayal of Christ. Valid baptism was an unconditional requirement for salvation, he said, and it was not possible to make any concession regarding that truth even in the interests of love. God has determined in advance that those who have not received the grace of baptism, for whatever reason, and in whatever period of history or culture, are destined for damnation.

Even the meeting with the head of all Sunni Muslims, the Great Mufti of Egypt and Grand Sheikh of Al-Azhar, for which I had made the lengthiest preparations, turned out to be fairly formal. During our conversation, the Grand Sheikh consulted notes that were probably prepared by his advisers. He was informed that I had spoken in favor of the construction of the first mosque in our country and thanked me for my support for "the return of a mosque." In response to my statement about how important it would be for him to meet with John Paul II at Mount Sinai in the jubilee year of 2000, as proposed by the pope, he replied simply: Inshallah—we shall see; if it is the will of Allah. Of all my visits to religious representatives in Cairo, the most cordial was breakfast with the papal nuncio, a jovial elderly Roman with a wise and kindly gaze and an abundance of useful advice and witty comments.

On the day after we arrived in Cairo, I was taken to the pyramids by my oldest colleague from the Arts Faculty of Prague University, a professor of Egyptology, who initiated me into the rare discoveries of Czech explorers. He noticed that my gaze kept shifting to the desert and that my questions focused on the ancient story of the Jewish people's migration from the Book of Exodus. He proposed that we make a trip to the Sinai Peninsula the following weekend. We would spend the night in one of the oldest and most memorable monasteries of Christianity, the monastery of St. Catherine, and then we would climb Mount Sinai together. He would also take me to some old Coptic monasteries in the desert, and if I liked, he would take me on a day trip deep into the desert, where there is nothing to be seen in any direction but endless plains of sand, and he would leave me there to meditate, in the hope that he would return for me with his jeep before nightfall. Naturally I agreed with everything immediately, without knowing at that moment that that single day in the desert would become my most striking association with the word *Africa*.

At the end of the first week we climbed Mount Sinai together. The ascent was rather demanding because of the heat, and we had to hurry in order to be back at St. Catherine's monastery by nightfall. As we walked up the stone steps of an ancient pilgrims' stairway, I meditated on the Ten Commandments with sweat on my face; and on the return journey, the scenery of Elijah's hermitage, with a little lake and a broad vista of the surrounding landscape through rocky gorges, imprinted itself forever on my heart.

For my "day in the desert" I chose the liturgically most suitable day of my remaining time in Egypt: Ash Wednesday, the beginning of Lent, the time of repentance before Easter. The sun did not beat down so mercilessly that day, and a breeze blew from deep in the endless desert, gently ruffling the sand. I was surrounded on all sides by the desert, the setting of God's great trials, the site of the forty-year wanderings of the chosen people, the place where Jesus fasted for forty days, and to which the ascetics and hermits retreated in the first centuries of Christianity—like an enormous "Nothing." A silence beyond comparison with anything—because even silence comes in many forms—slowly entered me. I had finally found myself in the place where, according to scripture, the Lord led his people—his bride—in order to remonstrate with her heart.

I sat for a long while on a small mat. After a few hours I got up to stretch my legs a little and take a walk in the desert. The landscape around me in all directions was identical, apart from slight changes in the waves of sand. Without an ability to take bearings from the sun and stars, one could change direction slightly and lose one's way hopelessly. For a moment the imprint of my footsteps remained in the sand, but then the wind swept them away. Vanity of vanities!

I recalled the gospel story about Christ and the woman accused of adultery, which I expect everyone likes, except for Pharisees who consider themselves just. Jesus sat down and wrote in the sand. I always wondered what he wrote and why. I tried writing something in the sand with my finger, but a moment later it was all covered up. "The letter killeth, but the Spirit giveth life," I remembered from St. Paul. Didn't Jesus have something similar in mind? The Law is the letter, but the Spirit is a gentle wind, which covers it in love and mercy, like golden sand.

I imagined the moment of Judgment as an enormous desert of pure divinity, where all the twisted things inside us, who are burdened with pain and guilt, all those dark chasms in our life stories and our hearts, will be straightened out and covered up: God will be all in everything, as in that vast Nothing that now surrounded me on every side.

As evening approached, I stood up and tried to brush the fine sand from my face, my hair, and my beard. The sun was descending to the edge of the desert and my colleague's jeep was approaching from the distance.

THIRTEEN

On the Threshold of Old Age

"What's life like after fifty?," my students once asked me. "I can sincerely recommend it," I replied. "It's like a beautiful September afternoon. The sun no longer scorches you, but you can still sit outside in the garden and write." The sense that it is a marvelous and productive time, and that every year is better than the last, still remains with me, twenty years on. Only after I reached fifty did I have the feeling that it was now "the final draft."

I didn't mention writing by chance. Admittedly I still got enjoyment from everything I had been granted by the collapse of Communism, from public ministry as a priest: the sacred performance of the liturgy, and the opportunity to present the profundity of scripture through my sermons and accompany people spiritually in their problems and sorrows. I enjoyed my work with students and cooperation with colleagues in the university, as well as my frequent lectures in rural areas of the country and in major universities in other countries, not to mention my lecture and study tours all over the world. But what gave me the greatest enjoyment was my return to creative writing, for which I already had a propensity as a child.

During the summer vacation of 1998, I accepted an offer from a monastic community to spend a whole month in total isolation in a hermitage close to a contemplative monastery at the edge of a deep forest with a magnificent view of a landscape through which flows the majestic Rhine and where the mystic Hildegard von Bingen once walked. I needed to reflect with concentration on the first half century of my life and draw strength and inspiration for the decisive "final period of the match." Since then, I have returned to my hermitage every year for almost twenty years, spending four or five weeks there, and each time I have returned to Prague with an almost complete manuscript of another book, which is then published before Christmas by my permanent publisher, *Lidové noviny*. "I'm not good at thinking up what to give people for Christmas, so when I bring out a book in Advent it solves my problem," I would tell my readers at book signings, and add, "Through these books you see into my heart, and I can now look you in the eye." But the actual motive for writing was my deep enjoyment of the act of creation. After months of often hectic traveling and meeting a huge number of people requiring this, that, and the other from me, I was almost crawling by the time those weeks arrived; at moments of exhaustion I would often close my eyes and conjure up the picture of that room with its fireplace, writing desk, and altar while mentally counting down the days until my next departure.

Throughout the years and days, I maintained the same routine at the hermitage. After the first day, when I would make a pilgrimage to the tomb of the founder of the community, drawing the scent of the forest deep into my lungs or getting drenched by a summer rain shower, as I brushed from myself the dust of the past year, one day would be like the next. I would rise early and go for a run in the forest, though after that it would only be brisk walking. Then I would celebrate Mass alone—like during the days of clandestinity—in lengthy contemplative silence, praying the morning prayers from the breviary before the exposed sacrament on the altar. I would take my breakfast sitting on the window ledge with a view of the forest, then pray the

Hymn to the Holy Spirit before sitting down at the desk to write. Writing was a form of prayer and adoration for me: an altar stood opposite the desk, and the Eucharist lay on it permanently in a small monstrance. I wrote some of the pages literally kneeling. At half past twelve I would go to an agreed spot in the forest where a basket would be waiting for me with food for the next twenty-four hours. After lunch I would sleep for an hour. Then I would make myself a coffee and return to my writing until evening. Sometimes earlier, sometimes later, I would take another walk in the forest for an hour or two, reflecting, or silently praying the "Jesus prayer," that "pearl of Orthodoxy," which introduced into the culture of Eastern Christianity the practice of contemplation while rhythmically repeating a mantra. On my return, I would take a light supper and have time for spiritual reading—*lectio divina*. On weekends, I would light a fire in the grate and rejoice in the evening moment of holiday. On rare occasions, I would listen to music from recordings on my computer. The little cottage, which consisted of a porch, a living room, and a small bedroom, had electric current but no internet connection, no radio or television, no newspapers, and no books apart from the Bible and a breviary. I would always discover with amazement on my return to Prague—when I started neurotically to follow the news on the internet or browse the newspapers once more—that I had missed nothing during my month's media abstinence.

I was often aware, particularly during my early evening walks in the environs of the hermitage, how solitude, silence, fasting, and regular meditation improve not only one's thinking but also the responsiveness of the senses. I would have a more intense awareness of the color of flowers, the feel of the earth and tree bark, scents, and birdsong, and the wonderful music of the silent forest. I was happy and aware of it. I sensed it through all the pores of my skin, and the recesses of my soul. When I was writing and did not know how to continue—and sometimes I wrote well into the night—I would simply go to bed, and in the morning I would have a new chapter in my head. My dreams were quite different from those in my Prague apartment, where the aggressive noise from adjacent bars can be heard until the early hours. I understood those first pages of the Bible about Paradise, in which Adam walked with the Lord and conversed with him like with a friend.

The rest of the year I was able to write only articles, or the occasional angry polemic dictated by rage. But the quiet of the hermitage does not allow such emotions across the threshold. The hermitage is that "field hospital" that Pope Francis speaks of, in which wounds are bandaged and healed—the wounds that one has suffered oneself or the world's wounds that cannot leave one unaffected. The hermitage is a source of strength and energy. I found there something without which I would not have survived—physically, mentally, and, above all, spiritually—that noisy and demanding lifestyle.

■ WITHIN A FEW YEARS I HAD A SIZABLE readership not only at home but also around the world, thanks to translations. The first translations were into Polish. I was surprised that texts written for the "most secular country in Europe" were received equally well in the "most religious country in Europe." My Polish friends tell me that scarcely a week passes without someone in the Polish media quoting me. I have likewise become part of the debate about the religious and spiritual questions of our time in Germany, Holland, and Portugal, and when I arrived at a conference in Angola, I discovered that the local bishops and Dominican theologians and seminarists had read my books in Portuguese. In addition to translations into many European languages, there are now translations in Chinese, Korean, and Turkish. Three books published so far in English have found their way to India and other regions linked by the "Latin of our times."

Where possible, I have accepted invitations to meet my foreign readers at book readings in Krákow, the Hague, Miami, and Washington, even in Hong Kong and Rio de Janeiro. It interests me to know how my ideas are understood by people in often very different cultural contexts. Books—particularly in translation—start to have a life of their own. Writing and publishing them is just the beginning of their impact. I remember accompanying Václav Havel to a small theater in Manhattan for the premiere of one of his plays. As we walked down a spiral staircase to the basement, Václav told me excitedly that the atmosphere reminded him of the "apartment theaters" that we were familiar with during the period of "normalization" in our country. It was obvious that the director and the actors had interpreted this satire on the Stalinist regime in our country as a caricature of the administration of George W. Bush, but it aroused as much boisterous laughter as it had when we listened to the dissident author reading the text of this same play back in those times.

Cardinal Vlk once asked me to give a ceremonial lecture in his place at the beginning of the academic year at the University of Vienna. Seated alongside the academic officials in the auditorium were the Austrian chancellor and both Austrian cardinals, Schönborn and König. I think it was that lecture that convinced the former archbishop of Vienna, who was one of the main architects of the Second Vatican Council, to award me the prestigious Cardinal König Prize the following year. The laudatio at the König Prize award ceremony was written by President Havel and read by his former chancellor, Karel Schwarzenberg. Cardinal König, then in his ninety-ninth year, not only presented me with the prize in person, but he gave his speech without notes. He then spoke with equal spontaneity in front of the cameras for Austrian television news, after which he was present at the celebrations in a club late into the night. On that occasion he told me he was planning to come to Prague around the time of his forthcoming hundredth birthday and would like to celebrate Mass with me at our student chaplaincy (he himself had once been a university chaplain). I was the last person to receive the prize from his hands, however, as the cardinal died a few months later. I subsequently received further academic and church awards. In 2010 I received the Romano Guardini Prize from the Bavarian Catholic Academy, awarded for "outstanding merits in interpreting contemporary society," and the honorary title "Man of Reconciliation 2010" from the Polish Council of Christians and Jews. Shortly before, to my great surprise, Pope Benedict XVI awarded me the title "Monsignor, Second Class, Honorary Prelate of His Holiness." A few years later, in 2015, by which time he was "pope emeritus," Benedict remembered me again and invited me to lecture to a group of his former students at the papal summer residence at Castel Gandolfo. But the greatest surprise was yet to come.

The tenth anniversary of the death of Fr. Jiří Reinsberg fell on the eve of the Epiphany in January 2014. I was to give the sermon that evening at an anniversary Mass at the Týn Church. Just as I was leaving my apartment and locking the door, I heard the telephone ring. After hesitating for a moment, I went back and picked up the receiver. The voice at the other end sounded frail and elderly. "This is John Templeton. Is that Monsignor Halík? Monsignor, I have the honor to inform you that it was decided today that you will receive this year's Templeton Prize."

The floor rocked slightly beneath me and I was obliged to take several deep breaths. The Templeton Prize is known as the Nobel Prize in the sphere of spirituality. Its founder, Sir John Templeton, whose son it was on the telephone, thought it unjust that the Nobel Prize only rewarded merit in the fields of science, literature, and peace and totally ignored outstanding figures in the fields of the humanities and spirituality. He was convinced that the civilization of the future must be built on the interaction of science and faith, technology and spirituality, rationalism and ethics, so this prize, which used to be presented by Prince Philip at Buckingham Palace, sought to redress Nobel's omission. Some of the recipients of the Templeton Prize had previously received the Nobel Prize, or would later, including Mother Teresa of Calcutta, Alexander Solzhenitsyn, the physicist Charles H. Townes, and my two predecessors among the forty-three prizewinners, the Dalai Lama and Bishop Desmond Tutu.

I can't remember what I uttered in response, but I do recall that John Templeton told me that the matter must remain top secret until the official announcement, which would be in several months' time. Until that moment I could tell only one other person, who must take an oath of silence; that person would assist me with administrative and organizational matters. I was to prepare myself for plenty of those, including at least one preparatory meeting in London. I would shortly receive a letter with all the necessary details. He himself would come to London from Philadelphia to meet me in person. However, I heard nothing more for several weeks. It occasionally occurred to me that someone was playing a joke on me.

But then I received the news that the announcement of the award would take place in March at the British Academy. It coincided with the anniversary of the death of my teacher Jan Patočka and also the election of Pope Francis. On that day—March 14, 2014—John Templeton announced my name to the invited guests and representatives of the world's media at Carlton House, headquarters of the British Academy. There followed several speeches, and finally my own.

At the outset I expressed what I truly deeply felt at that moment:

When St. Augustine was asked which three paths led most surely to God, he replied "the first is humility, the second is humility and the third is humility." Becoming a Templeton Prize winner is a great test of humility. When I read the list of all previous winners' names, which, for years, I have spoken with respect and admiration, I certainly felt small and humble when compared with them. Thank you for this opportunity to experience humility so profoundly. I would like to recall with gratitude today my teachers of philosophy and theology, many of whom spent long years in Communist prison camps and had very little opportunity to write or publish. I am grateful to them for their intellectual, spiritual, and moral inspiration, for their witness of faith, courage, perseverance, and wisdom. They each bore a cross, while I today am able to experience the joy and light of the Easter morning, the resurrection of freedom.

I then ended my speech with the words:

> If I understand rightly the intention of Sir John Templeton,
> he wanted to create a community of men and women from gen-
> eration to generation, across frontiers of nations, cultures, and
> religions, who, in their time, and in their situations, have tried
> to understand the signs of the times, and open their minds
> and hearts to the movement of the Spirit. I enter humbly and
> with gratitude into the company of men and women whose
> first members included such saintly individuals as Mother
> Teresa and Brother Roger Schutz. There is one thing maybe
> that unites us all in spite of our differences. It is the idea that
> inspired Sir John Templeton's noble purpose, namely, the
> awareness that it is necessary for the life of individuals and
> society constantly to cultivate the spiritual dimension. The
> common dwelling of our civilization would be cold and inhos-
> pitable were the fire of the spirit absent from it. Reason is a
> great gift from God, and science and technology are among the
> pillars of our civilization. But rationality without any spiritual
> and moral impulses from the depths of faith could be a dan-
> gerous explosive. In a novel by the Czech writer Karel Čapek,
> the inventor of an explosive substance eventually receives an
> instruction: "You wanted to do big things and you'll do small
> things instead. You will do something that will bring light
> and warmth." At the time of the Velvet Revolution, twenty-
> five years ago, my friend Václav Havel expressed the hope
> that "truth and love must prevail over lies and hatred." This
> is an enormous and difficult task for the entire remainder
> of history. In the remaining years of my life I would like to
> do some small things that would bring light and warmth to
> people in our world. So help me God.

That was only the beginning, of course. Traditionally each prize-
winner gives a series of Templeton Lectures. I gave my first lecture at

the Scottish University of St. Andrews and then in Berlin, Paris, and Oxford and at the Pontifical Academy of Sciences in Vatican, where I met Pope Francis briefly and gave him copies of my books; then twice, together with another recipient of the Templeton Prize, Charles Taylor, at the congress of the American Academy of Sciences in San Diego, California; and finally in the aula of Charles University in Prague. I also received my first honorary doctorate; it was awarded by the oldest German university at Erfurt, the city where I was secretly ordained.

The culmination, of course, was the actual presentation of the Templeton Prize in May in the very heart of London, at the Church of St Martin-in-the-Fields. The ceremony was attended by many guests from universities and the church: our church was represented by both Czech cardinals, Miloslav Vlk and Dominik Duka, the Catholic church in England by the auxiliary bishop of Westminster, the Anglican church by the vicar of St Martin-in-the-Fields, and the German Bishops' Conference by their general secretary, Hans Langendörfer. Also present were members of the British House of Lords and members of the diplomatic corps, headed by the papal nuncio. The Czech Republic was represented by the minister of culture, the vice-speaker of the upper house of the Czech Parliament, and the Czech ambassador in London, while Charles University was represented by its pro-rector. In addition there were many guests of honor and a number of Czech and Slovak students studying in London, not to mention many of my friends from Britain and the Czech Republic. I received the medal and diploma from John Templeton in person. It was the last time he presented the award, because he died shortly afterward. Splendid musical accompaniment was provided by a large choir, which had performed in the film *Amadeus* and flew in from the United States especially for the occasion, and also by the excellent Czech pianist Martin Kasík. There followed speeches by John Templeton and a representative of the House of Lords, then finally my Templeton Lecture.

My starting point was the original purpose of the Templeton Prize as an award for "progress in religion," and I reflected on the relationship between those two concepts. Secularization had not gotten rid of religion but transformed it. I spoke about the new forms and social roles of religion, including those that misuse religion to justify violence. I also touched on a number of topical issues, such as the recent militantly atheist campaign in London encouraged by the contemporary apostle of atheism, Richard Dawkins. I said that the God of Dawkins's atheism—God as a naive scientific hypothesis—was not the God of the faith for whose freedom we fought against atheism linked to political power; atheism was no more immune to the temptations of power than religion. In an obvious reference to a recent statement by the then British prime minister, David Cameron, that Britain is a Christian country, or statements such as "Europe is a Christian continent," I asked what conclusions should be drawn from them. "What can religions (and specifically Christianity) do *to transform the globalization process into a culture of communication*?" I spoke of the need for a united Europe in the face of the dangers of nationalism, xenophobia, isolationism, and Putin's Russia, which was again trying to bring back into the sphere of its dominant influence the states of the former Soviet empire in particular. I said that "Christianity does not need to be a flag flying over Europe, but Europe and the world needs people who restore to the word *love* the profound meaning that it had in the radical message of the gospel. . . . Tolerance is the secular translation of the gospel injunction to love one's enemies. But when religious concepts are translated into secular language and concepts, something is usually lost. . . . A certain model of 'multiculturalism' based on the principle of tolerance results not in a *polis*, i.e., a community of citizens, or neighbors, but in a conglomeration of ghettos." I said that that the classical understanding of tolerance as people living undisturbed alongside each other was no longer valid; we had to learn to live *together*. I spoke about the challenges and pitfalls of interreligious dialogue and the need to identify and heal the wounds of our world. Finally I returned to the first recipient of the Templeton Prize, Mother Teresa of Calcutta, whose surprising spiritual diary had been recently published: "She bore the cross of a dual solidarity. In the daytime she was sister to those who needed their bodily wounds healed, and the hunger of their empty stomachs assuaged. At night she shared the darkness of those who feel themselves far from the light of God and suffer emptiness of the soul. Yes, therein lies true 'progress in religion.' It is the courage to combine spiritual depth with the open embrace of solidarity with all those who suffer. Alexander Solzhenitsyn, another Templeton Prize winner, once answered the question what would follow Communism. He replied: a very, very long period of healing. My answer to the question what will come after the period when many believers and non-believers thought it was easy to talk about God is, I expect a very, very long journey into the depths. And I pin my hopes on it."

After those words, the entire audience stood up and applauded me. The world's media covered my address—apart from the Russian media, because the main Russian news agency censored an excerpt from my speech.

Something else came out of that brief stay in London. I made the acquaintance of the principal of Oxford University's Harris Manchester College, the theologian Ralf Waller, and I gave him copies of my two books in English. Professor Waller was so taken by my books that he agreed with the proposal of the Prague developer and philanthropist Luděk Sekyra that one of the lecture rooms of the new building of that Oxford college, which he was building and financing, should be named after me, and a portrait of me should hang there. I gave a lecture in Oxford on the occasion of the inauguration of that room, and after it Professor Waller invited me to a meeting with Oxford professors of theology, to whom I presented for discussion the main ideas of my academic work to date. I didn't realize that the meeting also had a hidden agenda. My presentation had interested them to such a degree that shortly afterward a proposal was made, probably from that group, that Oxford University should award me an honorary doctorate of divinity.

THE AWARD CEREMONY IN OXFORD was dignified and splendid. The bedels processed through the city with the university insignias, followed by the professors of the different colleges in gowns of various colors according to discipline, and, finally, Lord Patten, university chancellor (and, among other things, the last British governor of Hong Kong), the gold-embroidered train of whose gown was carried by others. I also was given the scarlet-and-black gown of doctors of divinity and walked at the head of the group of nine recipients of honorary doctorates, who included Paul Krugman, winner of the Nobel Prize for economics, Supreme Court Judge Lord Mance, the Japanese architect Kazuyo Sejima, and the Estonian composer Arvo Pärt. When we had signed the commemorative book at All Souls College and lined up to enter the Sheldonian Theatre, where the award ceremony commenced after the National Anthem, Arvo Pärt, who for years had been my favorite composer, leaned over to me and said, "You're a priest, aren't you? Bless me, please!"

The next evening I traveled to London for a television interview. It was the day of the referendum about whether or not the United Kingdom should remain in the European Union. All my Oxford colleagues had voted unanimously to remain, like many people with whom Scarlett and I had spoken in Oxford and London. Only the taxi driver who drove us to London and back and the cleaner at the college said they had voted to leave. When I looked at the news on my computer the next morning, I suffered the same shock as the professors with whom I later spoke. The majority—albeit small— of voters had succumbed to the fake assertions about the economic disadvantages of remaining in the European Union, and the authors of the lies cynically admitted to them after the referendum. That result decided a process whose harmful consequences would start to become apparent month by month. When I returned to Oxford for a conference a year later, the grave negative impact of that unfortunate "Brexit" could already be felt, particularly on the education system, including the two most famous universities. Many people were calling for a second referendum, and some admitted that they had not realized what their vote would bring about and wanted to change it, but it was too late.

Likewise, in the Czech Republic at that time, people manipulated by irresponsible demagogues, and particularly by fake news emanating from social networks in the service of the Russians' war of disinformation against the West, were becoming more and more vociferous. There were also Czechs who hoped that in an eventual referendum about European Union membership, the majority of the population would opt for the Czech Republic's suicidal shift from the West to the wild East of Putin's oligarchs. In summer 2017, I traveled from Oxford to London, and from there I flew to the United States for the second time in two years for a fellowship at the University of Notre Dame, the largest Catholic university in the world. That time of calm in America gave me the opportunity to access the unlimited resources of university libraries and clarify my views in discussions with foremost specialists in various disciplines. It was an ideal environment for my own reflection and writing.

When I returned from my first fellowship at Notre Dame before Christmas 2015, Czech society was already almost unrecognizable. Had something fundamental happened to the social climate, or was I maybe only noticing it now as a result of my months away from the country, when I was able to compare it with another type of society? There was more nervousness, animosity, vulgarity, and aggressivity—in public space, in communication between politicians, in much of the media, particularly the internet, and even between friends and in families. This atmosphere clearly grew out of fear, and now there was a clear motive for people's fear: refugees and Muslims in general. But there were virtually no refugees in our country, and they weren't even interested in seeking asylum here. I was convinced that migrants were playing a vicarious role and that the real cause of fear was much deeper—in the feeling of chaos, frustration, and uprootedness, in other words, in a climate similar to one that once gave rise to fascism, Nazism, and Communism. Migrants as such weren't the real problem; the problem was the loss of an awareness of cultural identity.

The most powerful source of fear- and hate-mongering were the muckraking internet servers, particularly those that had become tools of the "hybrid" propaganda war being waged against the West by the Putin regime, whose objective was and is to disrupt the European Union and NATO and to bring the former countries of the Soviet regime back under Russian influence once more. To that end scaremongering is used to create panic, chaos, and distrust of European institutions, as well as support for extremist, nationalist, and often out-and-out neo-Nazi political groups. People who have tried to counter this atmosphere with rational arguments have been hounded by the media and subjected to slander and vilification.

I WAS FACED WITH A NEW AND DIFFICULT task, and I knew that it would require much reflection, prayer, and study: how to link theologically, and in a responsible way, three dimensions of the radical renewal of Christianity, which in my view has begun with Pope Francis. These dimensions are spiritual deepening, a new theological reading of the Gospels, and revitalizing the social commitment of Christians.

My two fall semesters at the University of Notre Dame in 2015 and 2017 enabled me to think through and formulate the basic questions and hypotheses for a new book. Between my two sojourns at Notre Dame I visited, in rapid succession, Australia, Asia (Hong Kong and Vietnam), and Africa (a stimulating conference of European and African theologians in Angola), and then several other American universities, including Boston University and Harvard, the Catholic University in Washington, and the University of Chicago, as well as in Miami, Florida. Everywhere I had discussions with many interesting people.

I centered my reflections on the question how can philosophical theology nowadays fulfill a task that derives from the mission of the biblical prophets, which was "reading the signs of the times," recognizing God's call in history as it happens. The Catholic Church has sought to do this through its social teachings, and a similar goal is fixed by the "political theology" associated with the name of J. B. Metz and the liberation theology it inspired. I have met personally Metz and the founder of Latin American liberation theology, the Peruvian theologian Gustavo Gutiérrez, and had discussions with them. In my conversation with Gutiérrez, I proposed an "alternative liberation theology." Classic liberation theology tries to read the Gospels with the eyes of people on the fringes of society, the poor and exploited; I seek to understand the perspective of people on the fringes of the church and beyond its visible boundaries. My pastoral experience in the Czech Republic and discussions about surveys of Czech religiosity prompted me to turn my attention to "seekers," whose numbers are growing in the churches and outside of them, whereas the number of "dwellers," and those who identify totally with the present shape of the churches and their social practice, is rapidly dwindling. I am convinced that if the Christian church is to stand the test in the current transformation of civilizations and in the transition from the modern to the postmodern epoch, it cannot simply concern itself with the orderly sheep in its fold, or with traditional mission work whose aim is to turn seekers into dwellers and squeeze them into the existing institutional and mental confines of the churches. It has to step outside its boundaries and seek to "accompany seekers" with mutual respect, without proselytizing intentions, with the risk that not only they, but we too, will be transformed, because we do not possess the whole truth; the truth is our common goal. The truth that is given us in Christ is not a static object and set of formulas but the way and the life, something that is dynamic and constantly calls on us to "put out into deep water." Here I anticipate a need for a synthesis of ecclesiology (comprehending the church), political theology (comprehending the role of Christians in society), and spirituality (seeking a specific style of living and applying one's faith) for the coming age.

I am convinced that as a reformer, Pope Francis needs a broad support network of theologians and other thinkers to develop and think more deeply about his theological and pastoral stimuli in the context of different cultures. After all, Vatican II was preceded by the efforts of generations of theologians, who for a long time were confronted by misunderstanding and harassment within the church. They maintained their loyalty to the church, however, and enabled it to emerge from the narrow confines of nineteenth-century Catholicism, hag-ridden with fear of the modern world, toward an authentic catholicity, responsive to God's challenges "in the signs of the times." Pope Francis's ecumenical openness in the anniversary year of the Protestant Reformation and his exhortation to treat with generous and merciful love people whose marriages have failed (of which there are increasing numbers in the church) aroused a sharp negative reaction on the part of certain groups of traditionalist Catholics. At that time I contacted my friend, the eminent Austrian pastoral theologian Paul Zulehner, and we wrote an open letter of support to Pope Francis. Within a short time that "Pro Pope Francis" initiative received the support of tens of thousands of believers from all over the world, including some fifteen hundred men and women theologians from five continents. In this way an intercontinental network of theologians came into being that is willing to continue along this path and listen attentively to "what the Spirit is telling the churches." This where I feel my place to be in the near future, provided the Lord grants me a clear mind and enough strength in my declining years.

A Journey to Eternal Silence

FOURTEEN

Never before had I felt such utter solitude—
either in the hermitage above the Rhine or in
the Egyptian desert. Never before had I been
aware of such a strange silence as on that January day. I was alone in a tent on the edge of a
glacier on the shore of King George Island, at the precise spot where
the Atlantic and Pacific Oceans merge.

A windstorm blew the whole night, buffeting the canvas of my
tent, so I was a long time getting to sleep. Now it was a remarkable
calm Sunday morning. I walked alongside the glacier to a cliff, from
which I could see the vast flat ocean, covered in many ice packs. To
my right there soared dramatically jagged rocks against which the surf
broke. Directly opposite me, huge icebergs, with an incomparable hue
of pale shades of blue, rose from the ocean. The ground was muddy
everywhere and the going was hard. Yesterday I felt utterly exhausted
after walking several hours along the shore, where my feet were constantly getting stuck in the mud, while with my arms I had to fight
off attacking birds, who kept on violently flying into my face like in
that famous horror film. And on top of that, a gale started to blow
with the approach of evening, so that I finished my walk almost on

all fours, and it took me much longer than I expected to unfasten the tent entrance and then fasten it again. I ate very little, in order to conserve my stocks.

When Jaroslav Pavlíček, a Czech polar explorer, with whom I had flown into this bizarre world four days earlier from Chile in a military aircraft and then paddled to Nelson Island by kayak, left me two days before, he emphasized that he had no idea when the weather would allow him to return for me. If he did not return within a week, it meant something had happened to him, and I was to head for the Chinese base, where we had drunk tea while unloading our supplies. I didn't tell him that my back and all my muscles had ached so much when we were transporting our heavy load that I had totally failed to notice the direction we were traveling.

Most of my friends had no idea of my whereabouts. Those who heard about it mostly shook their heads or tapped their foreheads. A month ago I myself had been completing a trimester at Oxford and had absolutely no idea where I would find myself a couple of weeks later. A year earlier, after mature consideration, I agreed to take part—"one day"—in an Antarctic expedition aimed at researching the prerequisites for people to survive in conditions of extreme mental and physical stress. During the year, Scarlett and I prepared ourselves for the journey in various ways, mentally and physically. In the summer, under Jaroslav's guidance, we took part in "pre-Antarctic training" in the Austrian Alps and in Italy. We climbed to the summit of Dachstein, bivouacked on a rock wall at a height of over 2,500 meters above sea level, crossed a glacier, forded a wild river, and, in Italy, learned to cope with a boat on the sea. But fulfillment was still in the unforeseeable future—until I returned from Oxford, when a message awaited me: everything is prepared, we fly out in three weeks' time. Because of my fellowship in Oxford, I had arranged to be deputized at church and at the faculty for the winter semester, and the difference of several weeks between the end of the trimester at Oxford and the end of the semester in Prague provided a rare period of several free weeks, which wouldn't occur again soon. I had no excuse.

■ TWO SNAGS OCCURRED ON THE VERY first days of my sojourn on that most singular of the continents—the only one I had not yet visited. The small boat, which Jaroslav had prepared on Seal Beach during his last stay for our crossing to the Czech base on Nelson Island, was nowhere to be found. So Jaroslav had to go there alone in a small kayak, leaving me on my own for an unspecified length of time in a tent on the coast of King George Island. When he returned with a catamaran two days later and we finally crossed to our island, we were in for a shock after anchoring our craft and sitting down to lunch. A windstorm arose once more, and it was so strong that even though we had weighted the catamaran down with many heavy stones, it was carried away. We watched the boat—the only link with the continent and the most valuable possession of the Czech Antarctic station—disappear into the distance. Shortly afterward the powerful waves would decide, as we later joked, whether the craft would head for the shores of Australia or of Capetown.

When I saw Jaroslav dashing to a small boat to paddle after the lost vessel in the turbulent waves I shouted to him, "Are you crazy? It'll cost you your life!" "So join me," he shouted back. What happened next was like a very bad dream.

After about two hours of strenuous paddling in a windstorm through a heavy sea, we managed to reach the catamaran, climb aboard, and start the motor. Then, in the icy waves that totally drenched us, we managed to get both vessels back to shore. Jaroslav divulged to me that only twice during his fourteen years of sojourns in the Antarctic had he experienced anything as dangerous as that, and he admitted that if we hadn't reached the catamaran, or if its engine hadn't started, we would have had no chance, in such weather, to get back alive to shore in that little craft.

Such shared moments of danger lent an entirely new dimension to our friendship. From my position as trainee polar explorer, I immediately sprang several rungs up the ladder of the Antarctic hierarchy in Jaroslav's eyes: "I divide people into two sorts: the most numerous sort are those who would never have leapt into the sea like that with me in those circumstances, and there is another sort—and you are in it." From that moment, my attitude to that continent also changed entirely: I had undergone the baptism of wild nature, and I started to behave there with much greater confidence, because I got the impression that nothing worse could happen to me from then on.

Scarcely had we dried ourselves, than I celebrated my first Antarctic Mass in field conditions at the Czech station, probably the only Mass celebrated that day in that part of the world. I prayed especially for all those whose yearning to explore the beauty and mystery of the continent cost them their lives. A week later, our two-man expedition was to be joined by Scarlett and Dagmar Havlová, Václav Havel's sister-in-law, who were waiting in suspense at Punta Arenas on the Chilean coast for the next possible flight while diligently procuring supplies for the winter team, and in the little spare time left they explored Tierra del Fuego and got to know the beauties of Patagonia.

In the evening of my first, very adventurous day on Nelson Island I retired to my "Antarctic hermitage," a little wooden house, the size of a garden shed, whose furniture consisted solely of a plank bed under the window; but the view of the ocean from the window was magnificent. At that period of the Antarctic summer, the sun virtually does not drop below the horizon; only around midnight does it grow markedly dark, but in two or three hours' time the sky is bright again. Although I was understandably tired, I couldn't sleep; I gazed out of the window and pondered.

The stark and severe beauty of this land of ice has probably not changed in the past twenty million years. Nature here has triumphed over history: there is no record of anyone deliberately killing another person on this, the only continent unsullied by war. All around reigned the kind of silence that only happens when a windstorm drops. Never before, not even in the desert, had I learned to distinguish so clearly the various tonalities of silence, the different depths and colors of quietness. The hour arrived when one—and I believe it is everyone—thinks of God.

AN OLD LATIN PROVERB SAYS that the sea teaches us to pray. Yes, at those hours leaning into the maw of extreme danger, I really did pray incessantly, and I truly prayed differently than ever before. It was the strangest spiritual experience, and it brought me more than just confirmation that when their life is at stake, people quickly remember God. At such moments even those who have spent their lives bragging about their ungodliness often start to call on God. One wonders whether atheism is not simply a luxurious illusion, affordable only to those who have never known real need or have preferred to displace it totally from their consciousness.

When I tried to remember precisely how I prayed at those moments, I realized that it was not just an impassioned prayer for our deliverance. After all, there were moments on the sea when I almost wished for an end at last to that exhausting paddling and all the tension; for peace at last, even peace in the cold embrace of the water around and below me. Those curious moments, etched in my memory, gave way to some kind of awareness that it wasn't the end, that it couldn't be, that my story will have a continuation, and I mustn't give up.

At that moment something happened that is hard to describe; I sensed with enormous relief that I wasn't the one in charge of my life, that my strength to survive and persevere came from a much deeper source than the little bundle of my self, my muscles, my thoughts, and my nerves, and I had submitted myself totally to that source. "I'd switched over to God," handed God the tiller, and felt a great inrush of strength and enormous liberation. It involved a certain resignation but in no sense passivity. Rather I felt my activity intensified as it was no longer held back by fear for myself.

When I later reflected on those moments in those turbulent natural forces, I recalled St. Paul's words: "I live, no longer I, but Christ lives in me." That sentence, which I always had great affinity with, started from that moment on the ocean to be backed by experience. It was the counsel of St. Ignatius of Loyola: "Act as if everything depended on you; trust as if everything depended on God."

There are defining moments when people reach the limits of their capacity and, not wanting to give up, switch over to God and totally submit and surrender themselves to him. Maybe they heard or read many times previously that pious advice to abandon themselves, and maybe they have said in their prayers at a moment of devotion, "O God, I commit my life to you." But at a defining moment it shoots out of one like a flame, like the inhalation of one who is drowning or suffocating; without words or great reflection, like an immediate pure act of the spirit, in which one is totally whole—with body and soul, present, past, and future. I understood what is said about people at defining moments, that they experience—like when dreaming or probably also when dying—some kind of break in the time line, so that their entire past life and their future is with them.

And I would stress again that at such moments one recognizes that such "submission" is not an alibi for stopping what one is doing, that one can't stop paddling on a turbulent ocean—if I may use my own experience as a metaphor. If one has really gone beyond a certain limit and surrendered oneself, then one's activity immediately assumes a different character, a different quality—as if deriving strength from much deeper levels. At the beginning of this book I mentioned Eckhart's words about the unity of God and man and how beyond our "ego" there is something else, a deeper "inner person," a "deep self," *das Selbst*—and beyond the "god of theism," the god of our human notions, is an "inner God," "God beyond god." I had reflected on these matters for many years, but this time I experienced it.

If I ever deeply felt that encounter, the blending and inner unity of freedom and grace, human endeavor and divine assistance, activity and submission, struggle and trust, work and prayer—then it was that time in the waves off the coast of Nelson Island in the Antarctic.

■ IT IS VERY DIFFICULT TO SPEAK ABOUT IT, and it is obvious to me that one could talk about the awakening of a hidden reservoir of strength at defining moments in a completely different way—such as in terms of a neurophysiological process. Of course I could describe my experience at sea as an example of how neuromodulators are created in an organism in situations of stress. Knowledge about the creation and effects of endorphins and other neurophysiological processes is not only interesting but also practical. No doubt my entire story could be told without a single reference to God: "etsi Deus non daretur." Besides, I did not experience God's presence there as an intervention from above perceptible to the senses, like some deus ex machina. I myself would consider it inappropriate to mention God when describing the scene to certain people, because in the absence of a certain context and "preunderstanding," these words are as devoid of sense as an explanation of human endorphins without elementary knowledge of natural science.

The experience of a defining moment can be described both in the language of faith and in the language of science. Is it simply dual speech about the same thing? And if it is about the same thing, can the one explanation fully substitute for the other? In modern times we have accepted the dominance of the scientific, "natural" explanation—whose legitimacy in the framework of certain discourse I do not challenge, and I have no wish to debate it. But is that explanation really as "natural" as it claims to be? Is it exhaustive? Does it fully explain the entire depth of our experience?

I tend to believe that the same phenomenon can be described from both angles, although both explanations—each of which is legitimate and understandable "within its discourse"—are not simply different words for the same thing. They mean the same, but the one approach cannot simply replace the other, because they both express a specific perspective and identify different aspects and levels of the experience.

What is lost when I don't express my experience in the language of faith? I fear that my sense of gratitude is lost. That is something more than a fleeting emotion, than a simple feeling of well-being or a mere superstructure of a certain neurophysiological event. I think that the gratitude that overwhelms one after such an experience is, in reality, what turns the entire event into a profound, valuable, and transformative human experience. The fact that after such an experience one starts—at least for a time—to value life as a gift that is not to be taken for granted and one has a very strong need to show gratitude—not only for one's rescue, but for life as such—is probably something that is best expressed in the language of faith. Expressions such as "stroke of luck" don't get to the heart of what we experienced. There is a subtle but important consideration to bear in mind. One need not be a "believer," in the sense of holding and asserting certain ready-made, predefined "religious beliefs," to interpret "religiously" one's experience of being saved. The experience itself awakes in one gratitude, and by its very nature gratitude gravitates toward God, however we understand that word.

We should also bear in mind that even a "nonreligious" person at certain moments—whether at a moment of extreme danger or of joyful amazement or at a moment when danger and gratitude coalesce, will shout spontaneously, "My God!" Of course we can trivialize that reaction in various ways, as an unintentional activation of a certain cultural relic in our language; after all the person "didn't mean anything by it." But wasn't it a breakthrough to a deeper level than the one we generally "think" in? Do our language, our culture, and our soul truly have other more appropriate expressions available than the forgotten word *God*?

Isn't it rather the case that it is a moment of truth, when our emotions and our words instinctively reveal what is buried and forgotten in our surroundings but is entirely real? I can only thank *someone*: "fate," "luck," or "nature" is too abstract to receive gratitude. I would even make so bold as to say that only in the light of defining moments, at a moment of horror, amazement, or gratitude, can we get an inkling of what the word *God* means.

In the face of an experience that arouses profound "gratitude for life in general," it turns out that it makes no fundamental difference whether we were previously "believers" or "nonbelievers" or whether the words *God* and *faith* were at home in our vocabulary. It is only when one has been "rescued" that one starts to realize, or at least "understand" in a different way, what underlies words like *salvation*, *God*, *faith*, and *grace*. Those who were "unbelievers" can become believers at that moment, while those who previously counted themselves believers can realize for the first time the difference between faith as holding a worldview and faith backed by such an experience. I know people who found a path to God because they had a fundamental need to express gratitude after some defining moment. Faith born of gratitude, as a response to an experience of being rescued, is not simply a matter of conviction, or accepting some particular opinions, notions, or theories; rather it is transforming the basic structure of our life's inner field. Nobody is "forced" into faith even by such an experience; people can interpret this experience quite differently, or they may not even reflect on it at all. But that possibility of experiencing faith as profound gratitude has opened to them for a moment like a hidden treasure—in the way that, according to legend, buried treasures reveal themselves when the Passions are sung on the afternoon of Good Friday.

▌BUT WHAT ABOUT EXPERIENCES OF a totally opposite nature: experiences of tragedy, absurdity, pain, the death of loved ones, or the imminence of one's own death, which are equally part of the human condition? I maintain that the affirmation of life, the expression of joy, and gratitude are—even when God is not mentioned—a fundamental part of human "religious experience."

But where does painful asking for meaning lead us when we are overwhelmed by the "meaninglessness" and absurdity of our situation? What about the pain, suffering, and death that undermine our "sense of meaning" and frustrate our need to understand the meaning of events around us? Was it not the case of Job, whose loss of property and loved ones, or infection with painful boils, possibly afflicted him less than the fact that nothing made sense anymore, that his sense of justice and his religious certainties had been shaken, that he could not find in all his pious wisdom an answer to the questions, "why?" and "why me?" When we encounter evil, suffering, and death, it arouses a sense of absurdity and protest in us. What is the spiritual and religious meaning of this protest?

These questions were whirling through my head the next day when I was given the job of walking along a lengthy section of the Antarctic shore collecting what was washed up by the tide and recording it in a notebook. The day was overcast, the ocean roared, and I saw for the first time a giant petrel circling above me in the sky; I was beginning to tell the difference between good-naturedly sprawling seals and treacherous sea lions, which one should steer clear of. I communicated with the penguins, which look like endless processions of little friars, in their huge colonies. Jaroslav Pavlíček and I were the only people on the entire great island and therefore did not expect to meet a human being here.

I reached the beach, abandoned even by animals, which was covered in bleached bones, including the vertebrae of whales, probably left by whalers at the beginning of the past century. Scavenging birds circled beneath the lowering sky, from which we could probably expect sleet before long.

I returned once more to the question, what about tragic experiences and religious practice? What do near-death experiences awaken in us, unless they are immediately followed by the joyful experience and relief of a remarkable rescue? Do they open the door to belief or, on the contrary, the door to skepticism, doubt, and "disbelief"? Why is comfort, based on the certainty of immortality—which would seem to have been very effective in the past—now so enfeebled? Can it be revived or reconceived—or must even believers seek another source of hope that is not beyond the bounds of this world?

■ THE LAST CENTURY OF THE SECOND millennium has been called the most violent and darkest of all. When I was called on to give some message of hope in its final minutes, I could think of nothing except to note that although humankind had been given the means to destroy itself and the planet in a single moment, it didn't happen in the end. But what does that bode for the future? Will someone in the new century hold back the finger from the button, like the messenger from heaven held back Abraham's hand with a knife raised above the future as it lay bound in the boy Isaac? Will someone tell us that they don't want us to sacrifice the future and hope to anything? Heaven seems to have fallen silent. The absolute future—eternity, that unimaginable "space" and "time" after death, seems to have faded into nothing. I'm not speaking here about nonbelievers; even for a large number of Christians, that part of doctrine that deals with life after death is no longer as relevant, meaningful, or significant as it used to be. They don't deny it, but they don't live by it. It embarrasses them, and they ignore it. When I once asked a group of young Christians if the foundations of their faith in Christ, and their determination to live according to the gospel, would be seriously shaken if somehow they discovered that nothing remains of people after death, most of them said no: their faith and their faith-based lives would be practically unchanged. Atheists' favorite notion that the strongest motivation of believers is a vision of posthumous bliss, or of eternal damnation, would seem to have ceased to be a reality long ago.

Is the world now so diverse, colorful, and interesting that it has outshone heaven and rendered it invisible? Have the horrors of our world, including the mass tragedies of the twentieth century, surpassed and mocked all our notions of hell? Was it the hegemony of materialist ideology and the reduction of life to a mere biological occurrence that forbade our hope, yearning, and imagination to soar above the narrow space of a tangible reality measurable by reason? Was it the naive notions in which belief in heaven, purgatory, and hell were clothed in the past that discredited, or at least complicated, that belief in the eyes of nonbelievers?

But even where all notions about life after death, and about articles of faith, have quietly expired or are explicitly denied, the longing for paradise has not disappeared from the human heart. There was a time when political promises of "shining tomorrows" capitalized on it by promising bliss here and now: pay up, and today you will be with me in paradise. People who do not believe in eternal life, and do not expect it at a rational level, nevertheless often do not stop yearning for it unconsciously. They simply transfer their expectation of absolute values to the realm of relative things. But doesn't this transfer lead to a vicious circle of unreal demands and expectations, to overexertion and subsequent frustration?

Belief in heaven and hell left an appropriate space for life on earth; it let the world be the world. But when we project demands and hopes of eternal bliss and the fear of hell onto life on earth, we turn the world into something like heaven and hell simultaneously.

Aren't our exaggerated expectations of the earth, and of life on earth, the cause of the disappointment, anxiety, and boredom that the existentialists speak of ? Just as Freud tried to gain space for the ego, oppressed by the inflation of the sphere of the superego and the id, could not belief and hope in an afterlife *free life to be earthly*? I once amazed a certain group of atheists by saying that because we Catholics believe in angels and devils, we do not need to turn people into angels or devils; when we reserve the absolute poles of angelic whiteness and diabolic darkness solely for the world of the spirit, we can perceive people in all their variety and contradictoriness, as a mixture of good and evil. Because no one is for us an angel or a devil, we are able more realistically and kindly to perceive the paradoxes of the natural humanity of each of us terrestrials.

■ THERE ARE TIMES WHEN SOME TRUTH of faith seems hard to believe, because it is in such contrast to our historical experience or the mentality of the times. Nowadays that applies to belief in life after death for many people.

Maybe it is not the actual readiness to believe in "the life of the world to come" that has failed but rather the *imagination* that often accompanies belief. Sometimes people confuse imagination with belief itself: for them believing means creating a vivid image of something and incorporating that image into their inner world. When people say they don't believe in something, the reason is generally not the fact that it can't be "rationally proven"; that is often a secondary explanation. On many occasions they mean that they simply can't imagine it; they don't know what is at issue; it is too remote for them.

One can object, however, that faith in the biblical sense is actually a way—the sole and irreplaceable way—to somewhere my imagination cannot reach, to a realm of things that "eye has not seen, and ear has not heard, and what has not entered the human heart." It is the naked faith without images and notions that the mystics—including Eckhart and John of the Cross—have extolled.

▮ IF WE STAND BEFORE THE GATES OF DEATH, we stand before a mystery; the only way forward is the way of faith and hope. Only faith, not knowledge, can see beyond the gates of death.

Even the atheists' conviction that biological death is the final end and that beyond it is the void, the chemical decomposition of the body and at most the fading imprint of the human personality on the memory of others, is a kind of "belief." When materialist nihilism claims science as an authority, it does so without justification. Natural science is not a competent authority in such matters. If we ask scientists as scientists about life after death we should be content with their only possible answer, namely, a humble "We don't know"; it always seemed to be totally dishonest to want to shift that honest neutrality to the "yes" or "no" of our philosophical or religious convictions. Therefore all those popular books about "life after life," which try to corroborate belief in the afterlife "scientifically," by reporting the experience of patients in a state of clinical death, seem to me as dishonest as "scientific materialism." Let us content ourselves with the fact that science can guide us to the physiological aspects of the process of dying and decomposition of the body, but it cannot offer us any bridge across the abyss of the mystery of death.

And, moreover, when materialists maintain that there is "nothing" beyond the gates of death, then they are betraying their own materialism and have entered the preserve of mysticism. If we maintain that God is impossible to imagine, then the same applies totally to "nothing." When Meister Eckhart, the prince of mystics—and in my view the profoundest Christian theologian after St. Paul—said that God is "nothing," he was expressing in other words the impenetrability of God's mystery.

■ WHEN I RETURNED TO THE BASE along the narrow path in the cliffs along the shore, it was beginning to get dark. The ocean roared darkly, the clouds hung threateningly low, and a wind was rising. The rocks and icebergs towering above the foaming waves looked like ruins of castles and cathedrals long abandoned. On the shore, seals and sea lions lounged about, and a cormorant flew from a nest in the cliffs and circled high above my head. This land is amazingly clean. In general even animals approach humans with disarming trust and curiosity. Between the gusts of wind a deep silence spoke, as if I was hearing the earth breathe. The rocky coves with their tongues of icy snow protruding from the shadow of the rocks into the muddy soil covered with a carpet of seaweed looked all alike. When would I finally see the little light in the window of our base, showing that there was still another person with me on the whole of this island?

Once more my thoughts returned to the theme of death and immortality. There is precious little I can say about life after death. But isn't all sincere talk on this theme obliged at some point to give way to silence, whether it is the silence of shy hesitation before the closed doors of unfathomable mystery or the silence of longing that eludes the power of words and images?

That evening before bed I turned to a marvelous place in the *Confessions*, in which St. Augustine describes his conversation with his mother, Monica:

> As the day now approached on which she was to depart this life . . . she and I stood alone, leaning in a certain window from which the garden of the house we occupied at Ostia could be seen. Here in this place, removed from the crowd, we were resting ourselves for the voyage after the fatigues of a long journey. . . . We were . . . discussing together what is the nature of the eternal life of the saints . . . and we gradually passed through all the levels of bodily objects. . . . And we came at last to our own minds and went beyond them that we might climb as high as that region of unfailing plenty. And while we were thus speaking and straining after her, we just barely touched her with the whole effort of our hearts. Then with a sigh, leaving the first fruits of the Spirit bound to that ecstasy, we returned to the sounds of our own tongue, where the spoken word had both beginning and end.

■ I HAVE ALREADY COMPLETED MANY JOURNEYS and already experienced so much—and I am still not at the end. I still have much to learn, much to bring to maturity, much to expiate, and much to be grateful for. I probably haven't fulfilled yet the task I was entrusted with, and maybe I haven't adequately understood it yet.

St. Exupéry says in *The Little Prince*, "What is essential is invisible to the eye." Seldom do we realize how God operates in our lives. I imagine it like the way an oriental carpet is woven. If we look at the back of a carpet all we see is a fairly unsightly maze of threads and knots. When the carpet is finally woven and turned over one is astounded by the upper side, with its symmetrical decoration and bright colors. That hope gave me strength at very knotted periods of my life.

When I returned once more to my dramatic experience in the Antarctic, the scene from the Gospels came to mind when the disciples start to panic on the stormy Sea of Galilee while Jesus slept peacefully in the midst. Jesus preaches by means of his sleep. It even occurs to me that his sleep in the scene is a profounder revelation of his mission than the subsequent miracle, which he is forced to perform because of the disciples' lack of faith. Jesus does not come in the name of some deus ex machina, a god behind the scenes, who will eliminate all storms and sort out our lives according to our wishes, if we are good and do this or that. Jesus negates such a God beyond the bounds of our world, one who could be drawn into the world by fulfilling the law, bringing sacrifices, holding the right doctrinal opinions, or other religious behavior. By being amidst us and our storms as a man free from fear, Jesus is capable of infecting us with his calm. This is not the calm of a stoic sage or hero who can ensure a happy end to every crisis thanks to his cleverness or strength. It is the peace of the one from whom hope and trust shine. Jesus's God is not a "god behind the scenes"; his God is the foundation and depth of our being. We alienate ourselves from him through the fear that naturally takes control of us when we think of ourselves in the middle of whirlpools and storms, but we come into contact with him when we leave a free space inside ourselves—albeit in order for him to be silent and sleep. Yes, God knows how to be silent—and also teaches us silence.

Theologians, religious specialists, and preachers must speak about God. It is even more important that they should also be capable of being silent about God, of being silent before God and with God, of being silent in God, and of listening to God's silence. If those of us who speak about God "professionally" are not to be immodest blasphemers, we must also cultivate silent communication with the inexpressible mystery, communication that is called spiritual life. Our words must proceed from silence and flow into it.

■ I AM IMMENSELY GRATEFUL that I have been allowed to live in a time that has been one of transition in several meanings of the word. A time of transition is a blessed time, in which we can hear the sound of eternity.

When the Roman world was collapsing under the onslaught of the "barbarians," St. Augustine stood in mystic wonderment with the shell of his heart on the shores of the ocean of the Trinity's mystery. When Europe was encountering new continents, there was ignited within the souls of John of the Cross and Teresa of Avila—as a counterweight to Spain's external violent expansion—a longing to quietly and courageously penetrate the center of the night, the castle within. When the century of wars and fatal discoveries was approaching, the prophet of the death of God expressed the hope that the *heart of the earth*, the essence of all reality, was "of gold." At the same period, the dying nun Teresa of Lisieux discovered a new path to God: we will reach God not by moral acts but by accepting ourselves with all our weaknesses—and trusting in merciful love.

Yes this is *kairos*, the opportune moment, the hour for faith. Not faith as possession of eternal truths, but faith as the courage to enter new spaces, silently, with a heart full of wonder, and with trust. And not losing or betraying the path entrusted to us, bringing it as an offering, a gift of welcome.

Maybe that was the instruction we received for entering the new age and for the hour of our death. For I believe that the NOTH-ING that we walk toward in death is simply another wonderful name for God.

TOMÁŠ HALÍK

is a Czech Roman Catholic priest, philosopher, theologian, and scholar. He is a professor of sociology at Charles University in Prague, pastor of the Academic Parish by St. Salvator Church in Prague, president of the Czech Christian Academy, and a winner of the Templeton Prize. His books, which are bestsellers in his own country, have been translated into nineteen languages and have received several literary prizes. He is the author of numerous books, including *I Want You to Be: On the God of Love* (University of Notre Dame Press, 2016, 2019), winner of the Catholic Press Association Book Award in Theology and Foreword Reviews' INDIES Book of the Year Award in Philosophy.

Gerald Turner

has translated numerous authors from Czechoslovakia, including Václav Havel, Ivan Klíma, and Ludvík Vaculík, among others. He received the US PEN Translation Award in 2004.